MCAT
MNEMONICS
30 DAY MCAT

600+ MEMORY TRICKS TO HELP YOU SCORE 520+ ON THE MCAT

Copyright © 2024 30 Day MCAT.

All rights reserved. No part of this book may be reproduced, distributed, or transmitted in any form or by any means, including photocopying, recording, or other electronic or mechanical methods, without prior written permission from the publisher, except for brief quotations in critical reviews or certain other noncommercial uses permitted by copyright law.

For permission requests, please contact: support@30daymcat.com.

Published by 30 Day MCAT

Authors note

Welcome, future doctor!

This book was born out of a journey we never expected to take. Like many of you, we once stood where you stand now—facing the MCAT, a test that seemed insurmountable. After a first attempt that ended in disappointment, we began to question everything we thought we knew about studying. We discovered that traditional methods weren't always effective and that hours of memorization alone weren't enough.

In searching for a way to make studying more efficient and less overwhelming, we uncovered the power of mnemonics. These memory aids helped us hold onto complex information while building a deeper understanding, rather than just memorizing facts. Using these techniques, we were able to tackle the MCAT and ultimately score in the 99th percentile. Since then, we've shared these strategies with friends and students, watching as they, too, transformed their approach to studying and boosted their scores.

This book is our way of sharing that discovery with you. We hope these mnemonics lighten your study load, make information easier to grasp, and, most importantly, help you feel more confident as you prepare. Remember, the goal isn't just to memorize—it's to understand, retain, and apply this knowledge on your path to becoming a physician.

Stay resilient, stay focused, and keep moving forward. You're capable of amazing things, and we're here to support you every step of the way.

With determination, The 30 Day MCAT Team.

Study Strategies

Developing effective study strategies is crucial for mastering the MCAT material. Consider the following approaches:

- **Set Specific Goals:** Break down your study sessions into clear objectives, such as mastering one chapter or completing a set number of practice questions. Establishing clear milestones helps track progress and keeps you motivated throughout your preparation journey.

- **Use Active Study Techniques:** Incorporate flashcards, practice questions, and teaching concepts aloud to strengthen retention and understanding. Engaging actively with the material promotes deeper learning and highlights areas that require more focus.

- **Review Regularly:** Revisit difficult topics and mnemonics periodically to keep them fresh in your memory. Consistent review helps reinforce knowledge and prevents last-minute cramming, which can lead to stress.

- **Incorporate Breaks:** Avoid burnout by scheduling regular breaks to maintain focus and energy throughout your study sessions. Use these breaks to recharge, whether by taking a walk, meditating, or enjoying a light snack, to ensure sustained productivity.

How to use

This book is designed to be your study companion as you prepare for the MCAT. Each mnemonic is organized by topic, allowing you to focus on one subject area at a time. The goal isn't just memorization, but deeper understanding and retention of the material. Use this book to help turn complex topics into manageable, memorable pieces.

To maximize your results, revisit the mnemonics regularly to reinforce your knowledge. Here are a few helpful features included throughout the book:

- **Tips Section**: Additional tips and important information about each topic appear in dedicated sections. These insights provide extra guidance and context to help you approach the material with confidence.
- **Cheat Sheets**: At the beginning of each chapter, you'll find tables of formulas, terms, and abbreviations, complete with definitions. Use these as quick references when studying or as a refresher before diving into practice questions.
- **Using MCAT Mnemonics**: Mnemonics transform complex information into memorable, bite-sized pieces. Use them to reinforce understanding, improve retention, and recall key concepts quickly. Regularly revisit the mnemonics to strengthen memory, apply them in practice questions to see them in action, and customize or adapt them to suit your learning style. These tools are designed to make studying more efficient and less overwhelming.

We hope these features make studying more engaging, helping you absorb and retain the material more effectively. Approach this book as an interactive tool and adapt it to fit your personal study needs.

Unlock Exclusive Access to Quizify Platforms!

Access **MCAT Quizify** and get your first month for only **$1**!

Use code:

AMAZONBUNDLE

Start practicing with high quality MCAT questions designed to build your confidence and help you crush your exam.

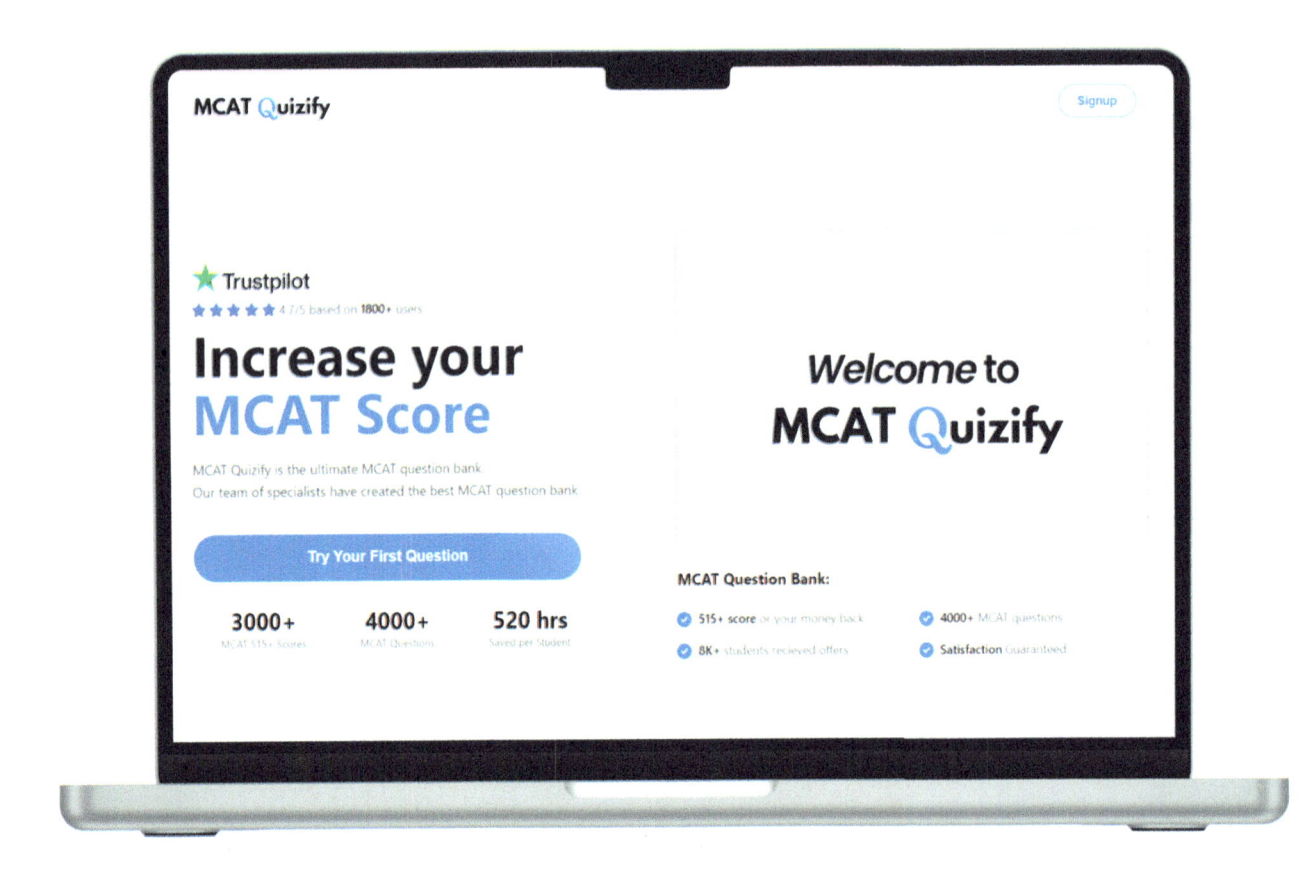

Join Our Free Skool Community!

Access free study resources! Get answers to your questions from a supportive community! And stay motivated with like-minded peers!

Join the 30 Day MCAT Skool Community, a free space where students share tips, resources, and motivation.

Visit: https://www.skool.com/30daymcat/about

🎁 Get a Free Gift From Us! 🎁

We value your feedback and would love to reward you for sharing your thoughts!

1️⃣ Email us a picture of you holding this book and a screenshot of the Amazon review you've posted.
2️⃣ We'll send you a FREE gift as a token of our appreciation.

How to Redeem Your Gift

1️⃣ Send your picture and Amazon review to: *support@30daymcat.com*
2️⃣ Include your name, shipping address, and a screenshot of your review.

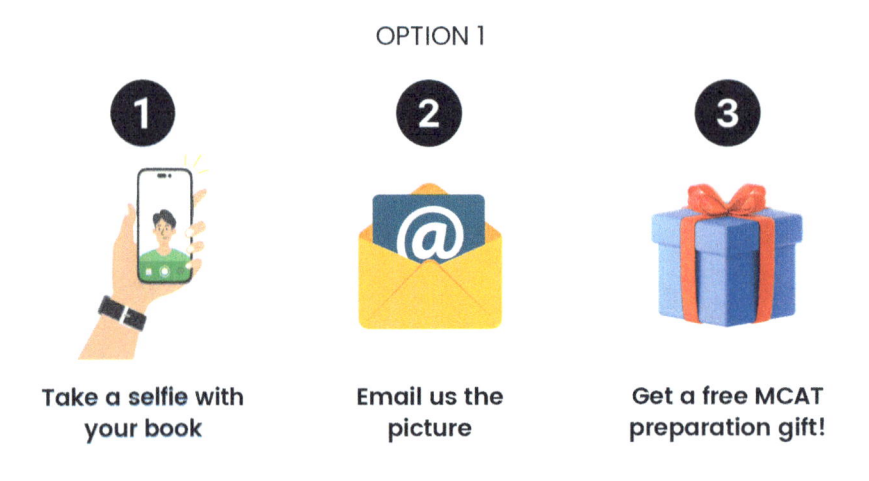

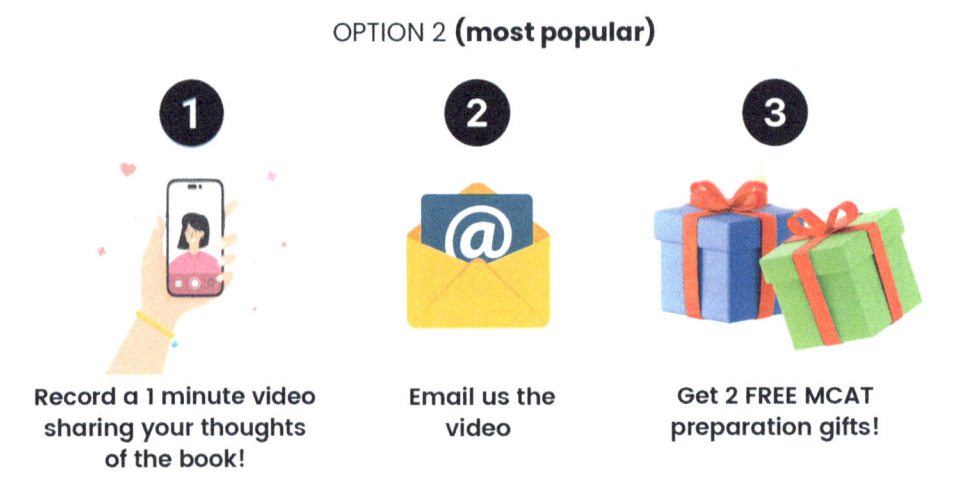

OPTION 1

1 Take a selfie with your book
2 Email us the picture
3 Get a free MCAT preparation gift!

OPTION 2 (most popular)

1 Record a 1 minute video sharing your thoughts of the book!
2 Email us the video
3 Get 2 FREE MCAT preparation gifts!

Explore More of Our High-Quality Resources

We offer a wide range of study materials to help you achieve your MCAT goals!

MCAT Complete Study Bundle

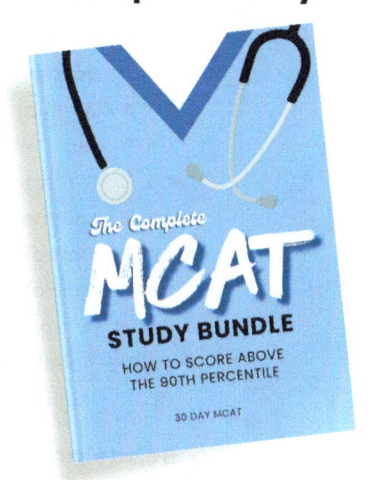

All-in-one book covering high-yield MCAT content.

MCAT Prep Courses

PREMIUM PACKAGE

STANDARD PACKAGE

Includes video lectures, study schedules, practice questions, plus coaching and accountability support.

- Visit Us Online: www.30daymcatshop.com
- Contact us anytime: support@30daymcat.com

Table of Contents

Biology
Tips for the MCAT (pg. 1)
Cheat sheet (pg. 5)
Chapters
Ch. 1 - The Cell (pg. 19)
Ch. 2 - Reproduction (pg. 22)
Ch. 3 - Embryogenesis & Development (pg. 25)
Ch. 4 - The Nervous System (pg. 28)
Ch. 5 - The Endocrine System (pg. 31)
Ch. 6 - The Respiratory System (pg. 34)
Ch. 7 - The Cardiovascular System (pg. 37)
Ch. 8 - The Immune System (pg. 40)
Ch. 9 - The Digestive System (pg. 43)
Ch. 10 - Homeostasis (pg. 53)
Ch. 11 - The Muscular System (pg. 49)
Ch. 12 - Genetics and Evolution (pg. 52)

Chemistry
Cheat sheet (pg. 55)
Chapters
Ch. 1 - Atomic Structure (pg. 73)
Ch. 2 - Periodic Table (pg. 76)
Ch. 3 - Bonding & Chemical Interactions (pg. 79)
Ch. 4 - Compounds & Stoichiometry (pg. 82)
Ch. 5 - Chemical Kinetics (pg. 85)
Ch. 6 - Equilibrium (pg. 88)
Ch. 7 - Thermochemistry (pg. 91)
Ch. 8 - The Gas Phase (pg. 94)
Ch. 9 - Solutions (pg. 97)
Ch. 10 - Acids & Bases (pg. 100)
Ch. 11 - Oxidation-Reduction Reactions (pg. 103)
Ch. 12 - Electrochemistry (pg. 106)

Biochemistry Chemistry
Cheat sheet (pg. 109)
Chapters
Ch. 1 - Amino Acids Peptides & Proteins (pg. 127)
Ch. 2 - Enzymes (pg. 130)
Ch. 3 - Non-Enzyme Protein Function & Analysis (pg. 133)
Ch. 4 - Carbohydrate Structure & Function (pg. 136)
Ch. 5 - Lipid Structure and Function (pg. 139)
Ch. 6 - DNA & Biotechnology (pg. 142)
Ch. 7 - RNA & Genetic Codes (pg.145)
Ch. 8 - Biological Membranes (pg. 148)
Ch. 9 - Metabolic Pathways (pg. 151)
Ch. 10 - Aerobic Respiration (pg. 154)
Ch. 11 - Lipid & Amino Acid Metabolism (pg. 157)
Ch. 12 - Bioenergetics & Metabolism Regulation (pg. 160)

Organic Chemistry
Cheat sheet (pg. 163)
Chapters
Ch. 1 - Nomenclature (pg. 179)
Ch. 2 - Isomers (pg. 182)
Ch. 3 - Bonding (pg. 185)
Ch. 4 - Analyzing Organic Reactions (pg. 188)
Ch. 5 - Alcohols (pg. 191)
Ch. 6 - Electrophilicity & Oxidation-Reduction (pg. 194)
Ch. 7 - Enolates (pg. 197)
Ch. 8 - Carboxylic Acid (pg.200)
Ch. 9 - Carboxylic & Derivatives (pg. 203)
Ch. 10 - Nitrogen & Phosphorus Compounds (pg. 206)
Ch. 11 - Spectroscopy (pg. 209)
Ch. 12 - Separations & Purifications (pg. 212)

Behavioral Science (Psychology & Sociology)
Cheat sheet (pg. 215)
Chapters
Ch. 1 - Biology & Behavior (pg. 227)
Ch. 2 - Sensation & Perception (pg. 230)
Ch. 3 - Learning & Memory (pg. 233)
Ch. 4 - Cognition, Consciousness & Language (pg. 236)
Ch. 5 - Motivation, Emotion & Stress (pg. 239)
Ch. 6 - Identity & Personality (pg. 242)
Ch. 7 - Psychological Disorders (pg. 245)
Ch. 8 - Social Processes, Attitude & Behaviours (pg. 248)
Ch. 9 - Social Interaction (pg. 251)
Ch. 10 - Social Thinking (pg. 254)
Ch. 11 - Social Structure & Demographics (pg. 257)
Ch. 12 - Social Stratification (pg. 260)

Math & Physics
Cheat sheet (pg. 263)
Chapters
Ch. 1 - Kinematics & Dynamics (pg. 275)
Ch. 2 - Work & Energy (pg. 278)
Ch. 3 - Thermodynamics (pg. 281)
Ch. 4 - Fluids (pg. 284)
Ch. 5 - Electrostatic and Magnetism (pg. 287)
Ch. 6 - Circuits (pg. 290)
Ch. 7 - Waves and Sounds (pg. 293)
Ch. 8 - Light and Optics (pg. 296)
Ch. 9 - Atomic Nuclear and Phenomena (pg. 299)
Ch. 10 - Mathematics (pg. 302)
Ch. 11 - Design Reasoning & Research Execution (pg. 305)
Ch. 12 - Data Base & Statistical Reasoning (pg. 308)

Tips for the MCAT

GENERAL TIPS FOR THE MCAT

- **Prioritize Active Recall**: Actively retrieving information strengthens memory retention. Use flashcards or cover up answers when reviewing notes to quiz yourself. This technique mimics test conditions, helping you recall information more effectively on exam day.

- **Approaching Full-Length Practice Tests**: Simulate test-day conditions with timed, full-length practice exams. These tests help you gauge your stamina, identify weak areas, and familiarize yourself with the MCAT format, ultimately boosting your confidence and accuracy for a higher percentile score.

- **Take Care of Yourself**: Rest, nutrition, and relaxation are essential before the MCAT. Quality sleep, a balanced diet, and regular breaks can boost focus and mental resilience, ensuring you're at your best on exam day.

HOW TO STUDY FOR THE BIOLOGICAL AND BIOCHEMICAL FOUNDATIONS OF LIVING SYSTEMS (BBLS)

- **Understand Key Biological Processes**: Focus on foundational topics like cellular respiration, photosynthesis, and enzyme activity. Conceptual understanding is crucial; avoid rote memorization and instead seek to understand how systems function.

- **Master the Basics of Biochemistry**: Study amino acids, protein structure, and biochemical pathways. Make mnemonics to remember metabolic cycles, and use diagrams to visualize complex pathways, reinforcing connections between concepts.

- **Use Practice Questions**: Apply what you learn through topic-specific questions. These questions reinforce your understanding and reveal which areas need more review, especially in complex biological pathways.

HOW TO STUDY FOR THE CHEMICAL AND PHYSICAL FOUNDATIONS OF BIOLOGICAL SYSTEMS (CPBS)

- **Grasp Core Chemistry Concepts**: Topics like acid-base balance, electrochemistry, and thermodynamics are essential. Practice applying formulas in a biological context to solidify your understanding and increase problem-solving speed.

- **Memorize Key Physics Equations**: Familiarize yourself with essential physics equations and practice using them in MCAT-style problems. Cheat sheets and formula tables can help you recall information more quickly.

- **Practice Applying Concepts**: Go beyond memorization by practicing questions that require analytical thinking and application of principles. Visual aids, like diagrams, are helpful for visualizing structures and reaction mechanisms.

HOW TO STUDY FOR THE PSYCHOLOGICAL, SOCIAL, AND BIOLOGICAL FOUNDATIONS OF BEHAVIOR (PSBB)

- **Understand Theories and Experiments**: Focus on major theories in psychology and sociology, such as learning theories and social interactions. Knowing key experiments and their implications can deepen your understanding of behavior and its biological basis.

- **Memorize Key Terms and Definitions**: Terms like "social stratification" or "class consciousness" are common in this section. Create flashcards for terminology and try to apply these terms in real-life examples for better retention.

- **Use Real-World Scenarios**: Apply psychological and sociological concepts to real-world scenarios, which can help in connecting theoretical knowledge with practical understanding, improving your ability to analyze passages on the exam.

HOW TO STUDY FOR CRITICAL ANALYSIS AND REASONING SKILLS (CARS)

- **Practice Reading Comprehension Daily**: Consistent practice with complex passages (even outside MCAT prep) can improve comprehension skills. Focus on reading actively—summarize main points and question the author's intent to build analytical skills.

- **Develop a Strategy for Answering Questions**: Techniques like eliminating obviously incorrect answers or predicting answers before reading choices can save time and increase accuracy.

- **Time Management**: Practice pacing to complete passages within a set time frame. Learn to quickly identify main ideas and conclusions to optimize your time, especially with dense, unfamiliar topics.

HOW TO STUDY FOR THE MCAT'S EXPERIMENTAL AND RESEARCH-BASED QUESTIONS

- **Understand Experimental Design:** Focus on experimental setups, variables (independent, dependent, and confounding), and controls. Practice identifying hypotheses and interpreting data from graphs and tables.

- **Practice Analyzing Data:** Familiarize yourself with common statistical methods and data interpretation. Learn to identify trends, outliers, and correlations in presented data.

- **Focus on Critical Thinking:** Develop skills to assess scientific claims critically. Understand how to evaluate the validity of experiments, identify flaws, and suggest improvements.

- **Review Scientific Journals:** Read summaries or abstracts of scientific articles to improve comprehension of research language and experimental frameworks, which mimic the MCAT's passage style.

- **Use Practice Passages:** Work on passages with experimental scenarios to hone your ability to apply theoretical knowledge to research-based contexts, a common feature of MCAT questions.

HOW THIS BOOK CAN HELP ON MCAT TEST DAY

- **Quick Recall with Mnemonics**: By using the mnemonics you've practiced, you'll have an easier time recalling complex information during the test. Familiar mnemonics can reduce stress and provide confidence when answering tough questions.

- **Simplified Review**: In the days leading up to test day, this book serves as a condensed review guide, allowing you to revisit key concepts without feeling overwhelmed by dense textbooks or scattered notes.

- **Confidence Boost with Cheat Sheets**: Use the cheat sheets to reinforce critical formulas, terms, and definitions that are likely to appear on test day. They offer quick refreshers to help you walk into the exam feeling prepared.

- **Strategic Focus on Weak Areas**: With practice and note-taking space, this book helps you focus on areas that need improvement. Use it to review those challenging topics one last time, so you can enter test day with a balanced understanding.

- **Stress Management through Familiarity**: Having reviewed and practiced concepts in a way that suits your learning style will make test day feel more manageable. Familiarity with the content and format can ease nerves, helping you perform your best.

CHEAT SHEET

THE CELL	
Cell Theory	• All living organisms are composed of cells, which are the basic units of life, and all cells arise from pre-existing cells.
Cell Structure	• The organized arrangement of the cell membrane, cytoplasm, nucleus, and organelles enables each cell to perform essential life functions.
Prokaryotic Cells	• Simple, single-celled organisms without a true nucleus or membrane-bound organelles, prokaryotic cells contain genetic material in a nucleoid region.
Eukaryotic Cells	• Characterized by a true nucleus and membrane-bound organelles, eukaryotic cells are found in multicellular organisms and carry out specialized functions within complex structures.
Cell Division	• The process by which cells reproduce, generating identical or genetically diverse cells.
Cell Communication	• Methods by which cells send and receive signals to coordinate actions.
Cell Specialization	• Process by which cells develop distinct forms and functions based on gene expression.
Cell Energy Production	• Cellular processes that generate energy, primarily in mitochondria or chloroplasts.
Eukaryotic Cell Structure	• Composition and organization of organelles within a eukaryotic cell.
Cell Membrane	• A phospholipid bilayer that controls the movement of substances in and out of the cell.
Nucleus	• The cell's control center, housing DNA and directing cellular activities.
Mitochondria	• Organelles responsible for ATP production, providing energy for the cell.

Endoplasmic Reticulum (ER)	• Network involved in protein and lipid synthesis, with rough and smooth regions.
Golgi Apparatus	• Modifies, sorts, and packages proteins and lipids for transport.
Lysosomes	• Organelles containing enzymes that break down waste materials and cellular debris.
Peroxisomes	• Organelles involved in detoxifying harmful substances and breaking down fatty acids.
Cytoskeleton	• A network of fibers that maintains cell shape, provides support, and enables movement.
Cell Cycle	• Series of phases that prepare a cell for division and replication.
Prokaryotic Cell Basics	• Characteristics of prokaryotic cells, which lack a nucleus and membrane-bound organelles.
Cell Envelope	• Protective layers around some cells, often including the cell wall and membrane.
Cell Wall	• A rigid structure providing support and protection in plant cells and bacteria.
Binary Fission	• Method of reproduction in prokaryotes, creating two identical cells.
DNA Replication	• Process by which DNA is copied to prepare for cell division.
Mutation	• A change in DNA sequence that may alter genetic expression.
Genetic Transfer in Bacteria	• Mechanisms by which bacteria exchange genetic material.
Virus Structure	• Composition of a virus, typically including genetic material and a protein coat.
Viral Replication Cycles	• The stages through which a virus infects a host and replicates.
Prions and Viroids	• Infectious agents, with prions being misfolded proteins and viroids affecting plants.

REPRODUCTION

Diploid vs. Haploid	• Describes cells with two chromosome sets (diploid) versus one set (haploid).
Stages of the Cell Cycle	• Phases a cell goes through during growth and division.
Mitosis Phases	• Stages of mitosis where a cell divides into two identical daughter cells.
Cell Cycle Checkpoints	• Control points that ensure proper cell division.
Key Regulatory Proteins	• Proteins that govern cell cycle progression.
p53 and Cancer Prevention	• A protein that prevents cancer by monitoring DNA integrity.
General Concept of Meiosis	• Explains the two-step process that produces gametes with half the usual chromosome number.
Meiosis I Phases	• The first division in meiosis that separates homologous chromosomes.
Meiosis II Phases	• The second division in meiosis that separates sister chromatids.
Spermatogenesis	• Process by which sperm cells are produced in males.
Oogenesis	• Formation of egg cells in females.
Male Sexual Development	• Organelles responsible for ATP production, providing energy for the cell.
Female Sexual Development	• Hormonal regulation of female reproductive development.
The Menstrual Cycle Phases	• Phases of the menstrual cycle that regulate female fertility.
Pregnancy and Menopause	• Describes gestation and the end of reproductive cycles in women.

EMBRYOGENESIS	
Fertilization	• Union of sperm and egg to form a zygote.
Twins	• Development of monozygotic (identical) or dizygotic (fraternal) twins.
Cleavage	• Rapid cell divisions without growth in an embryo.
Blastulation	• Formation of the blastocyst with differentiated cell layers.
Gastrulation	• Development of the three primary germ layers in the embryo.
Primary Germ Layers	• Layers (ectoderm, mesoderm, endoderm) that give rise to different tissues.
Differentiation	• Process where cells become specialized in structure and function.
Neurulation	• Formation of the neural tube, which becomes the nervous system.
Teratogens	• Substances that can cause developmental malformations.
Specialization and Determination	• Cells committing to specific functions.
Cell Specialization	• The process of cells taking on specific roles in the body.
Cell-to-Cell Communication	• Methods cells use to signal and influence each other.
Inducers and Reciprocal Development	• Molecules that guide cell differentiation.
Cell Migration, Cell Death, and Regeneration	• Processes involved in developing and maintaining tissues.
Senescence and Aging	• Cellular aging and its effects on the body.

Placenta and Umbilical Circulation	• Exchange of nutrients and waste between mother and fetus.
Shunts in Fetal Circulation	• Specialized fetal circulatory pathways.
Shunts Purpose and Pathway	• The function of fetal shunts in bypassing underdeveloped organs.
Gestation Milestones	• Key developmental events during pregnancy.
Trimester Overview	• Summary of fetal development by trimester
Birth Process (Parturition)	• The stages of labor and delivery.

NERVOUS SYSTEM	
Neuron Structure	• Components of a neuron, including dendrites, axon, and soma.
Myelin-Producing Cells	• Cells that produce the myelin sheath in the nervous system.
Glial Cells in the Nervous System	• Supportive cells in the nervous system with various roles.
Resting and Action Potential	• Electrical states that enable nerve impulses.
Na⁺/K⁺ Pump and Membrane Potential	• Mechanism that maintains cellular electrochemical balance.
Sodium Channel States	• The phases of sodium channels during nerve impulse transmission.
Action Potential Propagation	• How action potentials move along neurons.
Neurotransmitter Release and Removal	• Process of releasing and clearing neurotransmitters at synapses.

Nervous System Divisions	- Organization of the central and peripheral nervous systems.
Autonomic Nervous System (Sympathetic vs. Parasympathetic)	- The division controlling involuntary functions.
White and Gray Matter Location (Brain vs. Spinal Cord)	- Arrangement of nerve tissue in the brain and spinal cord.
Reflex Arcs (Monosynaptic vs. Polysynaptic)	- Neural pathways involved in reflex actions.

ENDOCRINE SYSTEM	
Peptide Hormones	- Hormones made of amino acids that act via cell surface receptors.
First Messenger	- Hormone that binds to a receptor to trigger a cellular response.
Second Messenger	- Molecules that amplify signals inside cells after hormone binding.
Steroid Hormones	- Hormones derived from cholesterol that pass through cell membranes.
Amino Acid-Derivative Hormones	- Hormones derived from amino acids with varying speed and duration of action.
Direct Hormones	- Hormones that act directly on target tissues.
Tropic Hormones	- Hormones that stimulate other glands to release hormones.
Hypothalamus	- Brain region that controls the pituitary gland.

Anterior Pituitary Interactions	- Hormones released by the anterior pituitary gland.
Posterior Pituitary Interactions	- Hormones stored and released by the posterior pituitary.
Thyroid	- Gland involved in metabolism and calcium regulation.
Parathyroid Glands	- Glands that regulate calcium levels in the blood.
Adrenal Cortex	- Produces hormones related to metabolism, stress, and sex.
Adrenal Medulla	- Releases hormones involved in the fight-or-flight response.
Pancreas	○ Regulates blood glucose levels through insulin and glucagon.
Gonads (Testes and Ovaries)	- Produce sex hormones that influence reproductive functions.
Pineal Gland	- Gland that regulates sleep through melatonin production.
Other Endocrine Tissues	- Organs like the kidneys and heart that release hormones.

RESPIRATORY SYSTEM	
Anatomy of Air Flow Through the Respiratory Tract	- Pathway air takes from the nose to the lungs.
Function of the Diaphragm and Muscles in Breathing	- Role of muscles in controlling inhalation and exhalation.
Lung Capacities and Volumes	- Measurements of air volume in the lungs.

Breathing Control Centers in the Brain	- Brain areas that regulate breathing rate and depth.
Gas Exchange in the Respiratory System	- Process where oxygen and carbon dioxide are exchanged in the lungs.
Thermoregulation in the Respiratory System	- Methods by which the respiratory system regulates body temperature.
Immune Function in the Respiratory System	- The respiratory system's role in trapping and removing pathogens.

CARDIOVASCULAR SYSTEM

Components of the Cardiovascular System	- The heart, blood, and vessels.
Heart Chambers and Blood Flow Direction	- Pathway blood follows through the heart chambers.
Heart Valves	- Valves that regulate blood flow within the heart.
Electric Conduction Pathway of the Heart	- The sequence of electrical impulses for heart contractions.
Phases of Heart Contraction (Systole and Diastole)	- Phases of the heart's pumping cycle.
Arteries vs. Veins	- Differences between arteries and veins in structure and function.
Arteries and Veins that Carry Deoxygenated Blood	- Exceptions to the oxygenation rule in vessels.

Cardiac Output Formula	• Calculation of blood pumped by the heart per minute.
Blood Vessel Layers and Endothelial Cells	• Structure and function of blood vessel layers.
Blood Composition	• Components found in blood, including cells and plasma.
Serum vs. Plasma	• Differences between blood plasma and serum.
Blood Cell Types	• Types of cells in the blood, including red cells, white cells, and platelets.
Erythrocytes (Red Blood Cells)	• Cells that transport oxygen in the blood.
Thrombocytes (Platelets)	• Cells involved in blood clotting.
Blood Cell Production	• Process of creating blood cells in the bone marrow.
Blood Antigens and Antibodies	• Molecules that determine blood type and immune response.
ABO Blood Types	• Blood types based on antigen presence on red blood cells.
Rh Factor and Maternal-Fetal Medicine	• The importance of the Rh factor in pregnancy.
Blood Pressure and Resistance	• The relationship between blood pressure and vessel resistance.
Blood Pressure Equation	• Formula for calculating blood pressure.
Baroreceptors and Blood Pressure Regulation	• Mechanisms that help maintain blood pressure.
Hormonal Control of Blood Pressure	• Hormones that regulate blood pressure.
ANP and Blood Pressure Reduction	• Hormone that reduces blood pressure by promoting salt excretion.

Oxygen Binding to Hemoglobin	• Process by which oxygen attaches to hemoglobin.
Carbon Dioxide and the Bohr Effect	• How CO_2 influences hemoglobin's oxygen affinity.
Fetal Hemoglobin	• A type of hemoglobin with a higher affinity for oxygen.
Nutrient and Waste Transport	• How nutrients and wastes are carried in the blood.
Fluid Balance - Hydrostatic and Osmotic Pressure	• Forces that manage fluid movement in tissues.
Edema and Lymphatic Drainage	• Fluid buildup and how the lymphatic system removes it.
Coagulation Cascade and Platelet Aggregation	• Steps involved in blood clotting.
Fibrin and Clot Stabilization	• Role of fibrin in forming stable blood clots.
Clot Breakdown by Plasmin	• The process by which blood clots are broken down.

IMMUNE SYSTEM	
Innate vs. Adaptive Immunity	• Differences between immediate and specific immune responses.
Main Immune System Organs	• Organs involved in producing and supporting immune cells.
Gut-associated Lymphoid Tissue (GALT)	• Lymphoid tissue in the gut protecting against pathogens.

Leukocytes (Types and Functions)	• Types of white blood cells and their immune roles.
Response Types: Nonspecific vs. Specific	• Differences in immunity based on specificity.
Noncellular Nonspecific Defenses	• Physical and chemical barriers that prevent infections.
Complement System	• Protein system that assists in destroying pathogens.
Interferons	• Proteins that hinder viral replication and boost immune defense.
Cells of the Innate System	• Immune cells involved in rapid, nonspecific responses.
Natural Killer Cells	• Cells that attack virus-infected or cancerous cells.
The Adaptive Immune System	• Immune system that targets specific pathogens.
Humoral Immunity (B-cells)	• Part of the immune system that produces antibodies.
Cytotoxic Immunity (T-cells)	• T-cells that kill infected cells.
Helper T-cells (CD4+) and Cytotoxic T-cells (CD8+)	• T-cells with roles in immune signaling and direct attack.
Memory T-cells and Regulatory T-cells (Treg)	• T-cells involved in immune memory and suppression.
Lymphatic Structure and Function	• he role of the lymphatic system in fluid balance and immunity.
Lacteals and Chyle	• Lymphatic vessels in the intestines that absorb fats.

DIGESTIVE SYSTEM

Alimentary Canal Pathway	• The pathway food follows through the digestive system
Parts of the Small Intestine	• Segments of the small intestine for nutrient absorption.
Layers of the GI Tract	• Tissue layers in the digestive tract wall.
Accessory Organs	• Organs aiding digestion without directly contacting food
Processes of Digestion	• Stages from food intake to waste excretion
Types of Digestion	• Physical and chemical breakdown of food
Secretions in Digestion	• Fluids aiding in food breakdown and absorption
Functions of the Liver in Digestion	• Liver's roles in digestion and metabolism.
Pancreas Functions	• Enzyme production and pH balance in the digestive system.
Gallbladder Function	• Storage and release of bile for fat digestion
Absorption and Defecation	• Nutrient uptake and waste removal processes.
Nutrient Absorption in the Small Intestine	• How nutrients are absorbed in the intestines
Process of Defecation	• Final stage of digestion where waste is expelled

HOMEOSTASIS

Anatomy of the Excretory System	• Organs involved in waste removal and fluid regulation.
Kidney Structure	• Parts of the kidney that filter blood and produce urine.
Osmoregulation: Filtration, Secretion, and Reabsorption	• rocesses that maintain water and electrolyte balance.
Nephron Function	• Functions of the kidney's filtering units
Blood Pressure Regulation in the Excretory System	• Kidney's role in managing blood pressure
Acid-Base Balance	• How the kidneys help regulate blood pH.
The Skin	• Skin functions in protection and temperature control.
Epidermis Layers (Strata)	• Layers of the outer skin
Dermis Layers	• Deeper layers of skin that provide structure and sensation
Temperature Regulation	• Mechanisms that control body temperature through the skin

MUSCULOSKELETAL SYSTEM

Skeletal Muscle Characteristics	• Traits of voluntary muscle tissue.
Smooth Muscle Traits	• Properties of involuntary muscle in organs.

Cardiac Muscle Features	- Specialized muscle of the heart.
Bone Composition and Types	- Structural and functional bone types.
Microscopic Bone Structure	- Microstructure of compact bone.
Bone Remodeling	- Ongoing bone formation and resorption.
Types of Joints and Movements	- Joint types and their associated movements.

GENETICS AND EVOLUTION	
Fundamentals and Concepts of Genetics	- Basic terms and ideas in genetics.
Mendel's Laws	- Principles of inheritance observed by Gregor Mendel.
Genetic Material Experiments	- Experiments that demonstrated DNA's role in heredity.
Nucleotide Mutation	- Types of genetic mutations that change DNA sequences
Analytical Approaches in Genetics	- Methods for studying genetic traits and inheritance.
Evolution	- Changes in species traits over generations due to natural selection.
Natural Selection	- The process where organisms better adapted to their environment survive and reproduce more successfully.
Genetic Drift	- Random changes in allele frequencies in a population, especially significant in small populations.

THE CELL

CELL THEORY BASICS

Mnemonic: **Old Reliable Partner**

- **O** Organisms
- **R** Reproduce
- **P** Pre-existing

Explanation:
- Remember that **O**rganisms are made of cells, **R**eproduction happens at the cellular level, and cells come from **P**re-existing cells.

ANIMAL CELL ORGANELLES VS. PLANT CELL ORGANELLES

Mnemonic: **Animals Lack Chlorophyll, Plants Have Vacuoles**

- **A** Animals
- **C** Chloroplasts
- **P** Plants
- **V** Vacuoles

Explanation:
- Animal cells lack chloroplasts and large central vacuoles, which are unique to plant cells. Plant cells also have a cell wall, providing extra structure and support.

CELL COMMUNICATION

Mnemonic: **Dial Connections Swiftly**

- **D** Direct Contact
- **C** Chemical Signaling
- **S** Surface Receptors

Explanation:
- Cells communicate by **direct contact**, **chemical signaling** (such as hormones), and through **surface receptors** that detect and respond to external signals from other cells.

PROKARYOTIC VS. EUKARYOTIC CELLS

Mnemonic: **Pros Lack Extras; Euks Are Organized**

- **P** Prokaryotic
  - **L** Lack nucleus
  - **E** Extremely simple structure
- **E** Eukaryotic
  - **A** Advanced
  - **O** Organized complexity

Explanation:
- Prokaryotic cells are simpler, lacking a nucleus and complex organelles. Eukaryotic cells, in contrast, have a nucleus and various specialized organelles, making them more complex.

MEMBRANE TRANSPORT

Mnemonic: **Always Enter and Exit**

- **A** Active Transport
- **E** Endocytosis
- **E** Exocytosis

Explanation:
- Membrane transport mechanisms include **Active Transport** (movement against the concentration gradient), Endocytosis (taking substances into the cell), and Exocytosis (releasing substances out of the cell).

GENETIC TRANSFER IN BACTERIA

Mnemonic: **Three Common Tricks**

- **T** Transformation
- **C** Conjugation
- **T** Transduction

Explanation:
- Bacteria can transfer genetic material through **Transformation** (uptake of DNA from the environment), **Conjugation** (direct transfer between bacteria via a pilus), and **Transduction** (transfer via bacteriophages, or viruses).

VIRAL REPLICATION CYCLES

Mnemonic: **All Penguins Sail And Leave**

- **A** — **A**ttachment
- **P** — **P**enetration
- **S** — **S**ynthesis
- **A** — **A**ssembly
- **L** — **L**ysis (or Release)

Explanation:
- The viral replication cycle involves **Attachment** to the host cell, **Penetration** of viral genetic material, **Synthesis** of new viral components, **Assembly** of new viruses, and **Lysis or Release** from the host cell.

CELL SIGNALLING PATHWAYS

Mnemonic: **Learn Real Tricks Inside Cells**

- **L** — **L**igand Binding
- **R** — **R**eceptor Activation
- **T** — **T**ransduction
- **I** — **I**ntracellular Response
- **C** — **C**ellular Response

Explanation:
- Cell signaling begins with **L**igand binding to a receptor, leading to **R**eceptor activation. The signal is then **T**ransduced, triggering an **I**ntracellular response that results in a specific **C**ellular outcome.

CYTOSKELETON

Mnemonic: **I Make cells Move**

- **I** — **I**ntermediate Filaments
- **M** — **M**icrotubules
- **M** — **M**icrofilaments

Explanation:
- The cytoskeleton includes **I**ntermediate filaments (structural stability), **M**icrotubules (cell division and transport), and **M**icrofilaments (cell shape support and movement).

REPRODUCTION

DIPLOID VS. HAPLOID

Mnemonic: **Double vs. Half**

DOUBLE — **D**iploid
HALF — **H**aploid

Explanation:
- Diploid cells contain two sets of chromosomes (one from each parent), while Haploid cells have only one set, typically found in gametes (sperm and egg cells).

STAGES OF THE CELL CYCLE

Mnemonic: **Go Sleep, Go Make Cells**

- G_1 — **G**rowth Phase 1
- **S** — **S**ynthesis Phase
- G_2 — **G**rowth Phase 2
- **M** — **M**itosis
- **C** — **C**ytokinesis

Explanation:
- The cell cycle stages include G_1 (cell growth), **S** (DNA synthesis), G_2 (preparation for mitosis), **M** (mitosis for division of the nucleus), and **C** (cytokinesis, dividing the cell into two).

HORMONAL REGULATION OF THE MENSTRUAL CYCLE

Mnemonic: **Four Ladies Enjoying Periods**

- **F** — **F**SH (Follicle-Stimulating Hormone)
- **L** — **L**H (Luteinizing Hormone)
- **E** — **E**strogen
- **P** — **P**rogesterone

Explanation:
- **FSH** stimulates follicle development, **LH** triggers ovulation, **Estrogen** helps thicken the uterine lining, and **Progesterone** maintains the uterine lining for potential pregnancy.

SPERMATOGENESIS

Mnemonic: **Some People May Seek Testes**

- **S** — **S**permatogonia
- **P** — **P**rimary Spermatocytes
- **M** — **M**eiosis I (producing Secondary Spermatocytes)
- **S** — **M**eiosis II (producing Spermatids)
- **T** — **T**ransformation (Spermatids mature into Spermatozoa)

Explanation:
- The process of spermatogenesis begins with **Spermatogonia** (stem cells), progresses to **Primary Spermatocytes** that undergo **Meiosis I** (yielding Secondary Spermatocytes), followed by **Meiosis II** to form Spermatids, which then mature into **Spermatozoa**.

OOGENESIS

Mnemonic: **Oh People Often Overreact**

- **O** — **O**ogonia
- **P** — **P**rimary Oocyte
- **O** — **O**vulation (Secondary Oocyte)
- **O** — **O**vum (mature egg, after fertilization)

Explanation:
- Oogenesis begins with **Oogonia** (stem cells) developing into a **Primary Oocyte**. After maturation and **Ovulation**, a Secondary Oocyte is released, which completes development into an **Ovum** if fertilized.

FERTILIZATION

Mnemonic: **Can All Fuse**

- **C** — **C**apacitation
- **A** — **A**crosomal Reaction
- **F** — **F**usion of Gametes

Explanation:
- During fertilization, **Capacitation** prepares the sperm to penetrate the egg, the **Acrosomal Reaction** releases enzymes to break down the egg's outer layers, and **Fusion of Gametes** combines the genetic material from both the sperm and egg.

EARLY EMBRYONIC DEVELOPMENT

Mnemonic: **Cute Babies Grow Nicely**

- **C** — Cleavage
- **B** — Blastulation
- **G** — Gastrulation
- **N** — Neurulation

Explanation:
- Early embryonic development involves **Cleavage** (cell division), **Blastulation** (formation of the blastula), **Gastrulation** (formation of germ layers), and **Neurulation** (development of the neural tube).

IMPLANTATION

Mnemonic: **Blast Trophies**

- **B** — Blastocyst Attachment
- **T** — Trophoblast Role

Explanation:
- During implantation, the **Blastocyst** attaches to the uterine wall, with the **Trophoblast** playing a key role in embedding the blastocyst and forming connections with maternal tissues.

PLACENTATION

Mnemonic: **Please Nourish Fetus**

- **C** — Placenta Structure
- **A** — Nutrient Exchange
- **F** — Fetal Gas Exchange

Explanation:
- Placentation involves the formation of the **Placenta**, which facilitates **Nutrient** and **Gas Exchange** between the mother and fetus, supporting fetal development.

EMBRYOGENESIS

GERM LAYERS

Mnemonic: **Every Man Eats**

- **E** — Ectoderm
- **M** — Mesoderm
- **E** — Endoderm

Explanation:
- The **Ectoderm** forms the nervous system and skin, the **Mesoderm** gives rise to muscles, bones, and the circulatory system, and the **Endoderm** develops into the digestive tract and internal organs.

INDUCTION

Mnemonic: **Influence Nearby Cells**

- **I** — Influence
- **N** — Nearby
- **C** — Cells

Explanation:
- Induction is the process where one group of cells, such as the **Notochord**, influences the development of nearby cells, like the formation of the **Neural Tube**.

APOPTOSIS

Mnemonic: **A Planned Departure**

- **A** — Apoptosis
- **P** — Programmed
- **D** — Departure (cell death)

Explanation:
- **Apoptosis** is a form of **Programmed Cell Death** that helps shape tissues and organs by removing unnecessary or damaged cells during development.

MORPHOGENS

Mnemonic: **Molecules Guide Patterns**

M	**M**olecules
G	**G**radients
P	**P**atterns

Explanation:
- **Morphogens** are signaling molecules that form **Gradients** across developing tissues, guiding **Pattern Formation** and influencing cell fate based on their concentration.

HOMEOTIC GENES

Mnemonic: **Help Organize Body Plan**

H	**H**omeotic
O	**O**rganize
B	**B**ody
P	**P**lan

Explanation:
- **Homeotic Genes** are responsible for o**rganizing** the **body plan** during development, determining the specific formation and arrangement of body parts.

NEURAL CREST CELL MIGRATION

Mnemonic: **I Don't Miss Destinations**

I	**I**nduction
D	**D**elamination
M	**M**igration
D	**D**ifferentiation

Explanation:
- Neural crest cells undergo **Induction**, then **Delaminate** from the neural tube, **Migrate** throughout the embryo, and finally **Differentiate** into various cell types.

ORGANOGENESIS

Mnemonic: **Organize Growth Carefully**

C		Organ formation
B		Growth
G		Cell differentiation

Explanation:
- **Organogenesis** is the process where organs form, involving **Growth** and **Cell Differentiation** to develop specific organs like the heart, lungs, and kidneys.

TERATOGENS

Mnemonic: **Danger Can Impact**

D	Drugs
C	Chemicals
I	Infections

Explanation:
- **Teratogens** are external factors, such as **drugs**, **chemicals**, or **infections**, that can disrupt normal development, potentially leading to birth defects.

POSTNATAL DEVELOPMENT MILESTONES

Mnemonic: **Progress Happens Always**

P	Puberty
H	Hormonal Factors
A	Aging

Explanation:
- **Postnatal Development** includes key milestones such as **Puberty** and **Aging**, influenced by **Hormonal** and **Genetic Factors** that regulate growth, maturation, and the aging process.

THE NERVOUS SYSTEM

NEUROGLIA

Mnemonic: **All Offer Mighty Encouragement**

- **A** Astrocytes
- **O** Oligodendrocytes
- **M** Microglia
- **E** Ependymal Cells

Explanation:
- The types of **Neuroglia** include **Astrocytes** (support and nutrient supply to neurons), **Oligodendrocytes** (form myelin sheaths in the CNS), **Microglia** (immune defense in the CNS), and **Ependymal Cells** (produce and circulate cerebrospinal fluid).

NEUROTRANSMITTER REUPTAKE

Mnemonic: **Recycle Neuro Signals**

- **R** Reuptake
- **N** Neurotransmitters
- **S** Synaptic Transmission

Explanation:
- Neurotransmitter **Reuptake** involves the reabsorption of **neurotransmitters** to regulate **Synaptic** Transmission. Drugs can target these mechanisms, either enhancing or inhibiting reuptake, to alter neural signaling.

NEUROMUSCULAR JUNCTION TRANSMISSION

Mnemonic: **ACh Receptor Activates Muscles**

- **A** Acetylcholine (ACh)
- **R** Receptors
- **A** Activation
- **M** Muscle Contraction

Explanation:
- At the Neuromuscular Junction, **Acetylcholine (ACh)** binds to **Receptors** on the muscle fiber, **Activating** ion channels that lead to **Muscle Contraction.**

SENSORY SYSTEMS

Mnemonic: **Very Helpful Tips Save Senses**

- **V** Vision
- **H** Hearing
- **T** Taste
- **S** Smell
- **S** Somatosensation

Explanation:
- The sensory systems involve specific receptors and pathways: **Vision** (photoreceptors in the retina), **Hearing** (hair cells in the cochlea), **Taste** (taste buds on the tongue), **Smell** (olfactory receptors in the nasal cavity), and **Somatosensation** (receptors for touch, temperature, and pain in the skin).

AUTONOMIC NERVOUS SYSTEM

Mnemonic: **Stress vs. Peace**

- **S** Sympathetic (Fight or Flight)
- **P** Parasympathetic (Rest and Digest)

Explanation:
- The **S**ympathetic system (norepinephrine) triggers "fight or flight" by increasing heart rate and dilating pupils, while the **P**arasympathetic system (acetylcholine) promotes "rest and digest," slowing heart rate and constricting pupils.

BRAIN REGIONS AND FUNCTIONS

Mnemonic: **Come Let's Help Find Places**

- **C** Cerebrum
- **L** Limbic System
- **H** Hypothalamus
- **F** Frontal Lobe
- **P** Pons

Explanation:
- The **cerebrum** handles thought and memory, the **limbic system** governs emotions, the **hypothalamus** controls hunger and temperature, the **frontal lobe** manages decision-making and personality, and the **pons** aids in breathing and sleep.

NEURODEGENERATIVE DISEASES

Mnemonic: **Aging Prompts Harm**

- **A** Alzheimer's
- **P** Parkinson's
- **H** Huntington's

Explanation:
- **Alzheimer's** affects memory and cognition, **Parkinson's** impacts motor control due to dopamine deficiency, and **Huntington's** causes uncontrolled movements and cognitive decline due to genetic mutation.

NEUROIMAGING TECHNIQUES

Mnemonic: **Many Find Pictures Enlightening**

- **M** MRI (Magnetic Resonance Imaging)
- **F** fMRI (Functional MRI)
- **P** PET (Positron Emission Tomography)
- **E** EEG (Electroencephalography)

Explanation:
- **MRI** provides detailed brain structure images, **fMRI** measures brain activity by detecting blood flow changes, **PET** scans show metabolic activity using radioactive tracers, and **EEG** records electrical activity in the brain, useful for studying brain waves.

NEUROENDOCRINE SYSTEM

Mnemonic: **Hormones Partner Nicely**

- **H** Hypothalamus
- **P** Pituitary Gland
- **N** Nervous System

Explanation:
- The **Neuroendocrine System** involves interactions between the **Hypothalamus** and **Pituitary Gland** in the **Nervous System** to regulate hormone production, forming the hypothalamic-pituitary axis that controls many body functions.

THE ENDOCRINE SYSTEM

HORMONE TRANSPORT AND REGULATION

Mnemonic: **Binding Feeds Control**

- **B** — **B**ound Hormones
- **F** — **F**ree Hormones
- **C** — **C**ontrol through Feedback Loops

Explanation:
- Hormones travel in the blood either **Bound** to proteins or as F**ree** molecules. **Feedback Loops**, primarily negative, regulate hormone secretion to maintain balance in the body.

HORMONE RECEPTOR TYPES & SIGNALING PATHS

Mnemonic: **Please Enter Cells Swiftly**

- **P** — **P**lasma Membrane Receptors
- **E** — **E**nzyme-Linked Receptors
- **C** — **C**ytoplasmic Receptors
- **S** — **S**teroid Hormone Pathways

Explanation:
- Hormone receptors include **Plasma Membrane Receptors** (for water-soluble hormones), **Enzyme-Linked Receptors** (triggering intracellular cascades), and **Cytoplasmic Receptors** (for lipid-soluble hormones). **Steroid Hormone Pathways** involve direct interaction with DNA to influence gene expression.

HYPOTHALAMIC PITUITARY CONTROL

Mnemonic: **Help Release Inhibitors**

- **H** — **H**ypothalamus
- **R** — **R**eleasing Hormones
- **I** — **I**nhibiting Hormones

Explanation:
- The **Hypothalamus** regulates the Pituitary Gland by releasing **Releasing Hormones** to stimulate pituitary secretion and **Inhibiting Hormones** to suppress it, maintaining hormonal balance in the body.

PITUITARY HORMONES

Mnemonic: **FLAT PEG Always Oxytocinates**

F FSH (Follicle-Stimulating Hormone)
L LH (Luteinizing Hormone)
A A - ACTH (Adrenocorticotropic)
T TSH (Thyroid-Stimulating Hormone)

P Prolactin
E Endorphins
G GH (Growth Hormone)
A ADH (Antidiuretic Hormone)
O Oxytocin

Explanation:
- The Anterior Pituitary releases **FSH, LH, ACTH, TSH, Prolactin, Endorphins,** and **GH** to target tissues like the ovaries, testes, adrenal cortex, thyroid, and more. The **Posterior Pituitary** stores and releases **ADH** (targeting kidneys) and **Oxytocin** (targeting uterus and mammary glands).

ADRENAL GLAND HORMONES

Mnemonic: **Salt, Sugar, Sex – All Emergency!**

S Salt (Mineralocorticoids, primarily Aldosterone
S Sugar (Glucocorticoids, primarily Cortisol)
S Sex (Androgens)
A Adrenaline (Epinephrine) and Norepinephrine

Explanation:
- The **Adrenal Cortex** produces **Mineralocorticoids** (like aldosterone for salt balance), **Glucocorticoids** (like cortisol for metabolism), and **Androgens** (sex hormones). The **Adrenal Medulla** releases **Adrenaline** and **Norepinephrine** for rapid stress responses.

PANCREATIC HORMONES

Mnemonic: **GIG's**

G Glucagon
I Insulin
G Gastrin
S Somatostatin

Explanation:
- The **Pancreas** produces **Glucagon** and **Insulin** to regulate blood glucose levels, while **Gastrin** aids digestion and **Somatostatin** balances hormone release and digestive processes.

THYROID HORMONES

Mnemonic: Take Care Today

- **T** — T3 (Triiodothyronine)
- **C** — Calcitonin
- **T** — T4 (Thyroxine)

Explanation:
- The **Thyroid Gland** produces **T3** and **T4** to control metabolic processes and **Calcitonin** to manage calcium levels in the blood.

ROLES OF THE PINEAL GLAND

Mnemonic: Sleep, Sync, Shield

- **S** — Sleep Regulation
- **S** — Synchronize Circadian Rhythm
- **S** — Shield Against Oxidative Stress

Explanation:
- The **Pineal Gland** regulates **Sleep** through melatonin, helps **Synchronize** the body's internal clock, and **Shields** cells from oxidative damage with its antioxidant properties.

ENDOCRINE SYSTEM DISORDERS

Mnemonic: Growth Troubles Hurt Daily

- **G** — Gigantism/Acromegaly
- **T** — Thyroid Disorders (e.g., Hypothyroidism, Hyperthyroidism)
- **H** — Hyperparathyroidism
- **D** — Diabetes Mellitus

Explanation:
- Endocrine disorders include **Gigantism/Acromegaly** (excess growth hormone), **Thyroid Disorders** (thyroid hormone imbalances), **Hyperparathyroidism** (elevated calcium levels due to parathyroid hormone), and **Diabetes Mellitus** (problems with insulin regulation).

THE RESPIRATORY SYSTEM

PULMONARY VENTILATION MECHANICS

Mnemonic: **Diving In and Out**

D — **D**iaphragm
I — **I**nhalation
O — **E**xhalation (Out)

Explanation:
- Pulmonary ventilation involves the **Diaphragm** contracting during **Inhalation** to draw air into the lungs and relaxing during **Exhalation** to expel air from the lungs.

ALVEOLAR GAS EXCHANGE

Mnemonic: **Oxygen Loads, Carbon Dioxide Leaves**

Oxygen Loads (enters the blood)
Carbon Dioxide Leaves (exits the blood)

Explanation:
- In **Alveolar Gas Exchange**, **Oxygen** diffuses from the alveoli into the blood, while **Carbon Dioxide** diffuses from the blood into the alveoli to be exhaled.

RESPIRATORY CONTROL CENTERS

Mnemonic: **Make Breathing Patterns**

M — **M**edulla Oblongata
B — **B**rainstem (specifically the Pons)
P — **P**neumotaxic Center (in the Pons)

Explanation:
- The **Medulla Oblongata** sets the basic respiratory rhythm, the **Pons** in the **Brainstem** fine-tunes breathing patterns, and the **Pneumotaxic Center** limits inhalation to protect the lungs.

FACTORS SHIFTING O2-HEMOGLOBIN CURVE

Mnemonic: **CADET, Face Right**

- **C** CO_2 (Increased carbon dioxide)
- **A** Acidity (Decreased pH, increased H+ concentration)
- **D** 2,3-DPG (Increased 2,3-diphosphoglycerate levels)
- **E** Exercise (Increased metabolic activity)
- **T** Temperature (Increased body temperature)

Explanation:
- A rightward shift in the O_2-hemoglobin curve, caused by higher CO_2, acidity (low pH), 2,3-DPG, exercise, and temperature, lowers hemoglobin's oxygen affinity, enhancing oxygen release to tissues.

RESPIRATORY DISORDERS

Mnemonic: **Always Bring Clear Lungs**

- **A** Asthma
- **B** Bronchitis
- **C** COPD (Chronic Obstructive Pulmonary Disease)
- **L** Lung Cancer

Explanation:
- Common respiratory disorders include **Asthma** (airway inflammation), **Bronchitis** (bronchial inflammation), COPD (chronic airflow limitation), and Lung Cancer (malignant growth in lung tissue).

RESPIRATORY DEFENSE MECHANISMS

Mnemonic: **Many Lungs Protect Against Invaders**

- **M** Mucociliary Escalator
- **L** Lymphatic System
- **P** Phagocytes (Alveolar Macrophages)
- **A** Antibodies
- **I** IgA (Immunoglobulin A)

Explanation:
- The respiratory system defends itself with the **mucociliary escalator** (traps particles), **lymphatic system** (immune support), **phagocytes** like alveolar macrophages (engulf pathogens), and **antibodies** like **IgA** (blocks pathogen attachment).

PULMONARY CIRCULATION

Mnemonic: **Right Around Lungs Left**

R — **Right Ventricle:** Pumps deoxygenated blood to the lungs.
A — **Arteries:** Carry deoxygenated blood from the heart to the lungs.
L — **Lungs:** Exchange carbon dioxide for oxygen in the alveoli.
L — **Left Atrium:** Receives oxygenated blood from the lungs.

Explanation:
- In **Pulmonary Circulation**, the **Right Ventricle** pumps deoxygenated blood through the **Pulmonary Arteries** to the **Lungs** for gas exchange, and oxygenated blood returns to the **Left Atrium**.

RESPIRATORY QUOTIENT (RQ)

Mnemonic: **Calculate Metabolic Exchange**

C — **Carbohydrates (RQ ≈ 1.0):** High RQ due to equal CO_2 produced and O_2 consumed.
M — **Mixed Diet (RQ ≈ 0.8):** Average RQ for a combination of nutrients.
E — **Energy from Fats (RQ ≈ 0.7):** Lower RQ due to more O_2 consumed relative to CO_2 produced.

Explanation:
- The **Respiratory Quotient (RQ)** is the ratio of **CO_2 produced to O_2** consumed during metabolism, with different values for **Carbohydrates (1.0)**, a **Mixed Diet (0.8)**, and **Fats (0.7)**, indicating which macronutrients are primarily being metabolized for energy.

VENTILATION-PERFUSION MATCHING

Mnemonic: **Very Perfect Balance**

V — **Ventilation:** Airflow reaching the alveoli.
P — **Perfusion:** Blood flow reaching the alveolar capillaries.
B — **Balance:** Matching ventilation to perfusion for optimal gas exchange.

Explanation:
- **Ventilation-Perfusion Matching** is the process of balancing **Ventilation** (airflow) with **Perfusion** (blood flow) in the lungs to ensure efficient oxygen and carbon dioxide exchange.

CARDIOVASCULAR SYSTEM

PHASES OF THE CARDIAC CYCLE

Mnemonic: **A Smart Veteran's Insight**

- **A** Atrial Systole
- **S** Ventricular Systole
- **V** Ventricular Diastole
- **I** Isovolumetric Relaxation

Explanation:
- The cardiac cycle includes **Atrial Systole** (atria contract), **Ventricular Systole** (ventricles contract), **Ventricular Diastole** (ventricles relax and fill), and **Isovolumetric Relaxation** (brief period of no blood flow as ventricles relax).

FACTORS AFFECTING CARDIAC OUTPUT

Mnemonic: **Heart Rate And Strength**

- **H** Heart Rate
- **R** Resistance (Peripheral Vascular Resistance)
- **A** Afterload
- **S** Stroke Volume (includes Preload and Contractility)

Explanation:
- Cardiac output is influenced by **Heart Rate**, **Resistance** (vessel resistance), **Afterload** (pressure the heart must pump against), and **Stroke Volume** (amount of blood ejected, affected by preload and contractility).

FACTORS INFLUENCING VASCULAR RESISTANCE

Mnemonic: **Very Large Pipe Length**

- **V** Viscosity of Blood
- **L** Length of the Vessel
- **P** Peripheral Diameter (Vessel Radius)

Explanation:
- Vascular resistance is affected by **Blood Viscosity**, **Vessel Length**, and **Vessel Radius** (diameter), with smaller vessel diameters increasing resistance significantly.

BLOOD PRESSURE REGULATION

Mnemonic: **Short Reflex, Long Hormones**

- **S** Short-Term (Baroreceptor Reflex)
- **R** Renin-Angiotensin-Aldosterone System (RAAS)
- **L** Long-Term (Kidneys and Hormonal Control)
- **H** Hormones (e.g., ADH, Aldosterone)

Explanation:
- Short-term blood pressure regulation involves the **Baroreceptor Reflex** for immediate adjustments, while long-term regulation relies on the **Renin-Angiotensin-Aldosterone System** (RAAS), **Kidneys, and Hormones** (e.g., ADH and Aldosterone) to maintain stability over time.

CORONARY CIRCULATION

Mnemonic: **Arteries Carry Vital Blood**

- **A** Coronary Arteries
- **C** Coronary Capillaries
- **V** Coronary Veins
- **B** Blood Flow to the Heart Muscle

Explanation:
- Coronary circulation involves **Coronary Arteries** delivering oxygen-rich blood, **Capillaries** providing exchange to the heart tissue, and **Veins** returning deoxygenated blood, ensuring heart muscle nourishment.

ELECTROCARDIOGRAM (ECG) COMPONENTS

Mnemonic: **Proper Quick Timing**

- **P** P Wave
- **Q** QRS Complex
- **T** T Wave

Explanation:
- In an ECG, the **P Wave** indicates atrial depolarization, the **QRS Complex** represents ventricular depolarization, and the **T Wave** shows ventricular repolarization. These components help assess heart rhythm, conduction, and electrical activity.

BLOOD COAGULATION

Mnemonic: **Factors Prompt Clotting**

- **F** — **F**ibrin Formation
- **P** — **P**latelet Plug Formation
- **C** — **C**oagulation Cascade

Explanation:
- Blood coagulation involves **Platelet Plug Formation** (initial plug), the **Coagulation Cascade** (series of reactions activating clotting factors), and **Fibrin Formation** to stabilize the clot, stopping bleeding effectively.

CARDIOVASCULAR-LYMPHATIC CONNECTION

Mnemonic: **Circulate and Cleanse**

- **C** — **C**apillaries
- **A** — **A**bsorption of Fluid
- **C** — **C**irculation of Lymph

Explanation:
- The **Cardiovascular System** and **Lymphatic System** are connected as blood **Capillaries** release fluid into tissues, which the lymphatic vessels **Absorb** and return to the bloodstream, maintaining fluid balance and aiding in immune response.

CARDIOVASCULAR DISEASES

Mnemonic: **Help Prevent Cardiovascular Attack**

- **H** — **Hypertension:** High blood pressure causing strain on the heart and arteries.
- **P** — **Peripheral Artery Disease (PAD):** Narrowing of peripheral arteries reducing blood flow.
- **C** — **Coronary Artery Disease (CAD):** Blocked coronary arteries leading to reduced blood flow to the heart.
- **A** — **Atherosclerosis:** Buildup of plaque in arteries, leading to narrowed and hardened vessels.

Explanation:
- In **Pulmonary Circulation**, the **Right Ventricle** pumps deoxygenated blood through the **Pulmonary Arteries** to the **Lungs** for gas exchange, and oxygenated blood returns to the **Left Atrium**.

THE IMMUNE SYSTEM

INNATE IMMUNITY

Mnemonic: **Protective First Immune Care**

- **P** — **P**hysical Barriers
- **F** — **P**hagocytosis
- **I** — **I**nflammation
- **C** — **C**omplement System

Explanation:
- **Innate Immunity** provides immediate defense with **Physical Barriers** (skin, mucous), **Phagocytosis** (engulfing pathogens), Inflammation (local immune response), and the **Complement System** (proteins that help destroy pathogens).

ADAPTIVE IMMUNITY

Mnemonic: **Antibodies Target Cells**

- **A** — **A**ntigen-Specific
- **T** — **T** Cells (Cell-Mediated Immunity)
- **C** — B **C**ells (Humoral Immunity for antibodies)

Explanation:
- **Adaptive Immunity** is **antigen-specific**, involving **B Cells** (humoral immunity, producing antibodies) and **T Cells** (cell-mediated immunity), providing a targeted defense against specific pathogens.

ANTIGEN PRESENTATION

Mnemonic: **APCs Teach T Cells**

- **A** — **A**ntigen
- **P** — **P**resentation by APCs (Antigen-Presenting Cells)
- **T** — **T** Cells

Explanation:
- **Antigen Presentation** involves **APCs** displaying antigens to **T Cells**, enabling the adaptive immune system to recognize and respond to specific pathogens.

T CELL ACTIVATION AND DIFFERENTIATION

Mnemonic: **Help Coordinate Responses**

- **H** — Helper T Cells
- **C** — Cytotoxic T Cells
- **R** — Regulatory T Cells

Explanation:
- **Helper T Cells** stimulate other immune cells, Cytotoxic **T Cells** directly kill infected cells, and **Regulatory T Cells** modulate the immune response to prevent overactivity.

B CELL ACTIVATION AND ANTIBODY PRODUCTION

Mnemonic: **Bind, Clone, Produce**

- **B** — Binding (Antigen binds to B cell receptor)
- **C** — Clonal Selection (Activated B cells multiply)
- **P** — Production (B cells produce antibodies)

Explanation:
- B cell activation involves **Binding** of an antigen to a B cell receptor, **Clonal Selection** where B cells multiply, and **Production** of antibodies to target the specific antigen.

IMMUNOLOGICAL TOLERANCE

Mnemonic: **Self-Protective Measures**

- **S** — Self-Antigen Recognition
- **P** — Peripheral Tolerance
- **M** — Mechanisms (like Central Tolerance in the thymus and bone marrow)

Explanation:
- **Immunological Tolerance** prevents immune responses against self-antigens through mechanisms like **Central Tolerance** (elimination of self-reactive cells in primary lymphoid organs) and **Peripheral Tolerance** (suppression of self-reactive cells outside primary organs).

HYPERSENSITIVITY REACTIONS

Mnemonic: **Allergic Triggers Can Delay**

- **A** — **Type I:** Allergic
- **T** — **Type II:** Tissue-Specific
- **C** — **Type III:** Complex-Mediated
- **D** — **Type IV:** Delayed

Explanation:
- The four types of hypersensitivity reactions include **Type I** (Allergic/Immediate), **Type II** (Tissue-Specific/Cytotoxic), **Type III** (Immune Complex-Mediated), and **Type IV** (Delayed, T-cell mediated), each involving different immune mechanisms and reactions.

AUTOIMMUNE DISEASES

Mnemonic: **My Immune Attacks Body**

- **M** — Multiple Sclerosis
- **I** — Inflammatory Bowel Disease
- **A** — Addison's Disease
- **B** — Systemic Lupus Erythematosus (SLE)

Explanation:
- Autoimmune diseases occur when the immune system mistakenly attacks the body's own tissues, as seen in conditions like **Multiple Sclerosis, Inflammatory Bowel Disease, Addison's Disease**, and **Systemic Lupus Erythematosus**.

TYPES OF IMMUNODEFICIENCY DISORDERS

Mnemonic: **Primary And Secondary Issues**

- **P** — Primary Immunodeficiency
- **A** — Acquired Immunodeficiency
- **S** — Secondary Immunodeficiency

Explanation:
- Immunodeficiency disorders include **Primary** (genetic/congenital), **Acquired** (developed later due to infections like HIV), and **Secondary** (caused by external factors such as medications or malnutrition).

THE DIGESTIVE SYSTEM

ENTERIC NERVOUS SYSTEM

Mnemonic: **Gut's Independent Control**

- **G** — **G**astrointestinal Motility
- **I** — **I**ndependent of CNS
- **C** — **C**ontrol of Secretion

Explanation:
- The **Enteric Nervous System** regulates **Gastrointestinal Motility** and **Secretion autonomously**, functioning **Independently** of the central nervous system to control digestive processes.

HORMONAL REGULATION OF DIGESTION

Mnemonic: **Get Some Chyme Going**

- **G** — **G**astrin
- **S** — **S**ecretin
- **C** — **C**holecystokinin (CCK)
- **G** — **G**astric Inhibitory Peptide (GIP)

Explanation:
- Hormones like **Gastrin**, **Secretin**, **Cholecystokinin (CCK)**, and GIP play key roles in regulating digestion by controlling acid production, bile release, enzyme secretion, and insulin response.

LIVER FUNCTION

Mnemonic: **Big Detox Makes Proteins**

- **B** — **B**ile Production
- **D** — **D**etoxification
- **M** — **M**etabolism of Nutrients
- **P** — **P**rotein Synthesis

Explanation:
- The liver supports digestion through **Bile Production**, removes toxins via **Detoxification**, manages **Nutrient Metabolism** for energy balance, and performs **Protein Synthesis** essential for blood health and coagulation.

30 Day MCAT

PANCREATIC ENZYMES FOR DIGESTION

Mnemonic: **All Cats Leap**

- **A** — Amylase
- **C** — Chymotrypsin and Trypsin
- **L** — Lipase

Explanation:
- The pancreas produces **Amylase** for carbohydrate digestion, **Chymotrypsin** and Trypsin for protein digestion, and **Lipase** for lipid digestion, aiding in nutrient breakdown and absorption.

ABSORPTION OF NUTRIENTS

Mnemonic: **Mostly Active Transport**

- **M** — Microvilli
- **A** — Active Transport
- **T** — Transport by Diffusion

Explanation:
- Nutrient absorption in the small intestine relies on **Microvilli** (to maximize surface area), **Active Transport** (for glucose and amino acids), and **Diffusion** (for lipids and other small molecules).

BACTERIAL FLORA OF THE LARGE INTESTINE

Mnemonic: **Bacteria Feed Gut**

- **B** — Bacteria
- **F** — Fermentation
- **G** — Gut Health

Explanation:
- The bacterial flora in the large intestine **break down** undigested carbohydrates, **ferment** fiber to produce gases and nutrients, and promote **gut health** by synthesizing vitamins and supporting immunity.

DISORDERS OF THE DIGESTIVE SYSTEM

Mnemonic: **Gastric Problems Can Upset**

- **G** Gastroesophageal Reflux Disease (GERD)
- **P** Peptic Ulcers
- **C** Celiac Disease
- **U** Ulcerative Colitis

Explanation:
- Digestive disorders include **GERD** (acid reflux), **Peptic Ulcers** (stomach sores), **Celiac Disease** (immune reaction to gluten), and **Ulcerative Colitis** (colon inflammation).

MALABSORPTION SYNDROMES

Mnemonic: **Poor Nutrient Absorption**

- **P** Pancreatic Insufficiency
- **N** Nutrient Deficiencies
- **A** Abnormal Intestinal Mucosa

Explanation:
- Malabsorption syndromes can be caused by **Pancreatic Insufficiency** (enzyme deficiency), **Nutrient Deficiencies** due to impaired absorption, and **Abnormal Intestinal Mucosa** from conditions like celiac disease, affecting the body's ability to absorb essential nutrients.

BILE ACID METABOLISM

Mnemonic: **Bile Assists Lipid Processing**

- **B** Bile Production
- **A** Absorption of Fats
- **L** Lipid Transport

Explanation:
- Bile acids, produced in the liver, help with **Fat Absorption** by emulsifying fats, enabling their digestion, and supporting **Lipid Transport** through micelle formation for efficient absorption

HOMEOSTASIS

NEGATIVE FEEDBACK LOOPS

Mnemonic: **Some Sensors React**

- **S** — **S**timulus
- **S** — **S**ensor
- **R** — **R**esponse

Explanation:
- In a negative feedback loop, a **Stimulus** triggers a **Sensor** that detects the imbalance and initiates a **Response** to restore homeostasis, such as insulin release by the pancreas to regulate blood glucose levels.

POSITIVE FEEDBACK LOOPS

Mnemonic: **Push Further Along**

- **P** — **P**ush
- **F** — **F**eedback
- **A** — **A**mplification

Explanation:
- Positive feedback loops amplify an initial Push, increasing the **Feedback** response until a physiological goal is achieved, as seen in Childbirth (enhanced contractions) and **Blood Clotting** (amplification of clotting factors).

THERMOREGULATION

Mnemonic: **Heat Maintained Properly**

- **H** — **H**ypothalamus
- **M** — **M**echanisms of Heat Loss
- **P** — Heat **P**roduction

Explanation:
- Thermoregulation involves the **Hypothalamus** as the control center, Mechanisms of **Heat Loss** like sweating and vasodilation to cool down, and **Heat Production** through shivering and metabolism to warm up. Together, these processes help maintain a stable body temperature for homeostasis.

FLUID AND ELECTROLYTE BALANCE

Mnemonic: **Kidneys Regulate Always**

- **K** — Kidneys
- **R** — Renin-Angiotensin-Aldosterone System
- **A** — Antidiuretic Hormone (ADH)

Explanation:
- The **Kidneys** maintain fluid and electrolyte balance using the **Renin-Angiotensin-Aldosterone System** (regulating blood pressure and sodium) and **Antidiuretic Hormone** (enhancing water reabsorption), ensuring homeostasis.

ACID-BASE BALANCE

Mnemonic: **Buffers Breathe Kindly**

- **B** — Buffers
- **B** — Breathing
- **K** — Kidneys

Explanation:
- **Acid-Base Balance** is achieved through Buffers (rapid pH control), **Breathing** (CO_2 regulation by the lungs), and the **Kidneys** (long-term pH adjustment through hydrogen and bicarbonate management).

OSMOREGULATION

Mnemonic: **Kidneys Manage Water**

- **K** — Kidneys
- **M** — Maintaining Osmolality
- **W** — Water Reabsorption

Explanation:
- The **Kidneys** maintain water balance by **Managing Osmolality** and adjusting **Water Reabsorption** based on hormone signals, ensuring stable fluid and solute levels in the body.

ENDOCRINE REGULATION OF HOMEOSTASIS

Mnemonic: **Hormones Control Stability**

- **H** — Hormones
- **C** — Cortisol
- **S** — Stability via Thyroid Hormones

Explanation:
- **Hormones** like **Cortisol** help the body respond to stress, while **Thyroid Hormones** ensure Stability by controlling metabolic rate, both crucial for maintaining homeostasis.

NEUROLOGICAL REGULATION OF HOMEOSTASIS

Mnemonic: **Hypothalamus Keeps Balance**

- **H** — Hypothalamus
- **K** — Key Control Center
- **B** — Balance

Explanation:
- The **Hypothalamus** acts as a **Key Control Center**, coordinating autonomic and endocrine responses to maintain **Balance** in body functions, such as temperature, hydration, and energy needs.

DISORDERS OF HOMEOSTASIS

Mnemonic: **Homeostasis Disruptions Persist**

- **H** — Hypertension
- **D** — Diabetes
- **P** — Pheochromocytoma

Explanation:
- **Disorders of Homeostasis** include conditions like **Hypertension** (blood pressure imbalance), **Diabetes** (glucose regulation disruption), and **Pheochromocytoma** (excess stress hormones), each affecting the body's ability to maintain stable internal conditions.

MUSCULOSKELETAL SYSTEM

MUSCLE FIBER TYPES

Mnemonic: **Slow Fibers, Fast Moves**

- **S** — Slow-Twitch (Type I)
- **F** — Fast-Twitch Type IIa
- **F** — Fast-Twitch Type IIb

Explanation:
- **Slow-Twitch (Type I)** fibers are aerobic and endurance-based, **Fast-Twitch Type IIa** fibers combine endurance and power, and **Fast-Twitch Type IIb** fibers are anaerobic, providing quick bursts of power but fatigues rapidly.

NEUROMUSCULAR JUNCTION TRANSMISSION

Mnemonic: **ACh Activates Contraction**

- **A** — Acetylcholine
- **A** — ACh Receptors
- **C** — Contraction Initiation

Explanation:
- At the **Neuromuscular Junction**, **Acetylcholine (ACh)** is released and binds to **ACh Receptors** on the muscle membrane, causing depolarization that initiates **Contraction**.

MUSCLE CONTRACTION MECHANISM

Mnemonic: **Calcium Slides Filaments**

- **C** — Calcium Ions
- **S** — Sliding Filaments
- **F** — Filament Binding

Explanation:
- In the **Sliding Filament Theory**, **Calcium Ions** allow actin-myosin **Filament Binding**, causing the Sliding of filaments that results in muscle contraction.

30 Day MCAT

MUSCLE METABOLISM

Mnemonic: **Always Act Energetic**

- **A** — Aerobic Metabolism
- **A** — Anaerobic Metabolism
- **E** — Energy Utilization Factors

Explanation:
- Muscle metabolism relies on **Aerobic** (oxygen-based, long-duration) and **Anaerobic** (quick, oxygen-independent) pathways, with utilization dependent on **Exercise Intensity**, duration, and oxygen availability.

BONE REMODELING

Mnemonic: **Bone Rebuilds Constantly**

- **B** — Bone Resorption
- **R** — Role of Osteoclasts
- **C** — Constant Formation by Osteoblasts

Explanation:
- **Bone Remodeling** involves **Bone Resorption** by osteoclasts, breaking down bone, and **Constant Formation** by osteoblasts, which build new bone, maintaining bone strength and mineral balance.

HORMONAL REGULATION OF BONE METABOLISM

Mnemonic: **Protect Calcium Density**

- **P** — Parathyroid Hormone (PTH)
- **C** — Calcitonin
- **D** — Vitamin D

Explanation:
- Bone metabolism is regulated by **Parathyroid Hormone** (increases calcium by promoting resorption), **Calcitonin** (reduces calcium by inhibiting resorption), and **Vitamin D** (boosts calcium absorption to strengthen bones).

JOINT STRUCTURE AND FUNCTION

Mnemonic: **Flexible Connections Strengthen**

- **F** — Fibrous Joints
- **C** — Cartilaginous Joints
- **S** — Synovial Joints

Explanation:
- **Fibrous Joints** provide immobility, **Cartilaginous Joints** allow slight movement, and **Synovial Joints** offer a wide range of motion, each suited to different functional needs in the body.

MUSCLE INJURIES AND DISORDERS

Mnemonic: **Sprains, Strains, and Cramps**

- **S** — Sprains
- **S** — Strains
- **C** — Cramps

Explanation:
- Muscle Injuries and Disorders include **Sprains** (ligament damage), **Strains** (muscle or tendon injury), and **Cramps** (painful muscle contractions), each impacting mobility and muscle function.

SKELETAL DISORDERS

Mnemonic: **Old Bones Ache**

- **O** — Osteoporosis
- **B** — Bone Fractures
- **A** — Osteoarthritis

Explanation:
- **Skeletal Disorders** include **Osteoporosis** (bone density loss), **Bone Fractures** (increased risk due to weakened bones), and **Osteoarthritis** (cartilage breakdown in joints), all contributing to reduced mobility and pain.

GENETICS AND EVOLUTION

EPIGENETICS

Mnemonic: **Environment Modifies Expression**

- **E** Environmental Factors
- **M** Methylation (DNA Methylation)
- **E** Expression Changes (Histone Acetylation)

Explanation:
- **Epigenetics** involves **Environmental Factors** that impact **Gene Expression** without changing the DNA sequence, primarily through mechanisms like **DNA Methylation** (gene silencing) and **Histone Acetylation** (gene activation).

POPULATION GENETICS

Mnemonic: **Hardy Genes Drift Far**

- **H** Hardy-Weinberg Equilibrium
- **G** Genetic Drift
- **F** Gene Flow

Explanation:
- **Population Genetics** studies factors like **Hardy-Weinberg Equilibrium** (stability model), **Genetic Drift** (random fluctuations), and **Gene Flow** (gene movement), all influencing the genetic makeup of populations.

MOLECULAR EVOLUTION

Mnemonic: **DNA Reveals Phylogeny**

- **D** DNA Sequencing
- **R** Relationships
- **P** Phylogenetic Analysis

Explanation:
- **Population Genetics** studies factors like **Hardy-Weinberg Equilibrium** (stability model), **Genetic Drift** (random fluctuations), and **Gene Flow** (gene movement), all influencing the genetic makeup of populations.

GENETIC DRIFT

Mnemonic: **Random Founders Bottle**

- **R** — Random Chance
- **F** — Founder Effect
- **B** — Bottleneck Effect

Explanation:
- **Genetic Drift** involves **Random Chance** affecting allele frequencies, with significant effects like the **Founder Effect** (limited variation in new populations) and **Bottleneck Effect** (loss of diversity after population decline).

NON-CODING DNA

Mnemonic: **Not In Genes**

- **N** — Non-coding Regulatory Sequences
- **I** — Introns
- **G** — Genome Evolution (Repetitive Elements)

Explanation:
- **Non-coding DNA** includes **Regulatory Sequences** (gene expression control), **Introns** (segments within genes), and Repetitive Elements that influence **Genome Evolution** and gene regulation, even though they don't code for proteins.

GENE LINKAGE AND RECOMBINATION

Mnemonic: **Linked Genes Recombine**

- **L** — Linked Genes
- **G** — Genetic Recombination
- **R** — Recombination Results

Explanation:
- **Gene Linkage** causes nearby genes to be inherited together, but **Genetic Recombination** during meiosis can separate linked genes, leading to **Recombination** Results that increase genetic diversity.

GENETIC DISORDERS

Mnemonic: **Single Chromosome Mix**

- **S** — Single-Gene Disorders
- **C** — Chromosomal Disorders
- **M** — Multifactorial Disorders

Explanation:
- **Genetic Disorders** include **Single-Gene Disorders** (mutations in one gene), **Chromosomal Disorders** (chromosomal abnormalities), and **Multifactorial Disorders** (influenced by multiple genes and environmental factors).

GENETIC ENGINEERING TECHNIQUES

Mnemonic: **Cut Genes Precisely**

- **C** — CRISPR-Cas9
- **G** — Gene Therapy
- **P** — Polymerase Chain Reaction (PCR)

Explanation:
- Genetic Engineering Techniques like **CRISPR-Cas9** enable precise genome editing, **Gene Therapy** repairs defective genes, and **PCR** amplifies DNA for further analysis, impacting fields like medicine and agriculture.

EVOLUTIONARY DEVELOPMENTAL BIOLOGY

Mnemonic: **Genes Shape Diversity**

- **G** — Genes
- **S** — Shape
- **D** — Diversity

Explanation:
- In **Evo-Devo**, changes in **Developmental Genes** affect morphology and physiology, shaping the **Diversity** of species through variations in gene expression during growth and development.

CHEAT SHEET

ATOMIC STRUCTURE	
Atomic structure	• refers to the arrangement of subatomic particles—protons, neutrons, and electrons—within an atom.
Isotopes	• are variants of a chemical element that have the same number of protons (atomic number) but different numbers of neutrons.
Isotopic abundance	• is the relative proportion of a specific isotope of an element found in a natural sample, expressed as a percentage or fraction of the total number of atoms of that element.
Effective nuclear charge	• is the net positive charge experienced by an electron in a multi-electron atom.
Quantum numbers	• are a set of four values that describe the unique quantum state of an electron in an atom. They define the electron's position, energy, shape of its orbital, and its orientation in space.
Principal Quantum Number (n)	• Specifies the main energy level (shell) of an electron and its distance from the nucleus.
Azimuthal (Angular Momentum) Quantum Number (l)	• also known as the angular momentum quantum number (l), is a quantum number that determines the shape of an orbital and the angular momentum of an electron within an atom.
Magnetic Quantum Number (ml)	• Specifies the orientation of the orbital in space.
Spin Quantum Number (ms)	• Represents the spin of an electron within an orbital.
Periodic trends	• refer to predictable patterns in the properties of elements that occur across periods (rows) and groups (columns) in the periodic table.
Atomic Radius	• the distance from the nucleus to the outermost electron.

30 Day MCAT

Ionization Energy	• The energy required to remove an electron from an atom in the gaseous state.
Electron Affinity	• The energy change when an atom gains an electron to form a negative ion.
Electronegativity	• A measure of an atom's ability to attract shared electrons in a chemical bond.
Metallic and Nonmetallic Character	• Metallic character refers to an element's ability to lose electrons, while nonmetallic character refers to the ability to gain electrons.
Photoelectric effect	• is the phenomenon where electrons are ejected from the surface of a material (usually a metal) when it is exposed to light or electromagnetic radiation of sufficient energy.
Atomic spectra	• are the patterns of light, or electromagnetic radiation, emitted or absorbed by atoms when their electrons transition between energy levels.
Quantum mechanical model of the atom	• is the modern theory of atomic structure, describing electrons as existing in probabilistic regions called orbitals rather than fixed paths around the nucleus.
Hybridization	• is the concept in chemistry where atomic orbitals mix to form new, equivalent hybrid orbitals that are used to form covalent bonds in molecules.
Molecular Orbital Theory	• is a theory that explains how atoms combine to form molecules, using the concept of molecular orbitals.
Bonding orbitals	• Lower in energy, formed when atomic orbitals combine constructively, stabilizing the molecule.
Antibonding orbitals	• Higher in energy, formed when atomic orbitals combine destructively, destabilizing the molecule.
Molecular Orbital Diagram	• MO theory uses a diagram to show how atomic orbitals combine to form molecular orbitals. The diagram helps predict the molecule's bonding and anti-bonding orbitals and its electronic configuration.

PERIODIC TABLE

d-block Elements	• These elements are characterized by the filling of ddd-orbitals.
Transition Metals	• A subset of d-block elements that commonly exhibit multiple oxidation states and have unique chemical properties.
f-block elements	• are a group of elements located in the periodic table in two distinct rows at the bottom: the lanthanides (elements 57–71) and the actinides (elements 89–103).
Lanthanides	• Elements filling the 4f orbitals, typically found in the period below the main table, known for their magnetic and luminescent properties.
Actinides	• Elements filling the 5f orbitals, many of which are radioactive and used in nuclear energy applications.
Metallic properties	• refer to the characteristics exhibited by metals, such as high electrical and thermal conductivity, malleability, ductility, and the ability to form positive ions (cations).
Non-metallic properties	• refer to the characteristics exhibited by non-metals, such as poor electrical and thermal conductivity, brittleness (in solid form), and the tendency to gain or share electrons during chemical reactions.
Allotropes	• are different forms of the same element, where the atoms are bonded together in different ways, resulting in distinct physical and chemical properties.
Diagonal relationships	• refer to the similarities in the properties of elements that are located diagonally to each other in the periodic table.
Periodic trends in acid-base properties	• refer to the predictable changes in the acidic and basic behaviors of elements and compounds as you move across a period or down a group in the periodic table.
Electronegativity	• is the ability of an atom to attract and hold onto electrons when it is part of a chemical bond.
Periodic trends in reactivity	• refer to the predictable changes in the chemical reactivity of elements as you move across a period or down a group in the periodic table.

Polarity	- refers to the distribution of electrical charge over the atoms in a molecule, which occurs when there is an uneven sharing of electrons in a bond or when a molecule has a net dipole moment.

BONDING & CHEMICAL INTERACTIONS

Bonding	- refers to the force that holds atoms together in molecules or compounds.
Chemical interactions	- refer to the forces and interactions that occur between atoms, ions, or molecules during chemical reactions.
Intermolecular forces	- are the forces of attraction or repulsion that exist between molecules.
Metallic bonding	- is the type of chemical bonding that occurs between metal atoms.
Ionic Bonding	- The transfer of electrons between a metal and a nonmetal, creating oppositely charged ions that are held together by electrostatic attraction.
Covalent Bonding	- The sharing of electron pairs between two nonmetals to form a stable bond.
Molecular Geometry	- The 3D arrangement of atoms in a molecule, determined by electron pairs around the central atom.
VSEPR Theory	- A theory that predicts molecular geometry by considering the repulsion between electron pairs around the central atom.
Hybridization	- The mixing of atomic orbitals to form new hybrid orbitals that determine molecular geometry.
Resonance Structures	- Different electron configurations for a molecule that reflect delocalized electrons; the actual structure is a hybrid of these forms.
Formal Charge	- A calculated value that helps determine the electron distribution in a molecule and its most stable form.

COMPOUNDS & STOICHIOMETRY

Empirical Formula	• The empirical formula represents the simplest whole-number ratio of elements in a compound.
Molecular Formula	• The actual number of atoms of each element in a compound.
Percent Composition	• The percentage by mass of each element in a compound.
Limiting Reactant	• The reactant that determines the amount of product in a chemical reaction because it is used up first.
Excess Reactant	• The reactant that remains after the reaction is complete.
Percent yield	• is a measure of the efficiency of a chemical reaction. It is the ratio of the actual yield (the amount of product actually obtained from a reaction) to the theoretical yield (the maximum possible amount of product predicted by stoichiometric calculations), expressed as a percentage.
Stoichiometry of solutions	• involves the calculation of the amounts of reactants and products in a chemical reaction occurring in solution.
Acid-base titrations	• are laboratory methods used to determine the concentration of an unknown acid or base by neutralizing it with a solution of known concentration.
Redox titrations	• A titration method where oxidation-reduction reactions are used to determine the concentration of a substance.
Gas Laws	• A set of laws that describe the behavior of gases, including relationships between pressure, volume, temperature, and number of moles.
Solubility Equilibria	• The equilibrium between a dissolved solute and its undissolved form in a saturated solution, governed by the solubility product constant (K_{sp}).

CHEMICAL KINETICS

Reaction Mechanisms	• A reaction mechanism is a step-by-step description of the pathway by which reactants are transformed into products. It includes a series of elementary steps, each representing a single molecular event, such as bond breaking or bond formation.
Rate Laws	• A rate law expresses the relationship between the reaction rate and the concentrations of the reactants.
Reaction Order	• The reaction order is the sum of the exponents in the rate law. It indicates how the rate is affected by the concentrations of the reactants.
Temperature Dependence of Reaction Rates	• The temperature dependence of reaction rates refers to how the speed of a chemical reaction changes with temperature.
Activation Energy	• Activation energy (E_a) is the minimum energy required for reactants to collide with sufficient force to overcome the energy barrier and form products. It determines how temperature influences the reaction rate; reactions with lower activation energy proceed faster.
Catalysts	• Catalysts are substances that increase the rate of a chemical reaction without being consumed in the process.
Le Chatelier's Principle	• Le Chatelier's Principle states that if a dynamic equilibrium is disturbed by a change in concentration, temperature, or pressure, the system will adjust to partially counteract the disturbance and re-establish equilibrium.
Kinetic Product	• The product that forms faster because it requires a lower activation energy. It is favored at lower temperatures and shorter reaction times.
Thermodynamic Product	• The product that is more stable and has lower overall energy. It is favored at higher temperatures and longer reaction times because it involves overcoming a higher activation energy.

Equilibrium Constant	• quantifies the ratio of the concentrations of products to reactants at equilibrium, each raised to the power of their stoichiometric coefficients
Reaction Rate	• The speed at which a chemical reaction proceeds, typically measured as the change in concentration of a reactant or product per unit time.
Transition State	• A high-energy, unstable configuration that represents the point of maximum energy along the reaction coordinate. The transition state occurs at the top of the activation energy barrier.
Intermediate	• A species formed during the reaction that is not present in the overall balanced equation. Intermediates exist temporarily and are consumed in subsequent steps of the reaction mechanism.
Molecularity	• The number of reactant molecules involved in an elementary step of a reaction.

EQUILIBRIUM

Solubility Equilibria	• Solubility equilibria refer to the equilibrium established when a slightly soluble ionic compound dissolves in water, forming ions, and the rate of dissolution equals the rate of precipitation.
Common Ion Effect	• The common ion effect occurs when the solubility of a salt decreases due to the presence of a common ion in solution.
Buffer Solutions	• A buffer solution resists changes in pH when small amounts of acid or base are added. It typically consists of a weak acid and its conjugate base, or a weak base and its conjugate acid.
Henderson-Hasselbalch Equation	• The Henderson-Hasselbalch equation relates the pH of a buffer solution to the concentration of the acid and its conjugate base.
Acid-Base Indicators	• Acid-base indicators are substances that change color depending on the pH of the solution.

Complex Ion Equilibria	• Complex ion equilibria involve the formation of complex ions, which are coordination compounds formed by a central metal ion and surrounding ligands.
Phase Equilibria	• Phase equilibria describe the equilibrium between different physical states (phases) of a substance, such as solid, liquid, and gas.
Dynamic Equilibrium	• A state in which the rate of the forward reaction equals the rate of the reverse reaction, resulting in no net change in the concentrations of reactants and products over time.
Le Chatelier's Principle	• A principle that predicts how a system at equilibrium will shift in response to changes in concentration, pressure, or temperature to partially counteract the disturbance.
Equilibrium Constant	• A dimensionless value that expresses the ratio of the concentrations of products to reactants at equilibrium, each raised to the power of their stoichiometric coefficients.
Reaction Quotient	• A mathematical expression similar to the equilibrium constant but calculated using initial or non-equilibrium concentrations.
Phase Equilibria	• The study of equilibrium between different physical states (phases) of a substance, such as solid-liquid equilibrium (melting/freezing), liquid-gas equilibrium (boiling/condensation), and solid-gas equilibrium (sublimation/deposition).

THERMOCHEMISTRY

Hess's Law	• Hess's Law states that the total enthalpy change of a chemical reaction is the same, regardless of the pathway taken, provided the initial and final states are the same.
Standard Enthalpy of Formation	• The standard enthalpy of formation is the change in enthalpy when one mole of a compound is formed from its elements in their standard states.
Standard Entropy (S°)	• The standard entropy is the absolute entropy of a substance at a standard state of 1 bar pressure and 298.15 K. It is a measure of the disorder or randomness of a system.
Gibbs Free Energy (ΔG)	• Gibbs free energy is a thermodynamic quantity that combines enthalpy (H) and entropy (S) to predict the spontaneity of a process. It is defined as.
Spontaneity	• A process is spontaneous if it can occur without external energy input. Spontaneity is determined by the sign of ΔG.
Equilibrium	• At equilibrium, ΔG=0, meaning there is no net change in the system, and the forward and reverse reaction rates are equal.
Calorimetry	• Calorimetry is the experimental technique used to measure the heat transferred during chemical or physical processes. It involves using a calorimeter and relies on the principle of conservation of energy.
Bond Energies	• Bond energy is the amount of energy required to break one mole of a particular bond in a gaseous molecule, or the energy released when the bond is formed.
Enthalpy	• Changes in enthalpy depend on the heat capacity of the system.
Entropy	• Entropy also depends on temperature, as it measures disorder, which typically increases with temperature.
Thermodynamic Cycles	• Thermodynamic cycles involve a sequence of processes that return a system to its initial state. They are used to analyze energy transfer, such as in heat engines and refrigerators.

THE GAS PHASE

Kinetic Molecular Theory of Gases	• A theory that explains the macroscopic behavior of gases based on the motion of gas particles
Ideal Gas Law	• It describes the behavior of ideal gases under various conditions.
Dalton's Law of Partial Pressures	• This law states that the total pressure of a mixture of non-reacting gases is the sum of their individual partial pressures
Graham's Law of Effusion	• Graham's law explains that the rate of effusion of a gas through a small hole is inversely proportional to the square root of its molar mass
Real Gases	• real gases experience intermolecular forces (attractive and repulsive) and occupy finite volumes. These deviations from ideal behavior become more pronounced at high pressures and low temperatures.
Deviations from Ideal Behavior	• refer to the ways in which real gases differ from the predictions of the ideal gas law under certain conditions.
Deviations from Ideal Behavior	• An equation that modifies the ideal gas law to account for intermolecular forces (a) and the finite volume of gas particles (b)
Gas Phase Reactions	• Gas phase reactions occur when reactants and products are in the gaseous state. These reactions can be described by chemical equations involving gases, and the behavior of the gases during the reaction can be understood using the ideal gas law or the appropriate real gas model.
Equilibrium	• occurs when the rates of the forward and reverse reactions are equal, and the concentrations (or partial pressures) of reactants and products remain constant over time.
Gas Phase Acid-Base Reactions	• Acid-base reactions that occur in the gas phase, often involving proton transfer or the formation of ionic species.
Gas Chromatography	• A technique used to separate and analyze compounds in a gaseous mixture.

Effusion	- is the process where gas particles pass through a tiny hole from one compartment to another. Graham's Law of Effusion explains the relationship between the rate of effusion and the molecular mass of gases.
Gas Phase Equilibria	- Gas phase equilibria deal with chemical reactions occurring in the gas phase that reach a dynamic equilibrium state, where the rate of the forward reaction equals the rate of the reverse reaction.
Molar Volume	- The volume occupied by one mole of a gas at a specific temperature and pressure.
Partial Pressure	- The pressure exerted by a single component of a gas mixture. According to Dalton's Law of Partial Pressures, the total pressure of a gas mixture is the sum of the partial pressures of each gas in the mixture.
Boyle's Law	- Boyle's Law states that the pressure and volume of a gas are inversely proportional at constant temperature.
Charles's Law	- Charles's Law states that the volume of a gas is directly proportional to its temperature, provided the pressure is constant.
Diffusion	- The process by which gas molecules move from an area of higher concentration to an area of lower concentration due to their random motion.
Gaseous Diffusion	- Gaseous diffusion refers to the process by which gas molecules spread and mix due to their random motion.

SOLUTIONS

Colligative Properties	• Colligative properties are properties of solutions that depend on the number of solute particles in a given amount of solvent, rather than the type of solute particles.
Raoult's Law	• Raoult's Law states that the vapor pressure of a solvent in a solution is directly proportional to the mole fraction of the solvent.
Solubility	• Solubility refers to the maximum amount of solute that can dissolve in a given amount of solvent at a specified temperature and pressure.
Factors Affecting Solubility	• Solubility refers to the maximum amount of solute that can dissolve in a given amount of solvent at a specific temperature and pressure.
Temperature	• For most solid solutes, solubility increases with temperature, while for gases, solubility decreases.
Pressure	• Pressure primarily affects the solubility of gases; higher pressure increases gas solubility (as described by Henry's Law).
Buffer Solutions	• Buffer solutions are aqueous solutions that resist changes in pH when small amounts of an acid or a base are added.
Henderson-Hasselbalch Equation	• The Henderson-Hasselbalch equation is used to calculate the pH of a buffer solution. It relates the pH of a buffer to the concentrations of the acid and its conjugate base
Redox Titrations	• Redox titrations are a type of titration where the analyte undergoes an oxidation-reduction reaction with the titrant. The equivalence point occurs when the amount of titrant added completely reacts with the analyte.
Colloids	• Colloids are mixtures in which one substance (the dispersed phase) is dispersed in another substance (the continuous phase), with the particles of the dispersed phase being between 1 nm and 1000 nm in size.
Colloidal Properties	• refer to the unique characteristics of colloidal systems

Brownian motion	- Random motion of particles due to collisions with solvent molecules.
Tyndall effect	- Scattering of light by colloidal particles, making the path of the beam visible.
Stability	- Colloidal particles tend to remain dispersed in the solvent due to repulsive forces between particles.
Colloidal Dispersions	- Colloidal dispersions are mixtures where the dispersed phase is finely distributed throughout the continuous phase. The dispersed particles do not settle out under normal conditions.
Electrolyte Solutions	- Electrolyte solutions are solutions that contain dissolved ions, allowing the solution to conduct electricity.

ACIDS & BASES

Arrhenius Theory	- Acids produce H^+ (or H_3O^+) ions in water, and bases produce OH^- ions.
Bronsted-Lowry Theory	- Acids are proton (H^+) donors, and bases are proton acceptors.
Lewis Theory	- Acids are electron-pair acceptors, and bases are electron-pair donors.
Acid Dissociation Constant (Ka)	- A measure of the strength of an acid, defined as the equilibrium constant for its dissociation in water.
Base Dissociation Constant (Kb)	- A measure of the strength of a base, defined as the equilibrium constant for its reaction with water.
ph	- pH is a measure of the acidity of a solution, representing the concentration of hydrogen ions or hydronium ions in the solution

pOH	• pOH is a measure of the basicity of a solution, representing the concentration of hydroxide ions in the solution
Strong Acids	• Acids that completely ionize in water, releasing all their H+ ions into the solution.
Weak Acids	• Acids that partially ionize in water, establishing an equilibrium between the undissociated acid and its ions.
Polyprotic Acids	• Acids that can donate more than one proton (H+) per molecule in a stepwise manner.
Polyprotic Bases	• Bases that can accept more than one proton (H+) in a stepwise manner.
Henderson-Hasselbalch Equation	• Relates the pH of a buffer solution to the ratio of conjugate base to weak acid.
Amphoteric Substances	• Substances that can act as either an acid or a base depending on the reaction.
Acidic Oxides	• Nonmetal oxides that react with water to form acids
Basic Oxides	• Metal oxides that react with water to form bases
Amphoteric Oxides	• React with both acids and bases
Neutral Oxides	• Do not exhibit acidic or basic properties

OXIDATION-REDUCTIONS

Oxidation Numbers	• A number assigned to an element in a compound that represents its charge or oxidation state.
Batteries	• Devices that convert chemical energy into electrical energy through redox reactions. They consist of one or more electrochemical cells.
Fuel Cells	• Electrochemical cells that continuously convert chemical energy into electrical energy using a fuel (e.g., hydrogen) and an oxidant (e.g., oxygen) without combustion.
Disproportionation Reactions	• Redox reactions in which a single species is simultaneously oxidized and reduced, forming two different products.
Comproportionation Reactions	• Reactions in which two species of the same element with different oxidation states react to form a single species with an intermediate oxidation state.
Redox Titrations	• Analytical techniques used to determine the concentration of an unknown substance by reacting it with a titrant that undergoes a redox reaction.
Electrochemical Cells	• Devices that generate electrical energy from chemical reactions (galvanic/voltaic cells) or drive chemical reactions using electrical energy (electrolytic cells).
Standard Reduction Potentials ($E°$)	• The voltage or potential difference associated with a reduction half-reaction measured under standard conditions (25°C, 1 M concentration, 1 atm pressure) relative to the standard hydrogen electrode (SHE).
Nernst Equation	• An equation that relates the cell potential to the standard electrode potential, temperature, and concentrations of the reactants and products.

Half-Reaction	- The separate equations representing the oxidation or reduction part of a redox reaction, showing the transfer of electrons.
Redox Reaction	- A chemical reaction in which one substance is oxidized (loses electrons) and another is reduced (gains electrons).
Reducing Agent	- The substance that gets oxidized by losing electrons, thereby causing another substance to be reduced.
Oxidizing Agent	- The substance that gets reduced by gaining electrons, thereby causing another substance to be oxidized.
Electron Transfer	- The movement of electrons from one species to another, which is the fundamental process underlying redox reactions.

ELECTROCHEMISTRY

Electrochemical Cells	- Devices that convert chemical energy into electrical energy (galvanic/voltaic cells) or use electrical energy to drive chemical reactions (electrolytic cells).
Second Law	- The masses of different substances deposited or dissolved by the same charge are proportional to their equivalent weights.
Concentration Cells	- Electrochemical cells where the electrodes are identical, but the concentrations of the electrolyte solutions differ, generating a potential difference

Electrochemical Cells	• Devices that convert chemical energy into electrical energy (galvanic/voltaic cells) or use electrical energy to drive chemical reactions (electrolytic cells).
Standard Reduction Potentials (E°)	• The potential difference of a reduction half-reaction under standard conditions (25°C, 1 atm, and 1 M concentration), measured relative to the standard hydrogen electrode (SHE).
Electrolysis	• A process where electrical energy is used to drive a non-spontaneous chemical reaction, such as splitting water into hydrogen and oxygen.
Faraday's Laws of Electrolysis	• Laws that describe the relationship between the amount of substance produced or consumed at an electrode and the total charge passed through the system.
Concentration Cells	• Electrochemical cells where the electrodes are identical, but the concentrations of the electrolyte solutions differ, generating a potential difference
Battery Types	• Categories of batteries based on chemistry and application, including primary (non-rechargeable), secondary (rechargeable), and specialized types like lithium-ion, alkaline, and lead-acid batteries.
Polarography	• An electrochemical technique that measures current as a function of applied voltage to analyze substances, often using a dropping mercury electrode.
Electrochemical Sensors	• Devices that use electrochemical reactions to detect and measure specific analytes, such as glucose sensors or oxygen sensors.

Bioelectrochemistry	- A field studying the interplay between electrochemical processes and biological systems, including electron transfer in cells and applications like biofuel cells and biosensors.
Electrode	- A conductor (usually metal) through which electrons enter or leave an electrochemical cell. Examples include anode (oxidation) and cathode (reduction).
Electrolyte	- A substance, typically in solution, that conducts electricity by allowing ions to move and participate in the electrochemical reaction.
Galvanic Cell	- A type of electrochemical cell where spontaneous redox reactions generate electrical energy.
Electrolytic Cell	- A type of electrochemical cell where electrical energy is used to drive a non-spontaneous redox reaction.
Redox Reaction	- A chemical reaction involving the transfer of electrons, comprising oxidation (loss of electrons) and reduction (gain of electrons).
First Law	- The mass of a substance is directly proportional to the charge passed
Second Law	- The masses of different substances deposited or dissolved by the same charge are proportional to their equivalent weights.

ATOMIC STRUCTURE

ISOTOPES AND ISOTOPIC ABUNDANCE

Mnemonic: **Isotopes Vary Weights**

- **I** Isotopes
- **V** Varying Abundance
- **W** Weight Calculation

Explanation:
- **Isotopes** have the same atomic number but differ in neutron count, leading to **Varying Abundances**. The **Atomic Weight** reflects the weighted average of each isotope's mass according to its abundance.

EFFECTIVE NUCLEAR CHARGE

Mnemonic: **Charge Affects Attraction**

- **C** Core Electrons
- **A** Attraction
- **A** Atomic Properties

Explanation:
- **Effective Nuclear Charge** is the net positive charge felt by valence electrons after shielding by **Core Electrons**, which strengthens **Attraction** to the nucleus and affects properties like **Ionization Energy** and **Electron Affinity**.

FOUR QUANTUM NUMBERS

Mnemonic: **Principal And Magnetic Spin**

- **P** Principal Quantum Number (n)
- **A** Azimuthal Quantum Number (l)
- **M** Magnetic Quantum Number (m_l)
- **S** Spin Quantum Number (m_s)

Explanation:
- The **Principal Quantum Number (n)** determines the energy level, **Azimuthal Quantum Number (l)** defines the orbital shape, **Magnetic Quantum Number (m_l)** indicates the orbital orientation, and **Spin Quantum Number (m_s)** specifies the electron's spin, collectively describing electron energy and spatial orientation.

PERIODIC TRENDS

Mnemonic: **Atoms Increase Energy Easily**

A — Atomic Size
I — Ionization Energy
E — Electron Affinity
E — Electronegativity

Explanation:
- **Atomic Size** decreases across a period and increases down a group, while **Ionization Energy**, **Electron Affinity**, and **Electronegativity** generally increase across a period and decrease down a group, reflecting the influence of nuclear charge and electron shielding.

PHOTOELECTRIC EFFECT

Mnemonic: **Photons Eject Electrons**

P — **Photons:** Light particles that strike a metal surface.
E — **Ejection of Electrons:** Electrons are ejected from the metal when hit by photons with sufficient energy.
E — **Energy Threshold:** Electrons are only ejected if the photon energy exceeds a certain threshold, supporting the particle nature of light.

Explanation:
- The **Photoelectric Effect** shows that **Photons** (light particles) can **Eject Electrons** from a metal surface when their energy surpasses a specific threshold, demonstrating that light behaves as particles and not just as waves.

ATOMIC SPECTRA

Mnemonic: **Excited Light Identifies**

E — Excited Electrons
L — Light Emission
I — Identification of Elements

Explanation:
- **Atomic Spectra** are created when **Excited Electrons** emit **Light** as they return to lower energy levels. This unique light emission pattern helps in the **Identification** of different elements.

QUANTUM MECHANICAL MODEL OF THE ATOM

Mnemonic: **Bohr Missed Waves**

- **B** — **B**ohr Model Limitations
- **M** — **M**odern Quantum Theory
- **W** — **W**ave-Particle Duality

Explanation:
- The **Quantum Mechanical Model** addresses **Bohr Model Limitations** by describing electron positions as probabilistic Waves rather than fixed orbits, acknowledging the **Wave-Particle Duality** of electrons.

HYBRIDIZATION

Mnemonic: **Hybrid Orbitals Bond**

- **H** — **H**ybrid Orbitals
- **O** — **O**rbital Geometry
- **B** — **B**onding

Explanation:
- **Hybridization** combines atomic orbitals into **Hybrid Orbitals** that determine **Orbital Geometry** and explain **Bonding** angles and shapes, helping to predict molecular structure.

MOLECULAR ORBITAL THEORY

Mnemonic: **Molecules Bond And Attract**

- **M** — **M**olecular Orbitals
- **B** — **B**onding Orbitals
- **A** — **A**ntibonding Orbitals
- **A** — **A**ttraction (Magnetism)

Explanation:
- **Molecular Orbital Theory** describes **Molecular Orbitals** as combinations of atomic orbitals, with **Bonding** and **Antibonding Orbitals** influencing **Attraction** properties like bond order and magnetism based on electron occupancy.

PERIODIC TABLE

D-BLOCK ELEMENTS AND TRANSITION METALS

Mnemonic: **Diverse States Create Compounds**

- **D** — **d**-block Elements
- **S** — **S**tates (Oxidation)
- **C** — **C**omplex Ion Formation

Explanation:
- **d-block Elements** (transition metals) exhibit **Variable Oxidation States** and readily form **Complex Ions**, which contribute to their diverse chemical properties and the creation of colorful compounds.

F-BLOCK ELEMENTS (LANTHANIDES AND ACTINIDES)

Mnemonic: **Fancy Metals Advance Technology**

- **F** — **f**-block Elements
- **M** — **M**agnetic and Luminescent Properties
- **A** — **A**pplications
- **T** — **T**echnology

Explanation:
- **f-block Elements,** including **Lanthanides** (known for magnetic and luminescent properties) and **Actinides** (notable for nuclear applications), play critical roles in modern **Technologies** like electronics, nuclear energy, and medical imaging.

METALLIC AND NON-METALLIC PROPERTIES

Mnemonic: **Metals Shine, Non-metals Don't**

- **M** — **M**alleability and Conductivity
- **S** — **S**hiny Appearance
- **N** — **N**on-metals
- **D** — **D**ull and Insulating

Explanation:
- **Metallic Properties** include **Malleability**, **Conductivity**, and **Shiny Appearance**, while **Non-metallic Properties** are characterized by being **Dull**, **Insulating**, and **Brittle**.

ALLOTROPES

Mnemonic: **Alternative Forms Exist**

- **A** Alternative Structures
- **F** Forms of Carbon
- **E** Existence of Oxygen Allotropes

Explanation:
- **Allotropes** are **Alternative Structures** of an element, such as **Forms of Carbon** (diamond, graphite, fullerene) and **Oxygen Allotropes** (O_2 for respiration, O_3 for UV protection), each with distinct properties and applications.

DIAGONAL RELATIONSHIPS

Mnemonic: **Like Elements Align**

- **L** Lithium and Magnesium
- **E** Electronegativity and Size
- **A** Aluminum and Beryllium

Explanation:
- **Diagonal Relationships** occur between elements like **Lithium** and **Magnesium** or **Aluminum and Beryllium**, where similarities in **Electronegativity and Size** lead to comparable chemical properties, despite being in different groups.

PERIODIC TRENDS IN IONIC RADII

Mnemonic: **Ions Reduces Strength**

- **I** Ionic Radii
- **R** Reduction in Radius
- **S** Strength and Lattice Energy

Explanation:
- **Ionic Radii** decrease for **Cations** (smaller size due to electron loss) and increase for **Anions** (larger size due to electron gain). Smaller radii enhance **Bond Strength** and **Lattice Energy** in ionic compounds.

PERIODIC TRENDS IN ACID-BASE PROPERTIES

Mnemonic: **Across Acids, Down Bases**

- **A** — **A**cross a Period
- **A** — **A**cidic Oxides
- **D** — **D**own a Group

Explanation:
- **Acid-Base Properties** of oxides shift **Across** a **Period**, becoming more acidic with non-metal oxides on the right. **Down a Group**, oxides and hydroxides become more basic, with metals forming basic oxides and hydroxides.

ELECTRONEGATIVITY AND POLARITY

Mnemonic: **Electrons Pull Polarity**

- **E** — **E**lectronegativity Differences
- **P** — **P**olarity in Bond
- **P** — **P**olarity in Molecules

Explanation:
- **Electronegativity Differences** determine **Bond Polarity** (greater differences create polar bonds), and **Molecular Polarity** results from both bond polarity and molecular shape, impacting the molecule's interactions.

PERIODIC TRENDS IN REACTIVITY

Mnemonic: **Reactivity Relates to Stability**

- **E** — **R**eactivity of Metals
- **P** — **R**eactivity of Nonmetals
- **P** — **S**tability through Oxidation States

Explanation:
- **Reactivity** of metals and nonmetals aligns with their electron **Stability**, with metals becoming more reactive down a group and nonmetals more reactive across a period.

BONDING & CHEMICAL INTERACTIONS

INTERMOLECULAR FORCES

Mnemonic: **Forces Determine Hydrogen Bonds**

- **F** — Forces (London Dispersion)
- **D** — Dipole-Dipole Interactions
- **H** — Hydrogen Bonding

Explanation:
- **Intermolecular Forces** like **London Dispersion Forces**, **Dipole-Dipole Interactions**, and **Hydrogen Bonding** influence physical properties such as **Boiling Point**, **Melting Point**, and **Solubility** based on the strength of these attractions.

METALLIC BONDING

Mnemonic: **Metals Conduct Easily**

- **M** — Metallic Bonding
- **C** — Conductivity
- **E** — Ease of Shaping (Malleability and Ductility)

Explanation:
- **Metallic Bonding** describes a **Sea of Delocalized Electrons** around metal ions, accounting for properties like **Conductivity and Ease of Shaping** (malleability and ductility) in metals.

IONIC BONDING

Mnemonic: **Ions Connect Strongly**

- **I** — Ionic Bonds
- **C** — Charge Influence
- **S** — Size (Ionic Radius)

Explanation:
- **Ionic Bonding** involves **Cations and Anions** attracting each other, with Lattice Energy affected by **Charge** (higher charges strengthen bonds) and **Size** (smaller ions increase bond strength).

COVALENT BONDING

Mnemonic: **Count Bonds Properly**

- **B** — **C**ovalent Bonds
- **D** — **B**ond Types
- **P** — **P**olarity

Explanation:
- **Covalent Bonding** involves **Electron Sharing** in **Single, Double**, or **Triple Bonds**, with **Polarity** occurring when atoms in a bond have differing electronegativities, resulting in partial charges.

MOLECULAR GEOMETRY AND VSEPR THEORY

Mnemonic: **Valence Shapes Predict**

- **V** — **V**alence Shell Electron Pair Repulsion (VSEPR)
- **S** — **S**hapes
- **P** — **P**redict Bond Angles

Explanation:
- **VSEPR Theory** helps predict **Shapes** and **Bond Angles** by arranging electron pairs to minimize repulsion, leading to distinct molecular geometries.

HYBRIDIZATION

Mnemonic: **Hybridize Bonds Shape**

- **H** — **H**ybridization
- **B** — **B**onding in Molecules
- **S** — **S**hape and Geometry

Explanation:
- **Hybridization** combines atomic orbitals to form **Bonding Patterns** in molecules, determining their **Shape**; for example, sp^3 hybridization gives methane a tetrahedral shape, while sp^2 hybridization gives ethene a planar geometry.

RESONANCE STRUCTURES

Mnemonic: Resonance Shares Electrons

- **R** — Resonance
- **S** — Sharing of Electrons
- **E** — Examples like Benzene

Explanation:
- **Resonance Structures** illustrate **Electron Delocalization** across a molecule, where electrons are **Shared** between multiple structures, as in **Benzene**, to achieve stability and uniform bond lengths.

FORMAL CHARGE

Mnemonic: Formal Calculation Simplifies

- **F** — Formula
- **C** — Calculate Charges
- **S** — Stability

Explanation:
- **VSEPR Theory** helps predict **Shapes** and **Bond Angles** by arranging electron pairs to minimize repulsion, leading to distinct molecular geometries.

OXIDATION-REDUCTION REACTIONS

Mnemonic: Oxidation Reduces Electrons

- **O** — Oxidation
- **R** — Reduction
- **E** — Electron Balance

Explanation:
- In **Redox Reactions, Oxidation** is the loss of electrons and **Reduction** is the gain of electrons. The **Half-Reaction Method** balances electrons in each half-reaction to ensure that total electrons lost equal electrons gained.

COMPOUNDS & STOICHIOMETRY

EMPIRICAL AND MOLECULAR FORMULAS

Mnemonic: **Essential Molecule Ratios**

- **E** — **E**mpirical Formula
- **M** — **M**olecular Formula
- **R** — **R**atios from Data

Explanation:
- The **Empirical Formula** provides the simplest ratio of atoms, while the **Molecular Formula** represents the actual atom count in a molecule. **Ratios** from experimental data help determine the empirical formula, which can then be scaled to find the molecular formula.

PERCENT COMPOSITION

Mnemonic: **Part Over Whole**

- **P** — **P**art (Element Mass)
- **O** — **O**ver Total Mass
- **W** — **W**hole Percentage

Explanation:
- To calculate **Percent Composition**, take the **Part** (mass of each element), divide it by the **Whole** (total compound mass), and multiply by 100 to get the percentage of each element.

LIMITING AND EXCESS REACTANTS

Mnemonic: **Limit React, Excess Left**

- **L** — **L**imiting Reactant
- **R** — **R**eact and Calculate
- **E** — **E**xcess Reactant

Explanation:
- The **Limiting Reactant** determines the **Theoretical Yield** of a reaction, as it's consumed first. **Calculate** product formation for each reactant; the one producing less product is the **Limiting Reactant**, while any remaining reactant is the **Excess**.

PERCENT YIELD

Mnemonic: **Actual Over Theoretical**

- **A** — Actual Yield
- **O** — Over Theoretical Yield
- **T** — Times 100

Explanation:
- **Percent Yield** measures reaction efficiency by comparing the **Actual Yield** to the **Theoretical Yield**. Calculated as (Actual Yield / Theoretical Yield) × 100, it shows the percentage of the expected product actually obtained.

STOICHIOMETRY OF SOLUTIONS

Mnemonic: **Moles Make Normality**

- **M** — Molarity (M)
- **M** — Molality (m)
- **N** — Normality (N)

Explanation:
- **Stoichiometry of Solutions** involves using **Molarity** (moles/liter), **Molality** (moles/kg), and **Normality** (equivalents/liter) to calculate solution concentrations and perform stoichiometric calculations, depending on the reaction requirements.

ACID-BASE TITRATIONS

Mnemonic: **Titration Curves End**

- **T** — Titration Principle
- **C** — Curves
- **E** — Endpoint Determination

Explanation:
- In **Acid-Base Titrations**, **Titration Curves** help visualize pH changes, and the **Endpoint** is identified by an indicator color change, indicating that the titration is complete.

30 Day MCAT

REDOX TITRATIONS

Mnemonic: **Redox Measures Unknowns**

R — Redox Reaction
M — Measurement with Standard Solution
U — Unknown Concentration

Explanation:
- **Redox Titrations** use a **Standard Solution** in a **Redox Reaction** to measure the **Unknown Concentration** of an analyte, with the endpoint determined by a change in oxidation state or color indicator.

GAS LAWS

Mnemonic: **Gases Behave Consistently Always**

G — Ideal **G**as Law (PV = nRT)
B — **B**oyle's Law (P ∝ 1/V)
C — **C**harles's Law (V ∝ T)
A — **A**vogadro's Law (V ∝ n)

Explanation:
- The **Ideal Gas Law** combines fundamental gas laws, including **Boyle's Law** (pressure and volume), **Charles's Law** (volume and temperature), and **Avogadro's Law** (volume and moles), to describe gas behavior under various conditions.

SOLUBILITY EQUILIBRIA

Mnemonic: **Ksp Predicts Saturation**

K — K_{sp} (Solubility Product Constant)
P — **P**redicting Precipitation
S — **S**aturated Solution Calculations

Explanation:
- The **Solubility Product (K_{sp})** helps in **Predicting Precipitation** and calculating **Saturated Solution** concentrations. When the ion product (Q) exceeds K_{sp}, a precipitate forms, indicating supersaturation.

CHEMICAL KINETICS

REACTION MECHANISMS

Mnemonic: **Elementary Reactions In Steps**

- **E** — **E**lementary Steps
- **R** — **R**ate-Determining Step
- **I** — **I**ntermediates

Explanation:
- A **Reaction Mechanism** consists of **Elementary Steps** that describe each part of the process, with the **Rate-Determining Step** controlling the reaction speed, and **Intermediates** forming temporarily within the sequence.

RATE LAWS

Mnemonic: **Rates Depend Constantly**

- **R** — **R**ate Law
- **D** — **D**etermine Exponents
- **C** — **C**alculate Rate Constant (k)

Explanation:
- The **Rate Law** relates the reaction rate to reactant concentrations, with exponents determined experimentally. After identifying the rate law, calculate the **Rate Constant (k)** based on observed data.

REACTION ORDER

Mnemonic: **Order Reveals Rate**

- **O** — **O**rder of Reactants
- **R** — **R**ate Law Relation
- **R** — **R**eaction Overall Order

Explanation:
- **Reaction Order** refers to the influence of each reactant on the rate, as represented by the **Rate Law** exponents. The **Overall Order** is the sum of these exponents, revealing the reaction's total order and its rate dependence on concentrations.

TEMPERATURE DEPENDENCE OF REACTION RATES

Mnemonic: **Arrhenius Increases Rate" or "A.I.R**

A — **A**rrhenius Equation
I — **I**ncreased Temperature
R — **R**ate Dependence

Explanation:
- The **Arrhenius Equation** shows that the **Rate Constant (k)** increases with **Increased Temperature**, as more molecules have enough energy to surpass the activation energy, accelerating the reaction rate.

ACTIVATION ENERGY

Mnemonic: **Energy Starts Reaction**

E — **E**nergy Barrier
S — **S**tart of Reaction
R — **R**ate Determination

Explanation:
- **Activation Energy** acts as an **Energy Barrier** that reactants must overcome to start a reaction. Reactions with lower activation energy occur faster, as more molecules meet the energy threshold to proceed.

CATALYSTS

Mnemonic: **Catalysts Lower Energy**

C — **C**atalysts
L — **L**ower Activation Energy
E — **E**nhanced Reaction Rate

Explanation:
- **Catalysts** work by **Lowering Activation Energy**, providing a pathway that requires less energy. This **Enhanced Reaction Rate** results from more molecules overcoming the energy barrier and reacting faster.

LE CHATELIER'S PRINCIPLE

Mnemonic: **Change Shifts Equilibrium**

- **C** — Concentration
- **S** — Stress Factors
- **E** — Equilibrium Position

Explanation:
- According to **Le Chatelier's Principle**, the **Equilibrium Position** adjusts in response to **Stress Factors** like **Concentration**, temperature, pressure, and volume changes, shifting to oppose and balance the applied change.

KINETIC PRODUCT VS. THERMODYNAMIC PRODUCT

Mnemonic: **Kinetics Faster, Thermo Stable**

- **K** — Kinetic Product
- **T** — Thermodynamic Product
- **S** — Stability

Explanation:
- The **Kinetic Product** forms quickly with lower energy but is less stable, while the **Thermodynamic Product** requires higher activation energy but results in greater **Stability**, favored at higher temperatures.

EQUILIBRIUM CONSTANT

Mnemonic: **Keep Calculating Direction**

- **K** — K Calculation
- **C** — Concentration or Pressure
- **D** — Direction of Reaction

Explanation:
- The **Equilibrium Constant (K)** provides insight into reaction direction: **Calculate** from concentrations or pressures to determine if the **Direction** favors products (K>1) or reactants (K<1).

EQUILIBRIUM

SOLUBILITY EQUILIBRIA

Mnemonic: **Ksp Predicts Saturation**

- **K** — **K**sp (Solubility Product Constant)
- **P** — **P**recipitation Prediction
- **S** — **S**aturation Calculation

Explanation:
- The **Solubility Product (Ksp)** helps in **Predicting Precipitation** by comparing the ion product (Q) to Ksp, and calculating **Saturation** concentrations in a solution, determining if it is saturated or supersaturated.

COMMON ION EFFECT

Mnemonic: **Ions Impact Solubility**

- **I** — **I**on Addition
- **I** — **I**mpact on Equilibrium
- **S** — **S**olubility Reduction

Explanation:
- The **Common Ion Effect** reduces **Solubility** by shifting equilibrium to favor precipitation of the solid when an Ion already present in the solution is added, decreasing the salt's solubility.

BUFFER SOLUTIONS

Mnemonic: **Buffers Balance pH**

- **B** — **B**uffer Components
- **B** — **B**alance pH
- **P** — **p**H Stability

Explanation:
- **Buffer Solutions** use a Weak Acid/Base Pair to **Balance pH** by absorbing added H^+ or OH^-, stabilizing the **pH** and resisting sudden changes upon the addition of acids or bases.

HENDERSON-HASSELBALCH EQUATION

Mnemonic: **pH Balances Ratio**

- **pH** — pH Calculation
- **B** — Balance of Acid/Base
- **R** — Ratio

Explanation:
- The **Henderson-Hasselbalch Equation** calculates **pH** by balancing the **Ratio** of the conjugate base to the weak acid, providing an efficient method to predict and control the pH of buffer solutions.

ACID-BASE INDICATORS

Mnemonic: **Indicators Show Transition**

- **I** — Indicator Color Change
- **S** — Select Proper Indicator
- **T** — Transition Range

Explanation:
- **Acid-Base Indicators** work by changing color within a **Transition Range** of pH values. Selecting the **Proper Indicator** ensures its color change aligns with the endpoint of the titration for accurate results.

COMPLEX ION EQUILIBRIA

Mnemonic: **Complex Ions Increase Solubility**

- **C** — Complex Ion Formation
- **I** — Increased Solubility
- **S** — Shifting Equilibrium

Explanation:
- **Complex Ion Formation** stabilizes metal ions in solution, **Increasing Solubility** by reducing free metal ion concentration and **Shifting Equilibrium** to dissolve more of the solid.

30 Day MCAT

PHASE EQUILIBRIA

Mnemonic: **Phases Depend on Pressure**

- **P** — Phase Diagram
- **D** — Determine Phase
- **P** — Pressure and Temperature Effects

Explanation:
- The **Phase Diagram** shows **Pressure and Temperature Effects** on phase changes, helping predict the phase of a substance at a given point. **Interpret** the diagram by locating temperature and pressure coordinates to identify whether the substance is solid, liquid, or gas.

COMMON ION EFFECT

Mnemonic: **Common Ions Shift Solubility**

- **C** — Common Ion Addition
- **S** — Shift in Equilibrium
- **S** — Solubility Reduction

Explanation:
- The **Common Ion Effect** involves adding a Common Ion to a solution, which **Shifts the Equilibrium** of a solubility reaction, reducing the **Solubility** of the sparingly soluble salt by driving the reaction towards the solid phase.

SOLUBILITY PRODUCT

Mnemonic: **Ksp Predicts Precipitation**

- **K** — Ksp (Solubility Product Constant)
- **P** — Predicting Precipitation
- **P** — Precipitation Conditions

Explanation:
- The **Solubility Product (K_{sp})** indicates the maximum product of ion concentrations in a saturated solution. By comparing the **Ion Product (Q)** to **K_{sp}** we can **Predict Precipitation**: precipitation occurs if Q exceeds K_{sp}.

THERMOCHEMISTRY

HESS'S LAW

Mnemonic: **Heat Equations Sum Simply**

- **H** — Hess's Law Principle
- **E** — Equation Manipulation
- **S** — Sum of Enthalpies

Explanation:
- **Hess's Law** states that the **Enthalpy Change** of a reaction can be determined by **Summing** the enthalpies of intermediate reactions, using **Equation Manipulation** to align them with the desired reaction.

STANDARD ENTHALPY OF FORMATION

Mnemonic: **Formation Helps Calculate**

- **F** — Formation of Compounds
- **H** — Hess's Law Application
- **C** — Calculate Enthalpy Change

Explanation:
- **Standard Enthalpy of Formation ($\Delta H_f°$)** values allow for **Calculation** of the overall enthalpy change by using the Formation enthalpies of products and reactants in a reaction, following **Hess's Law** principles.

STANDARD ENTROPY (S°)

Mnemonic: **Systems Seek Disorder**

- **S** — Standard Entropy ($S°$)
- **S** — Systems and Disorder
- **D** — Disorder Measurement

Explanation:
- **Standard Entropy ($S°$)** quantifies the **Disorder** in a system, with higher entropy indicating greater **Randomness**. Systems naturally progress toward increased entropy, as seen in phase changes and mixing.

GIBBS FREE ENERGY (ΔG)

Mnemonic: **Gibbs Helps Spontaneity**

- **G**   Gibbs Free Energy Equation
- **H**   Heat and Disorder
- **S**   Spontaneity

Explanation:
- **Gibbs Free Energy (ΔG)** combines **Enthalpy (ΔH)** and **Entropy (ΔS)** to predict **Spontaneity**: if ΔG is negative, the reaction proceeds spontaneously; if positive, the reaction is non-spontaneous.

SPONTANEITY AND EQUILIBRIUM

Mnemonic: **Gibbs Guides Equilibrium**

- **G**   Gibbs Free Energy (ΔG)
- **G**   Guiding Spontaneity
- **E**   Equilibrium Position

Explanation:
- **Gibbs Free Energy (ΔG)** determines **Spontaneity**: a negative ΔG indicates a spontaneous reaction moving toward equilibrium, while ΔG=0 signifies that the system has reached **Equilibrium**.

CALORIMETRY

Mnemonic: **Calorimeters Measure Heat**

- **C**   Calorimeter Setup
- **M**   Measure Temperature Change
- **H**   Heat Calculation

Explanation:
- **Calorimetry** involves using a Calorimeter to measure the **Temperature Change** of a reaction's surroundings. **Heat (q)** is then calculated using $q=mc\Delta T$ to determine the heat of the reaction.

BOND ENERGIES

Mnemonic: **Bonds Break, Energy Adds**

B   **B**ond Breaking
E   **E**nergy Release in Bond Formation
A   **A**dd Energies for ΔH

Explanation:
- **Bond Energies** are used to calculate the **Enthalpy Change (ΔH)** of a reaction by considering the energy needed to Break Bonds in the reactants and the energy released when **New Bonds** Form in the products.

TEMPERATURE DEPENDENCE & ENTROPY

Mnemonic: **Temperature Shifts Energy**

T   **T**emperature Influence
S   **S**hift in Entropy (ΔS)
E   **E**nthalpy Change (ΔH)

Explanation:
- **Temperature** impacts **Entropy (ΔS)** significantly, affecting reaction spontaneity, especially in processes with increased disorder. While **Enthalpy (ΔH)** is less temperature-sensitive, high temperatures can shift **Energy Balance** to make reactions more favorable depending on ΔS

THERMODYNAMIC CYCLES

Mnemonic: **Cycles Conserve Energy**

C   **C**ycle Process
C   **C**onservation of Energy
E   **E**fficiency and Work Output

Explanation:
- **Thermodynamic Cycles** involve a **Cycle Process** where a system returns to its starting state. The Conservation of Energy applies, with **Efficiency** determined by the work produced compared to heat absorbed, as in cycles used for engines and refrigeration.

THE GAS PHASE

KINETIC MOLECULAR THEORY OF GASES

Mnemonic: **Particles Move Constantly**

- **P** — Particles in Constant Motion
- **M** — Molecular Collisions
- **C** — Collisions and Temperature

Explanation:
- The **Kinetic Molecular Theory** assumes that gas **Particles Move Constantly** with **Elastic Collisions** and that **Temperature** affects their kinetic energy, explaining properties like pressure, volume, and temperature relationships in gases.

IDEAL GAS LAW

Mnemonic: **Properties Vary Naturally**

- **P** — Pressure (P)
- **V** — Volume (V)
- **N** — Number of Moles (n)
- **R** — Gas Constant (R)
- **T** — Temperature (T)

Explanation:
- $PV = nRT$, relates **Pressure (P)**, **Volume (V)**, **Moles (n)**, and **Temperature (T)**, allowing us to calculate any of these properties when the others are known.

DALTON'S LAW OF PARTIAL PRESSURES

Mnemonic: **Partial Pressures Add**

- **P** — Partial Pressure Calculation
- **P** — Pressure of Individual Gases
- **A** — Add for Total Pressure

Explanation:
- **Dalton's Law** states that in a gas mixture, each gas's **Partial Pressure** depends on its mole fraction, and the **Total Pressure** is the sum of all individual partial pressures.

GRAHAM'S LAW OF EFFUSION

Mnemonic: **Rates Relate by Roots**

- **R** — Rate of Effusion
- **R** — Relative Rates
- **R** — Roots of Molar Mass

Explanation:
- **Graham's Law of Effusion** states that the **Rates** of effusion of two gases are related by the square root of their molar masses, allowing calculation of how quickly a gas will effuse compared to another.

REAL GASES & DEVIATIONS FROM IDEAL BEHAVIOR

Mnemonic: **Real Gases Deviate**

- **R** — Real Gas Behavior
- **D** — Deviations from Ideal Conditions
- **I** — Intermolecular Forces

Explanation:
- **Real Gases** exhibit **Deviations** from **Ideal Behavior** due to **Intermolecular** Forces and the conditions of high pressure and low temperature, which impact how gases behave compared to the predictions of the ideal gas law.

VAN DER WAALS EQUATION

Mnemonic: **Adjust for Real Gases**

- **A** — Adjustments for Pressure
- **R** — Real Volume Consideration
- **G** — Gas Behavior

Explanation:
- The **Van der Waals Equation** modifies the ideal gas law by making **Adjustments** for **Pressure** and **Real Volume**, providing a better approximation of how **Real Gases** behave compared to ideal gases, especially under high pressures and low temperatures.

30 Day MCAT

GAS PHASE REACTIONS AND EQUILIBRIUM

Mnemonic: **Gases Balance Pressures**

- **G** — Gas Phase Equilibrium
- **B** — Balance of Concentrations
- **P** — Partial Pressures in K

Explanation:
- In **Gas Phase Reactions**, **Gases** achieve Equilibrium by balancing their concentrations, represented by partial pressures in the equilibrium constant expression, allowing for analysis and predictions of reaction dynamics.

GAS PHASE ACID-BASE REACTIONS

Mnemonic: **Gases Transfer Protons**

- **G** — Gas Phase Reactions
- **T** — Transfer of Protons
- **P** — Properties of Gaseous Acids and Bases

Explanation:
- In **Gas Phase Acid-Base Reactions**, **Gases** undergo **Proton Transfer** between molecules, allowing for analysis of their acid-base properties based on their behavior in the gas phase.

GAS CHROMATOGRAPHY

Mnemonic: **Gases Separate Clearly**

- **G** — Gas Phase
- **S** — Separation Principle
- **C** — Clear Analysis

Explanation:
- **Gas Chromatography** utilizes the **Gas Phase** of substances to achieve **Separation** based on how different compounds interact with a stationary phase, resulting in a **Clear Analysis** of the composition of gas mixtures.

SOLUTIONS

COLLIGATIVE PROPERTIES

Mnemonic: **Properties Depend**

- **P** — Properties
- **D** — Dependence

Explanation:
- **Colligative Properties** of solutions are influenced by the number of solute particles, which alters the physical properties of the solvent.

RAOULT'S LAW

Mnemonic: **Raoult Relates Pressures**

- **R** — Raoult's Law
- **R** — Relation to Mole Fraction

Explanation:
- **Raoult's Law** connects the vapor pressure of a solution to the vapor pressure of the pure solvent through the mole fraction, allowing predictions about vapor pressure changes in solutions.

SOLUBILITY AND FACTORS AFFECTING SOLUBILITY

Mnemonic: **Solubility Depends on Conditions**

- **S** — Solubility
- **D** — Dependence on Factors
- **C** — Conditions

Explanation:
- **Solubility** is affected by various **Conditions**, including temperature and pressure, impacting how much solute can dissolve in a solvent.

BUFFER SOLUTIONS

Mnemonic: **Buffers Resist Change**

B — Buffers
R — Resist Change

Explanation:
- **Buffer Solutions** are effective at **Resisting Change** in pH due to their composition, which allows them to neutralize small amounts of acids or bases.

HENDERSON-HASSELBALCH EQUATION

Mnemonic: **Henderson Helps Calculate pH**

H — Henderson-Hasselbalch Equation
H — Helps calculate the pH

Explanation:
- The **Henderson-Hasselbalch Equation** provides a simple way to **Calculate pH** in buffer solutions, linking pH to the ratio of conjugate base to weak acid concentrations.

REDOX TITRATIONS

Mnemonic: **Redox Determines Concentration**

R — Redox Titrations
D — Determining Concentration

Explanation:
- **Redox Titrations** measure the concentration of a substance based on **Redox** reactions, using standard solutions to facilitate the analysis.

COLLOIDS AND COLLOIDAL PROPERTIES

Mnemonic: **Colloids Display Unique Properties**

    C — Colloids
    D — Display Properties

Explanation:
- **Colloids** exhibit **Unique Properties** that distinguish them from true solutions and suspensions, including light scattering and particle movement behaviors

COLLOIDAL DISPERSIONS

Mnemonic: **Types of Colloids Matter**

    T — Types of Colloids
    M — Matter and Properties

Explanation:
- **Colloidal Dispersions** vary in **Types**, each exhibiting unique characteristics and behaviors, particularly in how they scatter light and react to environmental changes.

ELECTROLYTE SOLUTIONS

Mnemonic: **Electrolytes Vary Strength**

    E — Electrolyte Solutions
    V — Varying Strength

Explanation:
- **Electrolyte Solutions** differ in Strength, influencing their conductivity and the extent to which they affect colligative properties based on their dissociation behavior in solution.

ACIDS & BASES

ACID-BASE THEORIES

Mnemonic: Aunt Bessie Loves

A **Arrhenius Theory:** Defines acids as substances that increase H^+ in solution and bases that increase OH^-.

B **Brønsted-Lowry Theory:** Defines acids as proton donors and bases as proton acceptors.

L **Lewis Theory:** Defines acids as electron pair acceptors and bases as electron pair donors.

Explanation:
- The **Acid-Base Theories** classify substances based on their behavior in reactions.

ACID DISSOCIATION CONSTANT (KA)

Mnemonic: Ka Measures Acids

K Ka Calculation
M Measure Strength
A Acid Strength

Explanation:
- The **Acid Dissociation Constant (Ka)** helps in quantifying how well an acid dissociates in solution, providing insight into its Strength.

BASE DISSOCIATION CONSTANT (KB)

Mnemonic: Kb Measures Bases

K Kb Calculation
M Measure Strength
B Base Strength

Explanation:
- The **Base Dissociation Constant (Kb)** quantifies the degree to which a base dissociates in solution, providing insights into its Strength.

PH AND POH

Mnemonic:

pH & pOH Relation

p	**p**H Calculation
p	**p**OH Calculation
R	**R**elationship

Explanation:
- **pH and pOH** calculations reveal the **Relationship** between hydrogen and hydroxide ion concentrations, helping to determine acidity or basicity in solutions

STRONG AND WEAK ACIDS AND BASES

Mnemonic:

Strong Wins, Weak Fails

S	**S**trong Acids/Bases
W	**W**eak Acids/Bases
F	**F**ails to Ionize

Explanation:
- **Strong and Weak Acids** and **Bases** differ in their Ionization behavior in solution, directly impacting the pH based on their degree of dissociation.

POLYPROTIC ACIDS AND BASES

Mnemonic:

Polyprotic Steps Matter

P	**P**olyprotic Acids/Bases
S	**S**tepwise Ionization
M	**M**atter for Calculating pH

Explanation:
- **Polyprotic Acids** and **Bases** involve multiple **Steps** of ionization, each affecting the resulting pH of the solution based on their dissociation constants.

HENDERSON-HASSELBALCH EQUATION

Mnemonic: **Henderson Helps pH**

H   **H**enderson-Hasselbalch Equation

H   **H**elps in Buffers

p   **p**H Changes

Explanation:
- The **Henderson-Hasselbalch Equation** aids in calculating pH in buffer systems, showing how the ratio of acid to conjugate base affects the overall pH.

AMPHOTERIC SUBSTANCES

Mnemonic: **Amphoteric Acts Dual**

A   **A**mphoteric Nature

A   **A**cts According to Environment

D   **D**ual Functionality

Explanation:
- **Amphoteric Substances** exhibit Dual functionality, acting as either acids or bases based on the surrounding conditions, making them versatile in chemical reactions.

ACID-BASE PROPERTIES OF OXIDES & HYDROXIDES

Mnemonic: **Oxides and Hydroxides Vary**

O   **O**xides

H   **H**ydroxides

V   **V**ary Across Periodic Table

Explanation:
- The **Acid-Base Properties** of **Oxides** and **Hydroxides** depend on their composition, with properties Varying across the periodic table, influencing their behavior in reactions.

OXIDATION-REDUCTIONS

OXIDATION NUMBERS

Mnemonic: **Aunt Bessie Loves**

A — **Assigning Oxidation Numbers:** Follow specific rules to assign oxidation numbers to atoms in molecules and ions.
N — **Numbers Indicate Charge:** Oxidation numbers indicate the degree of oxidation or reduction of an atom within a compound.
E — **Easily Identified:** Common oxidation states for elements help in determining oxidation numbers in complex molecules.

Explanation:
- **Oxidation Numbers** are assigned to indicate the charge state of atoms in molecules, following specific rules for clear identification.

BATTERIES

Mnemonic: **Batteries Store Power**

B — **B**attery Types
S — **S**tore Electrical Energy
P — **P**ower Generation

Explanation:
- **Batteries** are devices that Store and convert energy, with different types functioning based on their design and chemical processes.

FUEL CELLS

Mnemonic: **Fuel Cells Generate Energy**

F — **F**uel Cell Operation
C — **C**lean Energy Source
G — **G**enerate Power

Explanation:
- **Fuel Cells** are efficient systems that **Generate** electrical energy from chemical reactions, offering a cleaner alternative to traditional energy sources.

DISPROPORTIONATION REACTIONS

Mnemonic: **Disproportionation Both Ways**

- **D** — **D**isproportionation Defined
- **B** — **B**oth Changes Occur

Explanation:
- In **Disproportionation Reactions**, one substance simultaneously undergoes **Both** oxidation and reduction, leading to products with different oxidation states.

COMPROPORTIONATION REACTIONS

Mnemonic: **Comproportionation Mixes States**

- **C** — **C**omproportionation Concept
- **M** — **M**ixing of Oxidation States

Explanation:
- **Comproportionation Reactions** involve substances of different oxidation states forming a product with an intermediate state, highlighting the mixing of oxidation states.

OXIDATION-REDUCTION

Mnemonic: **Titrations Define Chemistry**

- **T** — **T**itration Reactions
- **D** — **D**efine Redox Changes
- **C** — **C**hemistry of Electron Transfer

Explanation:
- **Oxidation-Reduction Titrations** are used to **Define** the concentration of substances through reactions based on **Chemistry** principles like electron transfer and standard solutions.

ELECTROCHEMICAL CELLS

Mnemonic: **Electrochemical Components Generate**

- **E** — Electrodes
- **C** — Components
- **G** — Generate Energy

Explanation:
- **Electrochemical Cells** consist of key Components that facilitate electron flow and Generate electrical energy through redox reactions.

STANDARD REDUCTION POTENTIALS ($E°$)

Mnemonic: **E° Indicates Spontaneity**

- **E** — Electrode Potentials
- **I** — Indicates Favorability
- **S** — Spontaneity Relation

Explanation:
- **Standard Reduction Potentials ($E°$)** provide insight into the **Spontaneity** of reactions, indicating how readily substances undergo reduction.

NERNST EQUATION

Mnemonic: **Nernst Calculates Potential**

- **N** — Nernst Equation
- **C** — Calculate Cell Potential
- **P** — Potential Adjustments

Explanation:
- The **Nernst Equation** enables **Calculation** of cell potential based on actual conditions, adjusting for concentration changes.

ELECTROCHEMISTRY

ELECTROCHEMICAL CELLS

Mnemonic: **Every Cell Generates Energy Salts**

- **E** — Electrodes
- **C** — Cell Types
- **G** — Generate Energy
- **E** — Electrolytes
- **S** — Salt Bridges

Explanation:
- **Electrochemical Cells** consist of **Electrodes**, electrolytes, and salt bridges that work together to Generate Energy through redox reactions, allowing for the flow of electrons and the production of electrical energy.

APPLICATION OF ELECTRODE POTENTIALS (E°)

Mnemonic: **E° Guides Feasibility**

- **E** — Electrode Analysis
- **G** — Guides Predictions
- **F** — Feasibility of Reduction

Explanation:
- The **Nernst Equation** enables **Calculation** of cell potential based on actual conditions, adjusting for concentration changes.

ELECTROLYSIS

Mnemonic: **Electrolysis Produces Products**

- **E** — **Electrolysis Process:** A method used to drive a non-spontaneous reaction using electrical energy.
- **P** — **Produces Compounds:** Converts reactants into their elements or simpler substances.
- **F** — **Factors Affecting Yield:** Includes current, time, and concentration of the electrolyte.

Explanation:
- **Electrolysis** is a **Process** that uses electricity to drive chemical reactions, **Producing** various products while being influenced by factors such as current and electrolyte concentration.

FARADAY'S LAWS OF ELECTROLYSIS

Mnemonic: **Faraday Calculates Mass**

- **F** — Faraday's First Law
- **C** — Calculates Charge
- **M** — Mass of Substance

Explanation:
- **Faraday's Laws of Electrolysis** state that the **Mass** of a substance produced or consumed during electrolysis can be calculated based on the amount of electric charge passed through the system.

CONCENTRATION CELLS

Mnemonic: **Concentration Creates Potential**

- **C** — Concentration Difference
- **C** — Creates Voltage
- **P** — Potential Calculation

Explanation:
- **Concentration Cells** generate electrical energy based on the Concentration difference of the same species in two half-cells, which Creates Potential driving the electrochemical reaction.

BATTERY TYPES

Mnemonic: **Primary and Secondary Power**

- **P** — Primary Batteries
- **S** — Secondary Batteries
- **P** — Power Sources

Explanation:
- **Battery Types** include **Primary** batteries, which are non-rechargeable and designed for single use, and Secondary batteries, which are rechargeable and can be reused multiple times, providing different options for powering devices.

POLAROGRAPHY

Mnemonic: **Polarography Analyzes Metals**

- **P** — Polarography Principle
- **A** — Analyzes Solutions
- **M** — Metal Ion Detection

Explanation:
- **Polarography** is a method that Analyzes Metals in solution by measuring the current response to voltage changes, helping to identify and quantify metal ion concentrations.

ELECTROCHEMICAL SENSORS

Mnemonic: **Sensors Measure Analytes**

- **S** — Sensors
- **M** — Measure Concentrations
- **A** — Analytes Monitored

Explanation:
- **Electrochemical Sensors** detect changes in electrical properties to Measure specific Analytes, playing a crucial role in various applications from medical diagnostics to environmental monitoring.

BIOELECTROCHEMISTRY

Mnemonic: **Bioelectrochemistry Bridges Applications**

- **B** — Basic Principles
- **B** — Bridges Disciplines
- **A** — Applications

Explanation:
- **Bioelectrochemistry** examines the principles of electron transfer in biological contexts, **Bridging** disciplines and leading to applications in medicine and biotechnology.

CHEAT SHEET

AMINO ACIDS & PROTEINS	
Non-standard Amino Acids	• Amino acids that are not among the 20 standard amino acids used during translation. These include selenocysteine and pyrrolysine (genetically encoded) and post-translationally modified amino acids like hydroxyproline.
Post-translational Modifications (PTMs)	• Covalent modifications of proteins after translation, such as phosphorylation, glycosylation, and acetylation, which regulate protein activity, localization, and stability.
Protein Folding	• The process by which a protein achieves its functional three-dimensional structure.
Protein Misfolding	• Incorrect folding that can lead to inactive proteins or aggregation, often implicated in diseases like Alzheimer's and Parkinson's.
Protein Domains	• Independently folding, functional regions of a protein, often associated with specific activities (e.g., kinase domain).
Protein Motifs	• Short, recurring sequences or structural patterns in proteins, often associated with a particular function (e.g., zinc finger motif).
Protein-Protein Interactions	• Specific physical contacts between proteins that are critical for cellular processes, including signaling, structural assembly, and enzymatic pathways.
Protein-Ligand Interactions	• Binding between a protein and a ligand (small molecule, ion, or another macromolecule), which is often central to the protein's function (e.g., enzyme-substrate binding).
Enzyme Kinetics	• The study of the rates of enzyme-catalyzed reactions and how they change in response to variables like substrate concentration, pH, and temperature.
Allosteric Regulation of Enzymes	• Modulation of enzyme activity through the binding of effectors (activators or inhibitors) at a site other than the active site, altering the enzyme's shape and function.

Protein-Nucleic Acid Interactions	• Specific binding between proteins and DNA or RNA, which is critical for processes like transcription, translation, replication, and repair. Examples include transcription factors and RNA-binding proteins.
Peptide Bond	• A covalent bond formed between the carboxyl group of one amino acid and the amino group of another, linking amino acids in a protein chain.
Polypeptide	• A long chain of amino acids linked by peptide bonds. Polypeptides fold to form functional proteins.
Primary Structure	• The linear sequence of amino acids in a protein, determined by the gene encoding the protein. This sequence dictates the protein's final shape and function.
Secondary Structure	• The localized folding of a protein into structures such as alpha-helices and beta-pleated sheets, stabilized by hydrogen bonds between backbone atoms.
Tertiary Structure	• The three-dimensional shape of a protein formed by interactions between the side chains (R groups) of amino acids, including hydrophobic interactions, hydrogen bonds, disulfide bonds, and ionic interactions.

ENZYMES	
Allosteric Regulation of Enzymes	• The regulation of an enzyme's activity through the binding of an effector molecule (allosteric modulator) at a site other than the active site.
Allosteric Activators	• increase activity.
Allosteric Inhibitors	• decrease activity.
Covalent Modification of Enzymes	• The regulation of enzyme activity through the addition or removal of chemical groups (such as phosphate, methyl, or acetyl groups) via covalent bonds.
Isozymes	• Isozymes are often found in different tissues or at different developmental stages of an organism.

Ribozymes	- RNA molecules that have catalytic activity, capable of speeding up specific biochemical reactions, similar to protein enzymes. Ribozymes are involved in processes such as RNA splicing and protein synthesis.
Cofactors	- Non-protein molecules that are essential for enzyme activity, often metal ions like magnesium (Mg^{2+}) or zinc (Zn^{2+}).
Coenzymes	- Organic cofactors, often derived from vitamins, that assist enzymes in catalyzing reactions. They often serve as carriers for chemical groups.
Enzyme Inhibition	- The process by which the activity of an enzyme is reduced or stopped.
Competitive inhibitors	- Compete with the substrate for the active site.
Non-competitive inhibitors	- Bind to a site other than the active site, changing the enzyme's shape.
Uncompetitive inhibitors	- Bind to the enzyme-substrate complex.
Enzyme Engineering	- The process of modifying an enzyme's structure, often through genetic engineering or directed evolution, to enhance its activity, stability, or specificity for industrial, medical, or research applications.
Enzyme Specificity	- The ability of an enzyme to selectively bind and catalyze the reaction of a particular substrate (or group of related substrates) while ignoring others.
Enzyme Mechanisms	- The detailed step-by-step process by which an enzyme catalyzes a specific reaction. This includes the binding of the substrate, the transition state, and the formation of the products.

NON ENZYME PROTEIN FUNCTION & ANALYSIS

Structural Proteins	• Proteins that provide support and shape to cells, tissues, and organs. They form the structural framework of cells and organisms, contributing to mechanical strength and stability.
Motor Proteins	• Proteins that convert chemical energy stored in ATP into mechanical work, enabling movement within cells and the body.
Transport Proteins	• Proteins that facilitate the movement of molecules or ions across membranes or within the bloodstream.
Storage Proteins	• Proteins that store nutrients or ions for later use. These proteins ensure the availability of essential substances when needed.
Hormonal Proteins	• Proteins that act as hormones, which are chemical messengers regulating physiological processes such as metabolism, growth, and immune function.
Receptor Proteins	• Membrane-bound or cytoplasmic proteins that bind to specific signaling molecules (ligands) and trigger a cellular response.
Protein Analysis Techniques	• Methods used to study proteins, including their structure, function, interactions, and expression.
Proteomics	• The large-scale study of proteins, particularly focusing on the identification, quantification, and analysis of their functions, interactions, and modifications within a biological system.
Protein Purification Techniques	• Methods used to isolate a specific protein from a mixture of proteins or biological samples.
Protein-Protein Interactions (PPIs)	• The study of how proteins interact with one another to form complexes that drive cellular processes such as signaling, gene regulation, and immune responses.
Protein Structural Analysis	• The determination of a protein's three-dimensional structure using techniques like X-ray crystallography, nuclear magnetic resonance (NMR) spectroscopy, and cryo-electron microscopy (cryo-EM) to understand how structure relates to function in non-enzymatic proteins.

Post-Translational Modifications (PTMs)	• Modifications that occur after protein synthesis, such as phosphorylation, glycosylation, and ubiquitination, which can regulate protein activity, localization, stability, and interactions, particularly in signaling and regulatory proteins.
Protein Localization and Trafficking	• The study of where proteins are located within a cell and how they move between different compartments (such as the nucleus, cytoplasm, and membrane-bound organelles), which is important for understanding their roles in cellular functions like transport, signal transduction, and regulation.
Protein-Ligand Binding	• The interaction between a protein and a small molecule (ligand), such as hormones, metabolites, or nucleic acids.

CARBOHYDRATE STRUCTURE & FUNCTION

Disaccharides	• Carbohydrates composed of two monosaccharide units joined by a glycosidic bond. These sugars are broken down into monosaccharides during digestion and serve as a source of energy.
Polysaccharides	• Long chains of monosaccharide units linked by glycosidic bonds, serving as energy storage or structural components in organisms.
Glycoconjugates	• Compounds in which carbohydrates (usually oligosaccharides) are covalently bonded to other molecules, such as proteins or lipids.
Carbohydrate Metabolism	• The set of biochemical pathways through which cells process carbohydrates to extract energy and build essential molecules.
Glycolysis	• The metabolic pathway in which one molecule of glucose is broken down into two molecules of pyruvate, producing energy in the form of ATP and NADH.
Gluconeogenesis	• The process of synthesizing glucose from non-carbohydrate precursors such as lactate, pyruvate, and amino acids.

Carbohydrate Metabolism Disorders	• Disorders resulting from defects in the enzymes or pathways involved in carbohydrate metabolism.
Dietary Fiber	• The indigestible portion of plant-based foods, primarily composed of cellulose, hemicellulose, pectin, and other polysaccharides.
Carbohydrate-Based Vaccines	• Vaccines that use carbohydrate antigens (often polysaccharides from bacterial capsules) to stimulate an immune response.
Glycosidic Bond Formation	• The chemical bond formed between two monosaccharides to create disaccharides, oligosaccharides, and polysaccharides.
Carbohydrate Recognition	• The ability of cells and proteins to specifically identify and bind to carbohydrate structures, often in the form of glycoproteins or glycolipids.
Signaling	• refers to the processes by which cells communicate and respond to external or internal stimuli to regulate various biological functions.
Glycobiology	• The study of the structure, function, and biology of carbohydrates and their derivatives, including how they influence cell function, gene expression, and development.
Glycogen	• A process in which carbohydrates, often attached to proteins or lipids (glycosylation), participate in the transmission of signals between cells.
Starch Metabolism	• The processes by which starch (the primary carbohydrate storage form in plants) is synthesized, stored, and broken down in plants.
Carbohydrate-Protein Interactions	• The interactions between carbohydrates and proteins, particularly in the form of glycoproteins and lectins, which play key roles in immune function, cell signaling, and molecular recognition.

LIPID STRUCTURE AND FUNCTION

Fatty Acid Structure	• Fatty acids are long hydrocarbon chains with a carboxyl group (-COOH) at one end.
Saturated fatty acids	• have no double bonds (e.g., stearic acid).
Unsaturated fatty acids	• have one or more double bonds (e.g., oleic acid with one double bond or linoleic acid with two double bonds).
Triacylglycerols (Triglycerides)	• A type of lipid composed of three fatty acids esterified to a glycerol molecule. Triacylglycerols are the primary form of stored fat in animals and serve as a concentrated energy source.
Phospholipids	• Lipids that contain a glycerol backbone, two fatty acid tails, and a phosphate group attached to the third carbon of glycerol.
Steroids	• A class of lipids characterized by a core structure of four fused carbon rings.
Eicosanoids	• A group of bioactive lipids derived from arachidonic acid, a 20-carbon polyunsaturated fatty acid.
Lipid Metabolism	• The process by which lipids (fats) are broken down, synthesized, and utilized by the body for energy production, cell structure, and signaling.
Beta-Oxidation	• the process by which fatty acids are broken down in the mitochondria to produce acetyl-CoA, which enters the citric acid cycle (Krebs cycle) to generate ATP.
Lipid Storage Diseases	• A group of inherited metabolic disorders in which abnormal storage of lipids (such as sphingolipids, cholesterol, or triglycerides) occurs within cells due to enzyme deficiencies.
Lipoprotein Metabolism	• The process by which lipoproteins (complexes of lipids and proteins) are synthesized, transported, and utilized in the body.

30 Day MCAT

Lipid Signaling Pathways	• Lipids play key roles in cell signaling, with molecules like eicosanoids and phosphoinositides acting as second messengers in pathways that regulate inflammation, immune responses, and cell growth.
Membrane Lipids and Membrane Fluidity	• his topic explores the role of lipids, particularly phospholipids, in forming cell membranes and how their structure (e.g., fatty acid composition) affects membrane fluidity, permeability, and function.
Fatty Acid Composition and Health	• The impact of different types of fatty acids (saturated, unsaturated, trans fats) on health, including their effects on cardiovascular health, inflammation, and metabolic disorders. This
Lipid Signaling Pathways	• Lipids play key roles in cell signaling, with molecules like eicosanoids and phosphoinositides acting as second messengers in pathways that regulate inflammation, immune responses, and cell growth.
Cholesterol Metabolism and Function	• This topic covers cholesterol synthesis, transport (e.g., LDL, HDL), and its roles in cellular processes, as well as its association with cardiovascular diseases.
Lipid Droplets and Lipid Storage	• Lipid droplets are dynamic organelles that store neutral lipids (triglycerides and sterol esters) in cells.

DNA & BIOTECHNOLOGY

DNA Structure	• DNA (Deoxyribonucleic Acid) is a double-stranded molecule composed of nucleotides, each containing a sugar (deoxyribose), a phosphate group, and a nitrogenous base (adenine, thymine, cytosine, or guanine).
DNA Function	• DNA functions as the genetic blueprint for all living organisms, storing and transmitting genetic information required for growth, development, and reproduction. It is the template for gene expression and cell division.
DNA Replication	• DNA replication is the process by which a cell duplicates its DNA to ensure that each daughter cell receives an identical copy of the genetic material.

Transcription	• Transcription is the process by which an RNA molecule is synthesized from a DNA template.
Translation	• Translation is the process by which the information encoded in messenger RNA (mRNA) is used to synthesize proteins.
Genetic Code	• The genetic code is the set of rules by which information encoded in the DNA or RNA sequence is translated into proteins.
DNA Repair Mechanisms	• DNA repair mechanisms are processes by which cells detect and correct damage to the DNA molecules.
DNA Sequencing	• DNA sequencing is the process of determining the exact sequence of nucleotides (adenine, thymine, cytosine, and guanine) in a DNA molecule.
CRISPR-Cas9 Gene Editing	• RISPR-Cas9 is a revolutionary gene-editing technology that allows precise modification of the DNA in living organisms.
Gene Therapy	• Gene therapy is a medical treatment that involves altering the genes inside a person's cells to treat or prevent disease.

RNA AND THE GENETIC CODE

RNA Structure and Function	• RNA (Ribonucleic Acid) is a single-stranded nucleic acid composed of a backbone of ribose sugar and phosphate groups, with nitrogenous bases (adenine, uracil, cytosine, and guanine).
RNA Transcription	• RNA transcription is the process by which a segment of DNA is copied into RNA, specifically messenger RNA (mRNA), by the enzyme RNA polymerase. This occurs in the nucleus of eukaryotic cells (or the cytoplasm in prokaryotes).

RNA Processing	• RNA processing refers to the modifications that a primary RNA transcript undergoes to become a mature, functional mRNA molecule.
Capping	• A 5' cap is added to the beginning of the RNA transcript, which protects it from degradation and assists in translation.
Splicing	• Non-coding regions (introns) are removed from the RNA transcript, and the coding regions (exons) are joined together to form a continuous sequence.
Polyadenylation	• A poly-A tail is added to the 3' end of the RNA, which enhances stability and facilitates export from the nucleus.
Genetic Code	• The genetic code is a set of rules that define how sequences of nucleotide bases (adenine, thymine, cytosine, and guanine) in DNA or RNA are translated into the amino acid sequence of proteins.
RNA Editing	• RNA editing is a post-transcriptional process in which the RNA sequence is altered after it has been transcribed from DNA.
Ribosome Structure and Function	• The ribosome is a molecular machine composed of ribosomal RNA (rRNA) and proteins. The ribosome reads the mRNA sequence and uses transfer RNA (tRNA) to add amino acids in the correct order, forming a polypeptide chain.
Ribozymes	• Ribozymes are RNA molecules that have catalytic properties, meaning they can facilitate chemical reactions without the need for proteins.
Non-coding RNA:	• Non-coding RNAs are RNA molecules that do not encode proteins but play vital regulatory roles in gene expression and cellular processes.
RNA Interference (RNAi)	• RNA interference is a biological process where RNA molecules inhibit gene expression by degrading specific mRNA molecules or by blocking their translation.

BIOLOGICAL MEMBRANES

Membrane Fluidity	• Membrane fluidity refers to the flexibility and movement of the lipid bilayer in biological membranes.
Membrane Transport:	• Membrane transport is the process by which substances move across the cell membrane.
Passive diffusion	• Movement of molecules from high to low concentration without energy.
Facilitated diffusion	• Movement of molecules across the membrane via carrier or channel proteins, still without energy.
Active transport:	• Movement of molecules against their concentration gradient, requiring energy, typically from ATP.
Membrane Protein	• Membrane proteins are proteins that are embedded in or attached to the cell membrane.
Integral (transmembrane) proteins	• Proteins that span the entire lipid bilayer, often serving as channels or transporters.
Peripheral proteins	• Proteins that are temporarily attached to the membrane surface, often involved in signaling or cell recognition.
Lipid Rafts	• Lipid rafts are specialized microdomains within the plasma membrane that are enriched with certain lipids (such as cholesterol and sphingolipids) and proteins.
Ion Channels:	• Ion channels are membrane proteins that allow the selective passage of ions (such as sodium, potassium, calcium, and chloride) across the cell membrane
Carrier Proteins:	• Carrier proteins are membrane proteins that facilitate the transport of specific molecules across the cell membrane.
Synaptic Transmission:	• Synaptic transmission is the process by which nerve cells (neurons) communicate with each other across synapses.

Action Potential:	• An action potential is a rapid, transient change in the membrane potential of a neuron or muscle cell that occurs when a cell's membrane becomes depolarized
Membrane Potential:	• The difference in electric charge across the cell membrane, typically between the inside and outside of the cell.
Endocytosis and Exocytosis:	• Processes by which cells internalize substances (endocytosis) or expel substances (exocytosis) by vesicles fusing with the plasma membrane.
Transmembrane Proteins:	• Proteins that span across the entire lipid bilayer, involved in various functions such as transport (channels and carriers), signaling, and maintaining cell structure.
Osmosis:	• The movement of water across a semipermeable membrane from an area of lower solute concentration to an area of higher solute concentration.
Membrane Receptors:	• Specialized proteins located on the cell membrane that bind to signaling molecules (like hormones or neurotransmitters), triggering intracellular signaling pathways that influence cellular behavior and responses.

CARBOHYDRATE METABOLISM I (GLUCOSE TRANSPPORT, GLYCOLYSIS, OTHER MONOSACCHARIDES, PYRUVATE DEHYDROGENASE, GLYCOGENESIS & GLYCOGENOLYSIS, GLUCONEOGENESIS)

Glucose Transporters (GLUTs):	• are a family of membrane proteins responsible for the facilitated transport of glucose across cell membranes.
Glycolysis Regulation:	• Glycolysis is a key metabolic pathway that breaks down glucose to produce energy in the form of ATP
Pyruvate Dehydrogenase Complex (PDC):	• The PDC is a multi-enzyme complex that converts pyruvate, the end product of glycolysis, into acetyl-CoA, which then enters the tricarboxylic acid (TCA) cycle for further energy production.

Cori Cycle:	• the Cori cycle is a metabolic pathway that involves the conversion of lactate produced by muscles during anaerobic metabolism into glucose in the liver.
Diabetes Mellitus:	• Diabetes mellitus is a group of metabolic disorders characterized by elevated blood glucose levels (hyperglycemia).
Hormonal Regulation of Glucose Metabolism:	• The regulation of glucose metabolism is controlled by hormones such as insulin and glucagon.
Galactose Metabolism:	• Galactose metabolism involves the conversion of galactose, a sugar found in milk and dairy products, into glucose through a series of enzymatic reactions
Glycogenolysis Regulation	• Glycogenolysis is the process by which glycogen is broken down into glucose-1-phosphate, which is then converted into glucose for energy use
Gluconeogenesis Regulation	• Gluconeogenesis is the synthesis of glucose from non-carbohydrate precursors like lactate, glycerol, and amino acids.

CARBOHYDRATE METABOLISM II (ACETYL-COA, REACTIONS OF THE CITRIC ACID CYCLE, ELECTRON TRANSPORT CHAIN, OXIDATIVE PHOSPHORYLATION)

Electron Transport Chain Complexes	• The Electron Transport Chain (ETC) consists of a series of protein complexes (I-IV) embedded in the inner mitochondrial membrane.
Oxidative Phosphorylation Coupling	• This process couples electron transport through the ETC with ATP synthesis. The movement of electrons drives the pumping of protons across the mitochondrial inner membrane, creating a proton motive force.
Electron transport	• The flow of electrons through the electron transport chain generates energy used to pump protons across the mitochondrial inner membrane.
Motive force	• Refers to the electrochemical gradient (proton motive force) created by the differential concentration of protons across the membrane.

ATP synthesis	- The process by which the energy stored in the proton gradient is harnessed by ATP synthase to produce ATP.
ATP Synthase	- is an enzyme complex located in the inner mitochondrial membrane that synthesizes ATP.
Respiratory Control	- refers to the regulation of oxidative phosphorylation by cellular energy demands.
Proton motive force	- The driving force for ATP synthesis, generated by the electron transport chain.
Uncoupling agents	- Molecules like DNP (dinitrophenol) that dissipate the proton gradient by allowing protons to re-enter the mitochondrial matrix without passing through ATP synthase.
Heat production	- Instead of producing ATP, the energy from the proton gradient is released as heat.
Reactive oxygen species	- Highly reactive molecules, such as superoxide and hydrogen peroxide, formed as byproducts of the electron transport chain.
Detoxify	- Cells use enzymes like superoxide dismutase and catalase to neutralize ROS.
Protect cells	- Antioxidants and detoxifying enzymes prevent cellular damage caused by oxidative stress.
Acetyl-CoA as a Metabolic Hub	- refers to the regulation of oxidative phosphorylation by cellular energy demands.
Brown adipose tissue	- A specialized type of fat tissue rich in mitochondria, involved in thermogenesis.
Ketogenesis	- is the biochemical process by which the liver produces ketone bodies (acetoacetate, β-hydroxybutyrate, and acetone) from acetyl-CoA.

LIPID AND AMINO ACID METABOLISM

Beta-Oxidation of Fatty Acids	• is the process by which fatty acids are broken down in the mitochondria to generate acetyl-CoA, NADH, and FADH2.
Fatty Acid Synthesis	• is the process of creating long-chain fatty acids from acetyl-CoA in the cytoplasm.
Cholesterol synthesis	• occurs primarily in the liver and involves the conversion of acetyl-CoA into cholesterol
Lipid Transport and Lipoproteins	• Lipid transport in the blood is mediated by lipoproteins, which are complexes of lipids and proteins.
VLDL (Very-Low-Density Lipoproteins)	• Deliver triglycerides synthesized in the liver.
Amino Acid Catabolism	• involves the breakdown of amino acids for energy or other metabolic processes.
Transamination	• Transfer of the amino group to form keto acids
Deamination	• Removal of the amino group as ammonia.
Urea cycle	• Conversion of ammonia into urea for excretion.
Essential Amino Acids	• are amino acids that the body cannot synthesize and must be obtained from the diet.
Ketogenic Amino Acids	• are amino acids that are metabolized into acetyl-CoA or acetoacetate, which can be used for ketone body production.
Amino Acid Neurotransmitters	• Certain amino acids act as neurotransmitters in the nervous system.
Eicosanoid Synthesis	• are signaling molecules derived from arachidonic acid, a polyunsaturated fatty acid

BIOENERGETICS AND REGULATION OF METABOLISM

Metabolic pathways	• are sequences of biochemical reactions within cells that convert substrates into products.
Glycolysis	• Breakdown of glucose to pyruvate, generating ATP and NADH.
Citric Acid Cycle	• Oxidation of acetyl-CoA to produce NADH, FADH2, and CO2.
Electron Transport Chain	• Utilization of NADH and FADH2 to generate ATP through oxidative phosphorylation.
Energy Coupling	• links exergonic (energy-releasing) reactions to endergonic (energy-requiring) reactions via molecules like ATP.
Redox Reactions in Metabolism	• (oxidation-reduction) involve the transfer of electrons between molecules.
Hormonal Regulation of Metabolism	• Metabolic pathways are regulated by hormones to maintain energy balance.
Insulin	• Promotes glucose uptake, glycogenesis, and lipogenesis.
Glucagon	• Stimulates glycogenolysis and gluconeogenesis during fasting.
Epinephrine	• Enhances glycogenolysis and lipolysis during stress.
Cortisol	• Regulates glucose and protein metabolism under prolonged stress.
Metabolic control analysis	• identifies the regulation points within metabolic pathways.
Flux	• The rate at which substrates flow through a pathway.

Metabolic Flux Analysis	• quantifies the rates of reactions within metabolic pathways, determining the flow of metabolites through cellular processes.
Obesity and Metabolic Disorders	• is characterized by excessive fat accumulation and is linked to metabolic disorders
Insulin resistance	• Reduced response to insulin, leading to hyperglycemia.
Type 2 diabetes	• Chronic condition associated with impaired glucose regulation.
Cardiovascular disease	• Resulting from dyslipidemia and inflammation.
Cancer Metabolism	• refers to the altered metabolic processes in cancer cells. A hallmark is the Warburg effect, where cancer cells preferentially use glycolysis for energy production even in the presence of oxygen.
Circadian Rhythms and Metabolism	• Circadian rhythms are 24-hour biological cycles that regulate metabolic processes, including glucose and lipid metabolism. The circadian clock aligns energy production and storage with periods of activity and rest, optimizing cellular functions and maintaining metabolic health.
Beta-Oxidation	• Breakdown of fatty acids in mitochondria to produce acetyl-CoA, NADH, and $FADH_2$.
Ketogenesis	• Formation of ketone bodies from acetyl-CoA during prolonged fasting or carbohydrate restriction.

Thermogenesis	• Generation of heat through metabolic activity, particularly in brown adipose tissue via uncoupling proteins.
mTOR Pathway	• Activated by low energy (high AMP/ATP ratio) to promote catabolic processes.
Oxidative Stress and Antioxidant Defense	• Imbalance between reactive oxygen species (ROS) production and elimination can damage cells. • Antioxidant systems like glutathione play a protective role.

AMINO ACIDS & PROTEINS

NON-STANDARD AMINO ACIDS

Mnemonic: **Non-Standard Players**

- **N** Non-proteinogenic (amino acids not used in proteins)
- **S** Selenocysteine (an essential non-standard amino acid)
- **P** Pyrrolysine (found in certain bacteria and archaea)

Explanation:
- Non-standard amino acids like **Selenocysteine** and **Pyrrolysine** play unique roles outside standard protein synthesis, contributing to specialized functions in certain organisms.

POST-TRANSLATIONAL MODIFICATIONS

Mnemonic: **Some Play It Cool**

- **S** Sumoylation
- **P** Phosphorylation
- **I** Iodination
- **C** Carboxylation

Explanation:
- Post-translational modifications like **Phosphorylation** and **Sumoylation** alter protein function, stability, and cellular location, influencing overall cellular activity.

PROTEIN FOLDING AND MISFOLDING

Mnemonic: **Fold Carefully, Stay Functional**

- **F** Folding
- **C** Chaperones (assist in folding)
- **S** Stress (can lead to misfolding)
- **F** Functional state (achieved by proper folding)

Explanation:
- Post-translational modifications like **Phosphorylation** and **Sumoylation** alter protein function, stability, and cellular location, influencing overall cellular activity.

30 Day MCAT

PROTEIN DOMAINS AND MOTIFS

Mnemonic: **Do Make Sense**

- **D** — Domains
- **M** — Motifs
- **S** — Specificity

Explanation:
- **Domains** and **Motifs** in proteins provide **Specificity** and modular functionality, enabling proteins to perform complex tasks efficiently.

PROTEIN-PROTEIN INTERACTIONS

Mnemonic: **Form Powerful Partnerships**

- **F** — Functional binding
- **P** — Protein complexes
- **P** — Pathways (cellular pathways influenced)

Explanation:
- **Protein complexes** formed through **Functional binding** are essential for regulating **Pathways** and coordinating cellular responses.

PROTEIN-LIGAND INTERACTIONS

Mnemonic: **Ligands Find Spots**

- **L** — Ligand (the molecule that binds)
- **F** — Fit (complementary shapes)
- **S** — Specificity (determines binding success)

Explanation:
- **Ligands** bind to proteins through Fit and Specificity, enabling precise molecular interactions critical for cellular functions.

ENZYME KINETICS

Mnemonic: **Michael Must Know**

M — Michaelis-Menten equation
M — Maximal rate (Vmax)
K — Km (affinity constant)

Explanation:
- The **Michaelis-Menten** equation describes the relationship between substrate concentration and reaction rate, where Vmax and Km reveal enzyme efficiency and affinity.

ALLOSTERIC REGULATION OF ENZYMES

Mnemonic: **Allosteric Sites Adjust**

A — Allosteric site
S — Site-specific (binding influences function)
A — Activator or Inhibitor

Explanation:
- **Allosteric** sites allow activators or inhibitors to bind, modulating enzyme function by altering its shape and activity without affecting the active site.

PROTEIN-NUCLEIC ACID INTERACTIONS

Mnemonic: **DNA Meets Proteins**

D — DNA-binding proteins
M — Motifs (recognize nucleic acids)
P — Protein-DNA/RNA interactions

Explanation:
- **Protein-nucleic acid interactions** involve specific Motifs in proteins that enable them to bind DNA or RNA, playing essential roles in gene expression and regulation.

30 Day MCAT

ENZYMES

ALLOSTERIC REGULATION OF ENZYMES

Mnemonic: **Allosteric Adjustments**

- **A** — Allosteric site
- **A** — Activator or Inhibitor (binds to allosteric site)

Explanation:
- **Allosteric regulation** involves effectors binding to a site other than the active site, allowing **Activators** or **Inhibitors** to modulate enzyme activity, either enhancing or reducing the enzyme's function.

COVALENT MODIFICATION OF ENZYMES

Mnemonic: **Covalent Change Control**

- **C** — Covalent modification (e.g., phosphorylation)
- **C** — Control (regulates activity)

Explanation:
- **Covalent modifications** like **Phosphorylation** add or remove functional groups, controlling enzyme activity by altering its structure and function in response to cellular signals.

ISOZYMES

Mnemonic: **I See Variety**

- **I** — Isozymes (enzyme variants)
- **S** — Specificity (vary by tissue)
- **V** — Variability in function

Explanation:
- **Isozymes** are different forms of an enzyme that catalyze the same reaction but differ in Specificity or kinetic properties, providing Variability across tissues.

RIBOZYMES

Mnemonic: **RNA Catalysts**

- **R** — Ribozyme
- **N** — Nucleotide (RNA-based structure)
- **C** — Catalysis (promotes reactions)

Explanation:
- **Ribozymes** are **RNA** molecules that can act as catalysts, facilitating reactions such as peptide bond formation, demonstrating that not all enzymes are proteins.

ENZYME COFACTORS AND COENZYMES

Mnemonic: **Co-Pilots for Reactions**

- **C** — Cofactors (metal ions or organic molecules)
- **P** — Partners in catalysis
- **R** — Reactions (facilitated by enzyme cofactors)

Explanation:
- **Cofactors** and **Coenzymes** like metal ions or vitamins act as partners in Reactions, assisting enzymes in achieving catalytic activity.

ENZYME INHIBITION

Mnemonic: **Can Not Unbind**

- **C** — Competitive inhibition
- **N** — Non-competitive inhibition
- **U** — Uncompetitive inhibition

Explanation:
- **Enzyme Inhibition** types include **Competitive** (competes with substrate), **Non-competitive** (binds to the enzyme alone), and **Uncompetitive** (binds only to enzyme-substrate complex), each affecting enzyme activity differently

ENZYME ENGINEERING

Mnemonic: **Enhance, Alter, Improve**

- **E** — Enhance stability
- **A** — Alter specificity
- **I** — Improve catalytic activity

Explanation:
- **Enzyme engineering** involves methods to **Enhance** stability, **Alter** substrate specificity, or **Improve** catalytic efficiency, tailoring enzymes for industrial and therapeutic applications.

ENZYME SPECIFICITY

Mnemonic: **Specific Substrate Selection**

- **S** — Specificity (unique to substrate)
- **S** — Substrate (only specific ones bind)

Explanation:
- **Enzyme specificity** ensures that each enzyme catalyzes only one specific reaction, recognizing only a particular **Substrate**, which is critical for precise biochemical pathways.

ENZYME MECHANISMS

Mnemonic: **Catalysis Methods Matter**

- **C** — Covalent catalysis (involves covalent bonds)
- **N** — Metal ion catalysis
- **U** — Methods (different ways enzymes catalyze)

Explanation:
- **Enzyme mechanisms** like **Covalent** catalysis and **Metal ion catalysis** are distinct methods by which enzymes facilitate chemical reactions, often improving reaction speed and efficiency.

NON ENZYME PROTEIN FUNCTION

STRUCTURAL PROTEINS

Mnemonic: **Keen Cats Enjoy Actively Climbing**

- **K** — Keratin
- **C** — Collagen
- **E** — Elastin
- **A** — Actin
- **C** — Cytoskeleton (structural role)

Explanation:
- **Structural proteins** like **Keratin, Collagen**, and **Actin** form the **Cytoskeleton** and provide essential support and stability to cells and tissues.

MOTOR PROTEINS

Mnemonic: **My Kin Moves**

- **M** — Myosin
- **K** — Kinesin
- **M** — Movement (Cell Transport & Muscle Movement)

Explanation:
- **Motor proteins** like **Myosin** and **Kinesin** enable cellular **Movement**, transporting cargo within cells and facilitating muscle contractions.

TRANSPORT PROTEINS

Mnemonic: **Hitch A Ride**

- **H** — Hemoglobin (oxygen transport)
- **A** — Albumin (transports various molecules)
- **R** — Ride (movement through the body)

Explanation:
- **Transport proteins** such as **Hemoglobin** and **Albumin** move essential molecules like oxygen and nutrients throughout the body, aiding in circulation and cellular function.

STORAGE PROTEINS

Mnemonic: **Feed Cats First**

- **F** — Ferritin (stores iron)
- **C** — Casein (stores amino acids)
- **F** — Fuel (stored nutrients)

Explanation:
- **Storage proteins** like **Ferritin** and **Casein** help maintain essential nutrients, providing a Fuel reserve for biological processes.

HORMONAL PROTEINS

Mnemonic: **Insulin Grows**

- **I** — Insulin (regulates blood sugar)
- **G** — Growth hormone (stimulates growth)

Explanation:
- **Hormonal proteins** like Insulin and Growth hormone regulate physiological processes, controlling metabolism and promoting growth in tissues.

RECEPTOR PROTEINS

Mnemonic: **Receive Signals Clearly**

- **C** — Receptor (binds signaling molecules)
- **S** — Signal transduction
- **C** — Cell communication

Explanation:
- **Receptor proteins** are involved in Signal transduction and play a crucial role in Cell communication by binding to specific signaling molecules.

PROTEIN ANALYSIS TECHNIQUES

Mnemonic: **Analyze Structure and Shape**

- **A** — **A**nalysis (of proteins)
- **S** — **S**tructure determination
- **S** — **S**hape (determines function)

Explanation:
- **Protein analysis techniques** focus on Structure and Shape determination to understand protein function and interactions.

PROTEOMICS

Mnemonic: **Proteomics**

- **P** — **P**rofiling (all proteins in a cell)
- **P** — **Pr**oteins
- **P** — **P**erfectly (accurate quantification)

Explanation:
- **Proteomics** involves **Profiling** proteins in a cell, identifying and quantifying them to understand cellular functions and pathways.

PROTEIN PURIFICATION TECHNIQUES

Mnemonic: **Can Precipitate Pure Protein**

- **C** — **C**hromatography
- **N** — **P**recipitation
- **U** — **P**urification (isolates desired protein)

Explanation:
- **Protein purification techniques** like **Chromatography** and Precipitation are used to Purify proteins for study or industrial use, separating them from complex mixtures.

CARBS STRUCTURE & FUNCTION

DISACCHARIDES

Mnemonic: **Silly Lazy Monks**

- **S** — Sucrose (glucose + fructose)
- **L** — Lactose (glucose + galactose)
- **M** — Maltose (glucose + glucose)

Explanation:
- **Disaccharides** like **Sucrose**, **Lactose**, and **Maltose** are crucial for Energy storage and transport, supplying sugars needed for cellular metabolism.

POLYSACCHARIDES

Mnemonic: **Sticky Giants Climb Cells**

- **S** — Starch (energy storage in plants)
- **G** — Glycogen (energy storage in animals)
- **C** — Chitin (structural support in fungi and exoskeletons)
- **C** — Cellulose (structural component in plants)

Explanation:
- **Polysaccharides** like **Starch** and **Glycogen** serve as **Energy storage**, while **Cellulose** and **Chitin** provide **Structural support**.

GLYCOCONJUGATES

Mnemonic: **Great Signals**

- **G** — Glycoproteins
- **S** — Signaling (cell-cell recognition)

Explanation:
- **Glycoconjugates** like **Glycoproteins** are involved in **Cell signaling** and recognition, allowing cells to communicate and respond to their environment.

CARBOHYDRATE METABOLISM

Mnemonic: **Great Gears Go Smoothly**

- **G** Glycolysis (breaks down glucose)
- **G** Gluconeogenesis (creates glucose from non-carb)
- **G** Glycogenolysis (breaks down glycogen)
- **S** Synthesis (builds glycogen)

Explanation:
- **Carbohydrate metabolism** involves processes like **Glycolysis** and **Gluconeogenesis**, regulated by enzymes that balance **Energy production** and storage.

GLYCOLYSIS

Mnemonic: **Get Energy Fast**

- **G** Glucose (starting molecule)
- **E** Energy investment phase (uses ATP)
- **F** Fructose-1,6-bisphosphate (key intermediate)

Explanation:
- **Glycolysis** is a metabolic pathway that converts **Glucose** to pyruvate, generating ATP and NADH in an **Energy payoff** phase following an initial investment.

GLUCONEOGENESIS

Mnemonic: **New Glucose Pathway**

- **N** Non-carbohydrate precursors (like amino acids)
- **G** Glucose production
- **P** Pathway for glucose synthesis

Explanation:
- **Gluconeogenesis** synthesizes **Glucose** from **Non-carbohydrate** sources, maintaining blood sugar levels during fasting or low-carb intake.

CARBOHYDRATE METABOLISM DISORDERS

Mnemonic: **Don't Give In**

- **D** — Diabetes mellitus
- **G** — Galactosemia
- **I** — Inborn errors like glycogen storage diseases

Explanation:
- **Carbohydrate metabolism disorders** include **Diabetes** and **Galactosemia**, where **Inborn errors** disrupt normal sugar processing and storage.

DIETARY FIBER

Mnemonic: **Fiber Fuels Gut**

- **F** — Fiber
- **F** — Fuel for gut bacteria
- **G** — Gut health

Explanation:
- **Dietary fiber** promotes **Gut health** by fueling beneficial bacteria and supports digestion, helping prevent diseases like colon cancer.

CARBOHYDRATE-BASED VACCINES

Mnemonic: **Carbs Fight Back**

- **C** — Carbohydrate antigens
- **F** — Fight infection
- **B** — Boost immunity

Explanation:
- **Carbohydrate-based vaccines** use **Carbohydrate antigens** to **Boost immunity** against pathogens, aiding in disease prevention.

LIPID STRUCTURE AND FUNCTION

FATTY ACID STRUCTURE

Mnemonic: **Saturated Smooth, Unsaturated Unstable**

- **S** Saturated (no double bonds, solid at room temp)
- **S** Smooth (stack tightly)
- **U** Unsaturated (one or more double bonds)
- **U** Unstable (kinks increase fluidity)

Explanation:
- **Saturated fatty acids** are solid and tightly packed, while **Unsaturated fatty acids** with double bonds are liquid and increase **Membrane fluidity**.

TRIACYLGLYCEROLS

Mnemonic: **Tri for Storage**

- **T** Triacylglycerols
- **S** Storage (energy storage form)

Explanation:
- **Triacylglycerols** are composed of three fatty acids linked to glycerol, serving as long-term **Energy storage** molecules.

PHOSPHOLIPIDS

Mnemonic: **Phospho Builds Barriers**

- **P** Phospholipids
- **B** Bilayer (forms cell membrane)

Explanation:
- **Phospholipids** arrange in a **bilayer**, forming the fundamental **Barrier** of cell membranes and allowing selective permeability.

STEROIDS

Mnemonic: **Strong Hormone Base**

- **S** — Steroids
- **H** — Hormones (steroid hormones)
- **B** — Bile acids (derived from cholesterol)

Explanation:
- **Steroids**, including **Cholesterol**, **Hormones**, and **Bile acids**, are derived from a common ring structure and serve as building blocks for vital **Physiological functions**.

EICOSANOIDS

Mnemonic: **Inflamed Pain Signals**

- **I** — Inflammation
- **P** — Pain
- **S** — Signaling molecules

Explanation:
- **Eicosanoids** like **Prostaglandins** and **Leukotrienes** are involved in **Pain** and **Inflammation** responses, acting as local **Signaling** molecules in tissues.

LIPID METABOLISM

Mnemonic: **Digest, Absorb, Deliver**

- **D** — Digestion (breakdown of lipids)
- **A** — Absorption (uptake by intestines)
- **D** — Delivery (transport via lipoproteins)

Explanation:
- **Lipid metabolism** includes **Digestion**, **Absorption**, and **Delivery** of lipids through **Bile acids** and **Lipoproteins** to cells for energy and storage.

BETA-OXIDATION

Mnemonic: **Burn Fat for Fuel**

- **B** — Beta-oxidation
- **F** — Fat breakdown to acetyl-CoA
- **F** — Fuel (produces energy)

Explanation:
- **Beta-oxidation** breaks down fatty acids into **Acetyl-CoA**, providing a major source of **Energy** through cellular respiration.

LIPID STORAGE DISEASES

Mnemonic: **Tough Genetic Burdens**

- **T** — Tay-Sachs disease
- **G** — Gaucher disease
- **B** — Burden on lipid storage and processing

Explanation:
- **Lipid storage diseases** like **Tay-Sachs** and **Gaucher** disease involve genetic mutations that impair **Lipid metabolism**, causing cell damage.

LIPOPROTEIN METABOLISM

Mnemonic: **Chylos Venture Lightly Here**

- **C** — Chylomicrons (transport dietary lipids)
- **V** — VLDL (very-low-density lipoproteins)
- **L** — LDL (low-density lipoprotein)
- **H** — HDL (high-dens lipoprotein, removes cholesterol)

Explanation:
- **Lipoproteins** like **Chylomicrons** and **HDL** transport lipids through the bloodstream, with each type having a specific role in **Lipid transport** and **Cholesterol** balance.

30 Day MCAT

DNA & BIOTECHNOLOGY

DNA STRUCTURE AND FUNCTION

Mnemonic: **Double Bases Store Genes**

- **D** — Double-helix structure
- **B** — Base pairing (A-T, C-G)
- **S** — Storage of genetic information
- **G** — Genes (units of heredity)

Explanation:
- **DNA** has a **Double-helix** structure with **Base pairing** (A-T, C-G) that stores Genetic information essential for heredity.

DNA REPLICATION

Mnemonic: **Initiate, Extend, End**

- **I** — Initiation (starting the process)
- **E** — Elongation (adding nucleotides)
- **E** — End (termination)

Explanation:
- **DNA replication** proceeds in **Initiation**, **Elongation**, and **Termination** steps, using enzymes like **DNA polymerase** and **Helicase** to ensure accurate copying.

TRANSCRIPTION

Mnemonic: **Start Writing RNA**

- **S** — Start (initiation)
- **W** — Writing RNA strand (elongation)
- **R** — RNA polymerase

Explanation:
- **Transcription** involves **RNA polymerase** synthesizing an RNA strand from DNA through **Initiation**, **Elongation**, and **Termination** phases.

TRANSLATION

Mnemonic: **Make Proteins Fast**

- **M** — mRNA (provides code)
- **P** — Proteins (end product)
- **F** — Function (produces proteins rapidly)

Explanation:
- **Translation** converts **mRNA** into Proteins using ribosomes, tRNA, and the genetic code, essential for cellular functions.

GENETIC CODE

Mnemonic: **Codes Specify Aminos**

- **C** — Codons (three-base units)
- **S** — Specify amino acids
- **A** — Amino acids (building blocks)

Explanation:
- The **Genetic code** consists of **Codons** that specify **Amino acids** during protein synthesis, providing instructions for protein structure

DNA REPAIR MECHANISMS

Mnemonic: **Base Needs Maintenance**

- **B** — Base excision repair
- **N** — Nucleotide excision repair
- **M** — Mismatch repair

Explanation:
- **DNA repair** mechanisms like **Base excision** and **Mismatch repair** correct errors in DNA, maintaining genome integrity.

DNA SEQUENCING

Mnemonic: Read Every Base

- **R** — Read (determining DNA sequence)
- **E** — Every nucleotide
- **B** — Base (identifying base order)

Explanation:
- **DNA sequencing** reads each **Base** in DNA, using techniques like **Sanger sequencing** and **Next-generation sequencing** to determine genetic information.

CRISPR-CAS9 GENE EDITING

Mnemonic: Precise Cut and Paste

- **P** — Precise (accurate editing)
- **C** — Cut (DNA cleavage)
- **P** — Paste (insert new DNA)

Explanation:
- **CRISPR-Cas9** provides a **Precise** method to **Cut** and edit DNA, allowing targeted gene modifications for medical and research applications.

GENE THERAPY

Mnemonic: Genes Treat Illness

- **G** — Gene insertion or modification
- **T** — Treatment of genetic diseases
- **I** — Illness targeting

Explanation:
- **Gene therapy** involves inserting or modifying genes to treat **Genetic diseases**, offering potential cures for inherited disorders.

RNA AND THE GENETIC CODE

RNA STRUCTURE AND FUNCTION

Mnemonic: **Messenger Transfers Ribosomes**

- **M** — mRNA (messenger RNA, carries genetic code)
- **T** — tRNA (transfer RNA, brings amino acids)
- **R** — rRNA (ribosomal RNA, part of ribosome structure)

Explanation:
- **mRNA, tRNA, and rRNA** are key types of **RNA** involved in **Protein** synthesis, each with specific functions to support translation.

RNA TRANSCRIPTION

Mnemonic: **Start Writing RNA**

- **S** — Start (initiation)
- **W** — Writing RNA (elongation)
- **R** — RNA polymerase (enzyme involved)

Explanation:
- **RNA transcription** begins with **Initiation**, progresses through Elongation as RNA is synthesized, and ends with **Termination** by **RNA polymerase**.

RNA PROCESSING

Mnemonic: **Cap, Splice, Tail**

- **C** — Capping (5' cap addition)
- **S** — Splicing (removal of introns)
- **T** — Tail (poly-A tail added at 3' end)

Explanation:
- **RNA processing** modifies primary RNA transcripts by **Capping**, **Splicing**, and adding a **Poly-A tail** to produce mature mRNA.

GENETIC CODE

Mnemonic: **Three Bases, One Amino**

- **T** — Three bases (codon)
- **B** — Base triplet (codes for one amino acid)
- **O** — One amino acid per codon

Explanation:
- The **Genetic code** uses **Three-base** codons to specify **Amino acids**, guiding protein synthesis.

RNA EDITING

Mnemonic: **Modify After Transcription**

- **M** — Modify RNA sequence
- **A** — After transcription
- **T** — Transcription (post-transcriptional changes)

Explanation:
- **RNA editing** involves **Post-transcriptional modifications** that **Modify RNA** sequences, altering genetic messages.

RIBOSOME STRUCTURE AND FUNCTION

Mnemonic: **Protein Building Site**

- **P** — Protein synthesis
- **B** — Building (site for assembly)
- **S** — Site (where mRNA and tRNA meet)

Explanation:
- The **Ribosome** is the **Site** of **Protein synthesis**, coordinating mRNA and tRNA interactions for amino acid assembly.

RIBOZYMES

Mnemonic: **Catalytic RNA Enzyme**

- **C** — Catalytic (acts as enzyme)
- **R** — RNA molecule
- **E** — Enzyme function

Explanation:
- **Ribozymes** are RNA molecules with **Catalytic** activity, functioning as **Enzymes** to facilitate reactions like peptide bond formation.

NON-CODING RNA

Mnemonic: **Long Micro Signals**

- **L** — lncRNA (long non-coding RNA)
- **M** — miRNA (microRNA)
- **S** — Signals (regulate gene expression)

Explanation:
- **Non-coding RNAs** like **lncRNA** and **miRNA** do not code for proteins but play crucial roles in **Gene regulation**.

RNA INTERFERENCE (RNAI)

Mnemonic: **Silence Interfering Genes**

- **S** — Silence gene expression
- **I** — Interfering with mRNA
- **G** — Genes targeted by siRNA and miRNA

Explanation:
- **RNAi** uses molecules like **siRNA** and **miRNA** to **Silence** specific **Genes**, regulating gene expression.

BIOLOGICAL MEMBRANES

MEMBRANE FLUIDITY

Mnemonic: **Temperature, Cholesterol, Chains**

- **T** — Temperature (affects fluidity)
- **C** — Cholesterol (maintains stability)
- **C** — Chains (fatty acid composition)

Explanation:
- **Membrane fluidity** is influenced by **Temperature**, **Cholesterol content**, and **Fatty acid chains**, impacting membrane flexibility and permeability.

MEMBRANE TRANSPORT

Mnemonic: **Passive, Facilitated, Active**

- **P** — Passive diffusion (no energy)
- **F** — Facilitated diffusion (requires carrier proteins)
- **A** — Active transport (uses energy)

Explanation:
- **Membrane transport** includes **Passive**, **Facilitated**, and **Active** mechanisms for moving substances across the cell membrane.

MEMBRANE PROTEINS

Mnemonic: **Integral and Peripheral**

- **I** — Integral proteins (span the membrane)
- **P** — Peripheral proteins (attach to surface)

Explanation:
- **Membrane proteins** include **Integral** proteins that span the bilayer and Peripheral proteins attached to the membrane's surface, both essential for cell functions.

LIPID RAFTS

Mnemonic: **Rafts Signal Order**

- **R** — Rafts
- **S** — Signal (cell signaling platforms)
- **O** — Order (membrane organization)

Explanation:
- **Lipid rafts** are specialized regions in the membrane that **Organize** molecules for **Cell signaling** and maintain structural **Order**.

ION CHANNELS

Mnemonic: **Ions Flow Freely**

- **I** — Ion channels
- **F** — Flow of ions
- **F** — Function in gradient maintenance

Explanation:
- **Ion channels** allow **Flow of ions** across membranes, crucial for maintaining **Ion gradients** and cellular signaling.

CARRIER PROTEINS

Mnemonic: **Carry Glucose and Ions**

- **C** — Carrier proteins
- **G** — Glucose transporters
- **I** — Ion pumps

Explanation:
- **Carrier proteins** like **Glucose transporters** and **Ion pumps** move molecules across the membrane, supporting nutrient uptake and ion balance.

SYNAPTIC TRANSMISSION

Mnemonic: **Neurotransmitters Activate Synapse**

- **N** — Neurotransmitters (chemical messengers)
- **A** — Activate ion channels
- **S** — Synapse (communication site)

Explanation:
- **Synaptic transmission** relies on **Neurotransmitters** that **Activate** ion channels, allowing signals to pass between neurons.

CELL SIGNALING

Mnemonic: **Signal, Transmit, Respond**

- **S** — Signal (received by receptors)
- **T** — Transmit message inside
- **R** — Respond to signal

Explanation:
- **Cell signaling** involves receiving an external **Signal**, **Transmitting** it within the cell, and initiating a cellular **Response**.

ACTION POTENTIAL

Mnemonic: **Spike and Spread**

- **S** — Spike in voltage
- **S** — Spread of electrical signal

Explanation:
- An **Action potential** is a rapid **Spike** in membrane potential that **Spreads** along neurons, enabling nerve signaling.

CARBOHYDRATE METABOLISM I

GLUCOSE TRANSPORTERS (GLUTS)

Mnemonic: **Tissues Go GLUT (1 to 4)**

- **T** — Tissues (specific transporter distribution)
- **G** — GLUT transporters (1 to 4, tissue-specific)

Explanation:
- GLUT transporters (1-4) have **Tissue-specific distribution**, with each type playing a unique role in **Glucose transport** across cell membranes.

GLYCOLYSIS REGULATION

Mnemonic: **Have Plenty of Phosphates**

- **H** — Hexokinase
- **P** — Phosphofructokinase-1 (PFK-1)
- **P** — Pyruvate kinase

Explanation:
- **Glycolysis regulation** is controlled by enzymes like **Hexokinase, PFK-1**, and **Pyruvate kinase**, each influenced by ATP levels and other metabolic signals.

PYRUVATE DEHYDROGENASE COMPLEX (PDC)

Mnemonic: **Pyruvate to Acetyl-CoA**

- **P** — Pyruvate (substrate)
- **A** — Acetyl-CoA (product)

Explanation:
- The **PDC** converts **Pyruvate to Acetyl-CoA** for entry into the TCA cycle, with regulation via phosphorylation and allosteric effectors.

GLYCOGENOLYSIS REGULATION

Mnemonic: **Phosphorylase for Breakdown**

- **P** — Phosphorylase (glycogen phosphorylase)
- **B** — Breakdown (of glycogen)

Explanation:
- **Glycogen phosphorylase** is the main enzyme in **Glycogenolysis**, activated by hormones like **Glucagon** to break down glycogen for energy.

GLUCONEOGENESIS REGULATION

Mnemonic: **New Pathway for Glucose**

- **N** — New glucose (production pathway)
- **P** — Pathway (regulated by enzymes)
- **G** — Glucose synthesis

Explanation:
- **Gluconeogenesis** produces **Glucose** from non-carbohydrate sources, regulated by enzymes like **Fructose-1,6-bisphosphatase** in response to fasting.

CORI CYCLE

Mnemonic: **Lactate to Liver Glucose**

- **L** — Lactate (produced by muscles)
- **L** — Liver (converts lactate back to glucose)
- **G** — Glucose

Explanation:
- The **Cori cycle** recycles **Lactate** from muscle cells to the Liver, where it's converted back into **Glucose** for energy.

DIABETES MELLITUS

Mnemonic: **Defective Insulin or Cells**

- **D** — Defective insulin production (Type 1)
- **I** — Insulin resistance (Type 2)
- **C** — Cells fail to absorb glucose

Explanation:
- **Diabetes mellitus** is caused by Defective insulin production (Type 1) or **Insulin resistance** (Type 2), leading to elevated blood glucose.

HORMONAL REGULATION OF GLUCOSE METABOLISM

Mnemonic: **Insulin and Glucagon Control**

- **I** — Insulin (lowers blood glucose)
- **G** — Glucagon (raises blood glucose)
- **C** — Control of blood sugar

Explanation:
- **Insulin** and **Glucagon** are key hormones that **Control** blood glucose levels, balancing glucose uptake and release.

GALACTOSE METABOLISM

Mnemonic: **Galactic Pathway Issues**

- **G** — Galactose
- **P** — Pathways (metabolized for energy)
- **I** — Issues (genetic disorders like galactosemia)

Explanation:
- **Galactose metabolism** is essential for energy production, but **Genetic disorders** like Galactosemia can cause toxic buildup of galactose in the body.

CARBOHYDRATE METABOLISM II

ELECTRON TRANSPORT CHAIN COMPLEXES

Mnemonic: **Never Forget Cytochrome Oxidase**

N — Complex I: **N**ADH dehydrogenase
F — Complex II: **F**ADH2 (succinate dehydrogenase)
C — Complex III: cytochrome bc1 **C**omplex
O — Complex IV: cytochrome c **O**xidase

Explanation:
- The **Electron Transport Chain** has four complexes that transfer electrons to **Oxygen** via **NADH** and **FADH2** to produce ATP.

OXIDATIVE PHOSPHORYLATION COUPLING

Mnemonic: **Electrons Make ATP**

E — **E**lectron transport
M — **M**otive force (proton gradient)
A — **A**TP synthesis (coupled process)

Explanation:
- **Oxidative phosphorylation** couples **Electron transport** with ATP synthesis through the **Proton gradient** created across the mitochondrial membrane.

ATP SYNTHASE

Mnemonic: **F0 F1 Spins ATP**

F0 — **P**roton channel (embedded in membrane)
F1 — **C**atalytic unit (synthesizes ATP)
S — **S**pins to produce ATP

Explanation:
- **ATP synthase** has **F0** and **F1** subunits; **F0** transports protons, while **F1** catalyzes ATP synthesis through rotational energy.

RESPIRATORY CONTROL

Mnemonic: **ADP Drives Proton Power**

- **A** — **A**DP availability
- **D** — **D**rives the process
- **P** — **P**roton motive force

Explanation:
- **Respiratory control** regulates Oxidative phosphorylation by **ADP availability** and the **Proton motive** force across the mitochondrial membrane.

UNCOUPLING AGENTS

Mnemonic: **Uncouple Heat Power**

- **U** — **U**ncoupling agents (like DNP)
- **H** — **H**eat production (instead of ATP)
- **P** — disrupts **P**roton gradient

Explanation:
- **Uncoupling agents** like **DNP** disrupt the Proton gradient, leading to **Heat** production instead of ATP synthesis.

REACTIVE OXYGEN SPECIES (ROS)

Mnemonic: **React, Detox, Protect**

- **R** — **R**eactive oxygen species
- **D** — **D**etoxify with antioxidants
- **P** — **P**rotect cells from damage

Explanation:
- **ROS** are generated during **Oxidative phosphorylation** and detoxified by antioxidants to **Protect** cells from oxidative damage.

ACETYL-CoA AS A METABOLIC HUB

Mnemonic: **Fuel for Fat, Cholesterol, Ketones**

- **F** — Fatty acid synthesis
- **C** — Cholesterol synthesis
- **K** — Ketone body formation

Explanation:
- **Acetyl-CoA** serves as a central **Metabolic hub** for processes like **Fatty acid** and **Cholesterol synthesis**, and **Ketogenesis**.

BROWN ADIPOSE TISSUE

Mnemonic: **Brown Burns Heat**

- **B** — Brown adipose tissue
- **B** — Burns fats
- **H** — generates Heat

Explanation:
- **Brown adipose** tissue generates **Heat** by burning fats, especially during cold exposure, due to its unique mitochondrial properties.

KETOGENESIS

Mnemonic: **Keto Makes Fuel**

- **K** — Ketone bodies
- **M** — Makes energy in fasting
- **F** — Fuel during low carbs

Explanation:
- **Ketogenesis** produces **Ketone bodies** as an alternative Fuel source during fasting or low-carbohydrate intake.

LIPID AND AMINO ACID METABOLISM

BETA-OXIDATION OF FATTY ACIDS

Mnemonic: **Activate, Transport, Break**

- **A** — Activation (fatty acid activated by CoA)
- **T** — Transport (carnitine shuttle into mitochondria)
- **B** — Breakdown (cyclic fatty acid degradation)

Explanation:
- **Beta-oxidation** includes **Activation** of fatty acids, **Transport** into mitochondria, and **Breakdown** into acetyl-CoA for energy production.

FATTY ACID SYNTHESIS

Mnemonic: **Acetyl Synthase Makes Fat**

- **A** — Acetyl-CoA carboxylase
- **S** — Synthase (fatty acid synthase)
- **M** — Makes fatty acids

Explanation:
- **Fatty acid synthesis** relies on **Acetyl-CoA carboxylase** and **Fatty acid synthase** to create long-chain fatty acids for storage.

CHOLESTEROL SYNTHESIS

Mnemonic: **HMG Builds Cholesterol**

- **H** — HMG-CoA reductase (key enzyme)
- **B** — Builds cholesterol

Explanation:
- **Cholesterol synthesis** is driven by **HMG-CoA** reductase, which catalyzes a key step in producing cholesterol.

30 Day MCAT

LIPID TRANSPORT AND LIPOPROTEINS

Mnemonic: **Carry Very Low High**

- **C** Chylomicrons (carry dietary fats)
- **V** VLDL (transports triglycerides)
- **L** LDL (carries cholesterol to cells)
- **H** HDL (removes excess cholesterol)

Explanation:
- **Lipoproteins** like **Chylomicrons**, **VLDL**, **LDL**, and **HDL** transport fats and cholesterol in the blood.

AMINO ACID CATABOLISM

Mnemonic: **Trans, Deaminate, Urea**

- **T** Transamination (transfer amino group)
- **D** Deamination (removal of amino group)
- **U** Urea cycle (excretes nitrogen)

Explanation:
- **Amino acid catabolism** involves **Transamination**, **Deamination**, and nitrogen disposal through the **Urea cycle**.

AMINO ACID NEUROTRANSMITTERS

Mnemonic: **Go Grab Glutamate**

- **G** GABA (inhibitory neurotransmitter)
- **G** Glycine (also inhibitory)
- **G** Glutamate (excitatory neurotransmitter)

Explanation:
- **Amino acids** like **Glutamate**, **GABA**, and **Glycine** serve as neurotransmitters, with Glutamate being excitatory and **GABA** and **Glycine** being inhibitory.

ESSENTIAL AMINO ACIDS

Mnemonic: **PVT. TIM HALL**

- **P** Phenylalanine
- **V** Valine
- **T** Threonine
- **T** Tryptophan
- **I** Isoleucine
- **M** Methionine
- **H** Histidine
- **A** Arginine
- **L** Leucine
- **L** Lysine

Explanation:
- The **Essential amino acids** must be obtained through diet as they cannot be synthesized by the body.

KETOGENIC AMINO ACIDS

Mnemonic: **Keep Leucine, Lysine**

- **K** Ketogenic amino acids
- **L** Leucine
- **L** Lysine

Explanation:
- **Ketogenic amino acids** like **Leucine** and **Lysine** contribute to **Ketone body production** during fasting or low-carb intake.

EICOSANOID SYNTHESIS

Mnemonic: **Eicosanoids from Arachidonic**

- **E** Eicosanoids
- **A** Arachidonic acid

Explanation:
- **Eicosanoids** like **Prostaglandins** and **Leukotrienes** are derived from **Arachidonic acid** and play roles in inflammation and signaling.

METABOLIC BIOENERGETICS

METABOLIC PATHWAYS

Mnemonic: **Glycolysis Connects Everything**

- **G** — Glycolysis
- **C** — Citric acid cycle
- **E** — Electron transport chain

Explanation:
- **Metabolic pathway**s like **Glycolysis**, the **Citric acid cycle**, and **Electron transport** are interconnected, supporting cellular energy production.

ENERGY COUPLING

Mnemonic: **Exer Meets Ender with ATP**

- **E** — Exergonic reactions
- **E** — Endergonic reactions
- **A** — ATP (couples the reactions)

Explanation:
- **Energy coupling** uses **ATP** to link **Exergonic** (energy-releasing) and **Endergonic** (energy-requiring) reactions, driving essential cellular processes.

REDOX REACTIONS IN METABOLISM

Mnemonic: **Redox Runs Energy**

- **R** — Redox reactions (oxidation-reduction)
- **R** — Runs energy production

Explanation:
- **Redox reactions** transfer electrons, essential in energy production, particularly within the **Electron transport** chain.

HORMONAL REGULATION OF METABOLISM

Mnemonic: **Insulin Gets Every Cell Control**

I Insulin
G Glucagon
E Epinephrine
C Cortisol

Explanation:
- Hormones like **Insulin, Glucagon, Epinephrine,** and **Cortisol** regulate Metabolic pathways, maintaining energy balance.

METABOLIC CONTROL ANALYSIS

Mnemonic: **Control Rates, Limit Flux**

C Control of metabolic rates
R Rate-limiting enzymes
F Flux through pathways

Explanation:
- **Metabolic control analysis** identifies **Rate-limiting enzymes** in metabolic pathways, helping to regulate **Flux** and pathway efficiency.

METABOLIC FLUX ANALYSIS

Mnemonic: **Measure Flow Rates**

M Measure rates of reactions
F Flux through metabolic pathways
R Rates of metabolic reactions

Explanation:
- **Metabolic flux analysis** quantifies **Reaction rates** within pathways, helping determine the metabolic flow in cells and tissues.

OBESITY AND METABOLIC DISORDERS

Mnemonic: **Obesity Brings Complications**

- **O** — Obesity
- **B** — Brings metabolic issues
- **C** — Complications (e.g., insulin resistance)

Explanation:
- **Obesity** leads to metabolic complications like **Insulin resistance**, Type 2 diabetes, and cardiovascular disease.

CANCER METABOLISM

Mnemonic: **Warburg's Altered Path**

- **W** — Warburg effect
- **A** — Altered metabolism
- **P** — Pathways in cancer cells

Explanation:
- **Cancer metabolism** involves the **Warburg effect**, where cancer cells rely on glycolysis, even in oxygen's presence, to support rapid growth.

CIRCADIAN RHYTHMS AND METABOLISM

Mnemonic: **Clock Controls Metabolism**

- **C** — Circadian clock
- **C** — Controls metabolic rhythms
- **M** — Metabolism (glucose, lipids)

Explanation:
- **Circadian rhythms** regulate **Metabolic processes**, including **Glucose** and **Lipid metabolism**, aligning them with daily activity patterns.

CHEAT SHEET

NOMENCLATURE	
Common Names of Simple Organic Compounds	• Simple organic compounds (alkanes) have traditional names based on prefixes indicating the number of carbon atoms.
Rules of IUPAC Nomenclature	• The IUPAC nomenclature system provides standardized guidelines for naming organic compounds to avoid ambiguity.
Types of Stereoisomers	• Stereoisomers have the same molecular formula and connectivity but differ in spatial arrangement.
Enantiomers	• Mirror-image isomers that cannot be superimposed.
Diastereomers	• Non-mirror-image isomers with different physical and chemical properties.
R/S Configuration	• The R/S configuration system assigns absolute configuration to chiral centers in molecules
E/Z Configuration	• Used for alkenes with two different groups attached to each carbon in the double bond.
E (Entgegen)	• High-priority groups are on opposite sides of the double bond.
Z (Zusammen)	• High-priority groups are on the same side of the double bond.
Nomenclature of Cyclic Compounds	• Cyclic compounds are named by adding the prefix cyclo- before the root name of the corresponding alkane, alkene, or alkyne.
Functional Groups	• Functional groups are specific groups of atoms in molecules that determine chemical properties and reactivity.
Naming Complex Molecules	• provide a clear, standardized, and systematic way to identify and communicate the structure of a compound.

Rules for Drawing Structures from IUPAC Names	• These rules ensure the drawn structure accurately corresponds to the provided IUPAC name.
Functional Groups	• Specific groups of atoms within molecules that determine the chemical properties and reactivity, essential in naming compounds.
Stereochemistry	• The study of the spatial arrangement of atoms in molecules, important for naming isomers (e.g., R/S and E/Z configurations).
Structural Isomers	• Compounds with the same molecular formula but different structural arrangements, requiring distinct names to differentiate them.
Parent Chain	• The longest continuous chain of carbon atoms in a compound, which serves as the basis for naming organic molecules.

ISOMERS	
Characteristics of Conformational Isomers	• are different spatial arrangements of atoms in a molecule that can be interconverted by rotation around single bonds.
Characteristics of Configurational Isomers	• cannot be interconverted by simple rotation around single bonds.
Characteristics of Enantiomers	• are stereoisomers that are non-superimposable mirror images of each other.
Characteristics of Diastereomers	• are stereoisomers that are not mirror images of each other.
Characteristics of Meso Compounds	• A meso compound is a molecule that has chiral centers but is optically inactive due to internal symmetry.
Characteristics of Cis-Trans Isomerism	• Cis-trans isomerism occurs in compounds where substituent groups are attached to a rigid structure, such as alkenes or cyclic compounds.
Rules for Drawing Fischer Projections	• Fischer projections are a way of representing three-dimensional molecules in two dimensions.

Rules for Drawing Newman Projections	• Newman projections are used to represent the conformation of a molecule, specifically around a single bond.
Factors Affecting Isomerization or Isomerization Reactions	• Isomerization reactions are processes where a molecule changes from one isomeric form to another.
Stereoisomerism	• This refers to isomers that have the same molecular formula and connectivity but differ in the spatial arrangement of atoms.
Chirality	• The concept of chirality deals with molecules that cannot be superimposed on their mirror image.
Structural (Constitutional) Isomerism	• This isomerism occurs when compounds have the same molecular formula but differ in the connectivity of their atoms, resulting in different structures.
Geometrical Isomerism	• A form of stereoisomerism, geometrical isomerism (such as cis-trans isomerism) occurs when molecules have restricted rotation (such as around a double bond or in a ring), leading to isomers with different spatial arrangements of substituent groups.
Optical Activity	• This refers to the ability of chiral compounds, such as enantiomers, to rotate plane-polarized light.

BONDING	
Types of Bonds Based on Polarity	• refer to the classification of chemical bonds depending on how electrons are shared between atoms, which is influenced by the difference in electronegativity between the atoms involved.
Nonpolar bonds	• involve equal sharing of electrons (e.g., in diatomic molecules like O_2).
Polar bonds	• involve unequal sharing due to differences in electronegativity (e.g., H_2O)

30 Day MCAT

Ionic bonds	- result from the complete transfer of electrons from one atom to another, creating charged ions (e.g., NaCl).
Steps on How to Determine Molecular Polarity	- To determine the molecular polarity of a molecule, evaluate the molecule's shape (geometry), the electronegativity differences between atoms, and the symmetry of the molecule.
Types of Intermolecular Forces	- are the forces that hold molecules together.
London dispersion forces	- weak forces that exist in all molecules, caused by temporary dipoles.
Dipole-dipole forces	- attractive forces between polar molecules.
Hydrogen bonding	- strong type of dipole-dipole interaction that occurs when hydrogen is bonded to electronegative atoms like oxygen, nitrogen, or fluorine.
Rules on How to Draw Resonance Structures	- represent different possible ways of arranging electrons in a molecule, with each structure contributing to the overall molecular description.
Types of Hybrid Orbitals	- are formed by mixing different atomic orbitals to produce new orbitals that are better suited for bonding.
Key Concepts in Molecular Orbital Theory (MOT)	- Molecular Orbital Theory explains bonding by describing how atomic orbitals combine to form bonding orbitals (lower energy) and antibonding orbitals (higher energy).
Steps to Calculate Formal Charge to Determine the Most Stable Lewis Structure	- To calculate the formal charge of an atom in a molecule, subtract the number of bonds (represented by "sticks") and lone pair electrons (represented by "dots") from the atom's valence electrons.
How Hyperconjugation Works	- Hyperconjugation refers to the delocalization of electrons in sigma bonds, particularly in molecules with adjacent empty or partially filled p-orbitals.
Factors Affecting Bond Dissociation Energy	- The energy required to break a bond, called bond dissociation energy.

ANALYZING ORGANIC REACTIONS

Analyzing Organic Reactions	• This process involves observing and understanding the reaction mechanisms, identifying the reactants and products, and considering factors that influence the reaction such as energy, rate, and selectivity.
Common Reaction Intermediates	• These are transient species that form during the course of chemical reactions and are crucial to understanding the reaction pathway.
Carbocations	• positively charged carbon species with an incomplete octet.
Carbanions	• negatively charged carbon species with a lone pair of electrons.
Free Radicals	• neutral species with an unpaired electron.
Carbenes	• neutral species with a divalent carbon atom that has two nonbonding electrons.
Nitrenes	• reactive intermediates containing a nitrogen atom with a lone pair and a singlet state.
Benzyne	• a resonance-stabilized intermediate in aromatic substitution reactions.
Factors Affecting Reaction Rates	• These are the conditions that influence the speed of a chemical reaction.
Key Thermodynamic Functions	• These are functions that help describe the energy changes and spontaneity of reactions
Enthalpy (H)	• A measure of the total heat content of a system, indicating whether a reaction releases or absorbs heat.
Entropy (S)	• A measure of the disorder or randomness in a system, affecting how much energy is available to do work.

30 Day MCAT

Gibbs Free Energy (G)	• A thermodynamic quantity that predicts the spontaneity of a reaction; if G is negative, the reaction is spontaneous
Common Electrophilic Aromatic Substitution Reactions	• These reactions involve the substitution of an atom or group on an aromatic ring by an electrophile.
Factors Affecting Nucleophilic Substitution Reactions	• Nucleophilic substitution reactions involve the displacement of a leaving group by a nucleophile.
Nature of Nucleophile	• A stronger nucleophile increases the reaction rate.
Factors Affecting Elimination Reactions	• Elimination reactions result in the removal of atoms or groups from a molecule.
Types of Pericyclic Reactions	• Pericyclic reactions involve concerted electron movements within a cyclic transition state.
Electrocyclic Reactions	• Reactions in which a single bond is formed or broken in a cyclic fashion.
Woodward-Hoffmann Rules	• These rules predict the stereochemistry of pericyclic reactions by considering the number of electrons involved (4n or 4n+2), the stereochemistry of reactants, and the mode of the reaction (conrotatory or disrotatory).

ALCOHOLS

Factors Affecting the Acidity of Alcohols	• The acidity of alcohols, or their ability to donate a proton.
Common Reactions of Alcohols	• reaction which includes oxidation, reduction, dehydration, and nucleophilic substitution.
Oxidation of Alcohols	• The process of oxidation of alcohols involves the loss of electrons or the addition of oxygen

Factors Affecting Dehydration of Alcohols	• The dehydration of alcohols, which typically leads to the formation of alkenes.
Common Protecting Groups for Alcohols	• Protecting groups are used to temporarily block the reactivity of alcohols during complex organic reactions.
Reactions of Grignard Reagents	• Grignard reagents (RMgX) are reactive compounds that can participate in a variety of reactions.
Types of Phenols	• Phenols are compounds with a hydroxyl group attached to a benzene ring.
Simple Phenols	• Contain one hydroxyl group on the aromatic ring.
Polyphenols	• Contain multiple hydroxyl groups attached to the aromatic ring.
Different Methods for Synthesizing Alcohols	• Alcohols can be synthesized through various methods, including hydration of Alkenes, Hydroboration-oxidation, and oxidation of Alkyl Halides
Spectroscopic Analysis of Alcohols	• This refers to the use of various spectroscopic techniques to identify and characterize alcohols.

ELECTROPHILLICITY & OXIDATION - REDUCTION

Types of Electrophiles	• Electrophiles are electron-deficient species that seek electrons to complete their valence shell, making them reactive in chemical reactions.
Carbocations	• Positively charged carbon atoms with an incomplete octet, making them highly electrophilic.
Carbonyl Compounds	• Molecules containing a carbonyl group (C=O), such as aldehydes and ketones, where the carbonyl carbon is electrophilic due to its partial positive charge.
Alkyl Halides	• Compounds with a carbon-halogen bond, where the carbon attached to the halogen is electrophilic due to the electron-withdrawing effect of the halogen.

Lewis Acids	• Electron-pair acceptors, such as metal ions or compounds like BF$_3$, which are highly electrophilic.
Types of Nucleophiles	• Nucleophiles are electron-rich species that donate electrons to electrophiles in chemical reactions:
Common Electrophilic Aromatic Substitution Reactions	• These reactions involve an electrophilic species substituting a hydrogen atom on an aromatic ring.
Types of Nucleophilic Acyl Substitution Reactions:	• These reactions involve the substitution of a leaving group with a nucleophile at a carbonyl carbon:
Rules for Assigning Oxidation States	• The oxidation state is a measure of the degree of oxidation of an atom in a molecule.
Common Redox Reactions	• These reactions involve the transfer of electrons, where one species is oxidized (loses electrons) and another is reduced (gains electrons).
Common Inorganic Oxidizing Agents	• Inorganic oxidizing agents facilitate the oxidation of other substances by accepting electrons.
Common Organic Oxidizing Agents	• Organic oxidizing agents are primarily used to oxidize organic compounds.

ENOLATES

Kinetic Enolate	• The enolate formed at the fastest rate, usually under conditions of low temperature or with bulky bases. It
Thermodynamic Enolate	• the more stable enolate formed at higher temperatures or with smaller bases.
Common Reactions of Enolates	• Enolates are reactive intermediates that can participate in several important reactions in organic synthesis. These reactions occur due to the nucleophilic nature of the enolate ion, which can attack electrophilic species.

Self-Aldol Condensation	• An aldol reaction where the enolate of one molecule reacts with the carbonyl group of the same molecule.
Types of Aldol Condensation	• Aldol condensation reactions involve the formation of a β-hydroxy carbonyl compound (aldol addition) followed by a dehydration step (aldol condensation) to yield an α,β-unsaturated carbonyl compound.
Crossed-Aldol Condensation	• An aldol reaction between two different carbonyl compounds, which can lead to a mixture of products unless one reactant is in excess.
Intramolecular Aldol Condensation	• A reaction where the enolate of a molecule reacts with another carbonyl group within the same molecule, forming a cyclic product.
Key Factors Affecting Claisen Condensation	• refer to the variables that influence the rate, efficiency, and outcome of the Claisen condensation reaction
Reduction of Carbonyl Compounds	• The process of reducing carbonyl compounds (like aldehydes, ketones, and carboxylic acids) to alcohols using reducing agents like $LiAlH_4$ (lithium aluminum hydride) or $NaBH_4$ (sodium borohydride).
Reduction of Alkynes to Alkenes and Alkanes	• Alkynes can be reduced to alkenes through partial hydrogenation (e.g., using Lindlar's catalyst), or further reduced to alkanes with complete hydrogenation, typically using hydrogen gas and a metal catalyst (e.g., palladium or platinum).
Mechanism of Catalytic Hydrogenation	• A reaction where a metal catalyst, such as Pd (palladium), Pt (platinum), or Ni (nickel), is used to facilitate the addition of hydrogen (H_2) to unsaturated compounds like alkenes or alkynes, turning them into saturated hydrocarbons (alkanes).
Achieving Stereoselectivity in Reduction Reactions	• The use of specific conditions to control the stereochemistry of a reduction reaction, such as using chiral reducing agents, chiral ligands, substrate control, temperature, solvent effects, or enzyme catalysis to favor one stereoisomer over another.

CARBOXYLIC ACID

Factors Affecting the Acidity of Carboxylic Acids	• The acidity of carboxylic acids is determined by several structural and electronic factors that influence how easily the proton (H^+) can dissociate from the carboxyl group (-COOH).
Resonance Stabilization	• The carboxylate anion ($RCOO^-$) formed when the proton dissociates is stabilized by resonance.
Inductive Effect	• Electron-withdrawing groups (such as halogens or nitro groups) near the carboxyl group can pull electron density away from the carboxyl group through the sigma bond.
Common Reactions of Carboxylic Acids	• Carboxylic acids are versatile compounds that undergo various chemical reactions due to their functional group (-COOH).
Steps of Esterification	• Esterification is the reaction between a carboxylic acid and an alcohol to form an ester.
Acidic Hydrolysis of Esters	• Acidic hydrolysis of esters involves the reverse of esterification, where the ester is broken down by water in the presence of an acid.
Basic Hydrolysis of Esters	• Basic hydrolysis of esters, also known as saponification, is the process where an ester is broken down by a strong base (such as sodium hydroxide, NaOH) into a carboxylate salt and alcohol.
Factors Affecting Decarboxylation	• Decarboxylation involves the removal of a carboxyl group (CO_2) from a carboxylic acid.
Common Carboxylic Acid Derivatives	• Carboxylic acid derivatives are compounds related to carboxylic acids in which the -OH group is replaced by another group, such as a halide, an ester, or an amide.
Common Nucleophilic Acyl Substitution Reactions	• Nucleophilic acyl substitution is a reaction in which a nucleophile attacks the electrophilic carbonyl carbon of a carboxylic acid derivative, replacing the leaving group.
Nucleophilic Attack	• The hydroxide ion (OH^-) from the base attacks the electrophilic carbonyl carbon of the ester, breaking the ester bond.

CARBOXYLIC ACID DERIVATIVES

Reactivity of Carboxylic Acid Derivatives	• Carboxylic acid derivatives differ in reactivity based on their ability to undergo nucleophilic acyl substitution, where a nucleophile attacks the carbonyl carbon and replaces the leaving group.
Nucleophilic Acyl Substitution	• This is the general mechanism for many reactions involving carboxylic acid derivatives.
Acid Chloride Reactions	• Acid chlorides are highly reactive compounds due to the excellent leaving group ability of chloride.
Ester Reactions	• Ester reactions encompass several important processes where esters undergo transformation due to the reactivity of the ester group (RCOOR').
Transesterification	• Esters can undergo transesterification, where one alcohol is substituted for another, forming a new ester and alcohol.
Amide Reactions	• Amides are relatively less reactive compared to esters, but they can still undergo important chemical reactions.
Nitriles	• Nitriles are compounds containing the functional group -C N (a carbon triple-bonded to nitrogen).
Spectroscopic Analysis of Carboxylic Acid Derivatives	• Spectroscopic techniques are used to identify and characterize carboxylic acid derivatives
Claisen Condensation Mechanism	• The Claisen condensation is a reaction where two esters (or an ester and a carbonyl compound) react in the presence of a base to form a β-keto ester.
Dieckmann Condensation Mechanism	• The Dieckmann condensation is an intramolecular version of the Claisen condensation.

NITROGEN & PHOSPHORUS COMPOUNDS

Amines	• Amines are compounds containing nitrogen atoms with a lone pair of electrons.
Basicity of Amines	• Amines are basic due to the lone pair of electrons on the nitrogen atom. This allows amines to accept protons (H^+) and form ammonium ions (RNH_3^+).
Amides	• Amides are organic compounds containing a carbonyl group (C=O) linked to a nitrogen atom (NH_2).
Nitriles	• Nitriles are compounds containing a cyano group (C N), which consists of a carbon triple-bonded to a nitrogen.
Reduction	• Nitriles can be reduced to amines by hydrogenation or using reducing agents like $LiAlH_4$. The triple bond (C N) is reduced to a single bond ($C-NH_2$), forming a primary amine.
Hydrolysis	• Nitriles can be hydrolyzed to carboxylic acids in the presence of water and either an acid or base.
Imines	• Imines are formed by the reaction of a primary amine with an aldehyde or ketone.
Enamines	• Enamines are derived from secondary amines and carbonyl compounds (usually ketones).
Phosphorus Compounds	• Phosphorus compounds include several different types of chemical species that contain phosphorus, such as phosphines, phosphates, and phosphites.
Phosphines	• Phosphines are compounds where phosphorus is bonded to three organic groups (R_3P). They are typically used as reducing agents or ligands in organometallic chemistry.
Phosphites	• Phosphites contain a phosphorus atom bonded to two alkyl or aryl groups and one oxygen atom. They are used in organic synthesis and as antioxidants.
Phosphate Esters	• Phosphate esters are compounds where a phosphate group (PO_4) is bonded to an alkyl or aryl group.

Nucleophilic Substitution Reactions of Phosphorus Compounds	• Phosphorus compounds, particularly phosphates and phosphites, undergo nucleophilic substitution reactions.
Arbuzov Reaction	• The Arbuzov reaction is a nucleophilic substitution where a dialkyl phosphite reacts with an alkyl halide to form an alkyl phosphonate.
Heterocyclic Compounds	• Heterocyclic compounds are cyclic compounds that contain atoms of at least one element other than carbon, such as nitrogen, oxygen, or sulfur.
Pyridine	• Pyridine is a six-membered aromatic compound containing one nitrogen atom. It is a basic compound and is often used as a solvent or ligand in chemical reactions.
Pyrrole	• Pyrrole is a five-membered heterocyclic compound with one nitrogen atom.
Biologically Important Nitrogen Compounds	• Nitrogen plays a crucial role in biological systems, and several important biological compounds contain nitrogen.
Amino Acids	• Amino acids are the building blocks of proteins, containing both an amine group ($-NH_2$) and a carboxyl group ($-COOH$).
Nucleotides	• Nucleotides are the building blocks of nucleic acids like DNA and RNA.
Neurotransmitters	• Neurotransmitters are chemicals that transmit signals across synapses in the nervous system.
Spectroscopic Analysis of Nitrogen and Phosphorus Compounds	• Spectroscopic techniques such as IR (Infrared) and NMR (Nuclear Magnetic Resonance) spectroscopy are essential tools for identifying and analyzing nitrogen and phosphorus compounds.
IR Spectroscopy	• the absorption of infrared radiation by molecules can be used to identify specific functional groups, such as N-H (amine) and P-H (phosphine) bonds.

SPECTROSCOPY

Infrared (IR) Spectroscopy	• is a technique used to analyze the vibrations of chemical bonds in a molecule.
Functional Group Regions in IR	• In IR spectroscopy, different functional groups absorb infrared light at characteristic frequencies.
Nuclear Magnetic Resonance (NMR) Spectroscopy	• NMR spectroscopy is used to determine the structure of organic compounds by observing the interactions of nuclear spins in a magnetic field.
Proton NMR (^{1}H NMR)	• proton NMR (^{1}H NMR) specifically analyzes the behavior of hydrogen atoms in a molecule.
Integration	• Integration gives information about the number of hydrogen atoms that are contributing to each signal, helping to identify how many protons are present in each environment.
Carbon-13 NMR (^{13}C NMR)	• Carbon-13 NMR (^{13}C NMR) analyzes the behavior of carbon atoms, specifically the ^{13}C isotope, which is present in small quantities in organic compounds.
Carbon-13	• The ^{13}C isotope is used in NMR because it has a nuclear spin, unlike the more abundant ^{12}C isotope. This makes it detectable in NMR spectra.
Mass Spectrometry (MS)	• Mass spectrometry (MS) is a technique that measures the mass-to-charge ratio (m/z) of ions produced from a sample.
UV-Vis Spectroscopy	• Ultraviolet-visible (UV-Vis) spectroscopy is a technique used to analyze the absorption of UV and visible light by molecules, primarily focusing on conjugated systems.
Chromophores	• Chromophores are parts of a molecule that absorb light in the UV or visible spectrum.
Spectroscopic Analysis of Mixtures	• When analyzing mixtures of compounds, it is essential to use spectroscopy to identify the individual components.
Correlation Tables	• Correlation tables are used in NMR spectroscopy to predict chemical shifts and splitting patterns for different functional groups.

SEPARATIONS & PURIFICATIONS

Extraction	• Extraction is a technique used to separate compounds based on their solubility in different immiscible solvents, typically in a liquid-liquid system.
Distillation	• Distillation is a separation technique that utilizes differences in boiling points to separate liquid mixtures.
Simple Distillation	• Used when the boiling points of components differ significantly (more than 25°C).
Vacuum Distillation	• Used for compounds with high boiling points or those that decompose at their boiling points.
Chromatography	• Chromatography is a method for separating and analyzing the components of a mixture based on their interactions with a stationary phase and a mobile phase.
Recrystallization	• Recrystallization is a method used to purify solid compounds by exploiting differences in solubility.
Sublimation	• Sublimation is a technique used to purify solids by exploiting their ability to transition directly from the solid to the gas phase without passing through a liquid phase.
Filtration	• Filtration is used to separate solids from liquids using a porous barrier.
Gravity Filtration	• Used for removing solid impurities from liquids under the force of gravity.
Centrifugation	• Centrifugation separates components in a mixture based on their density by spinning the sample at high speeds.

Drying Agents	• Drying agents are used to remove water from organic solvents, ensuring the sample is anhydrous.
Extraction Efficiency	• Extraction efficiency refers to how effectively a compound is separated between two solvents.
Phase Equilibria and Distribution	• This topic explores the principles of solubility, phase transitions, and the partitioning of substances between phases.
Characterization Techniques	• These methods are used to verify the purity and identity of separated compounds.

NOMENCLATURE

COMMON NAMES OF SIMPLE ORGANIC COMPOUNDS

Mnemonic: **Meth Eats Peanut Butter**

- **M** Methane
- **E** Ethane
- **P** Propane
- **B** Butane

Explanation:
- Use **Meth**, **Eth**, **Prop**, and **But** as prefixes for the first four simple organic compounds (alkanes), which are foundational in organic chemistry.

RULES OF IUPAC NOMENCLATURE

Mnemonic: **Find Long Chain Names**

- **F** Find the longest carbon chain
- **L** Locate the functional group(s)
- **C** Count and number the chain
- **N** Name according to prefixes and suffixes

Explanation:
- The **IUPAC nomenclature** system involves finding the longest carbon chain, numbering, and naming based on functional groups and their positions.

TYPES OF STEREOISOMERS

Mnemonic: **Enantiomers & Diastereomers Differ**

- **E** Enantiomers (mirror-image isomers)
- **D** Diastereomers (non-mirror image)

Explanation:
- **Stereoisomers** include **Enantiomers** (mirror images) and Diastereomers (non-mirror images), which differ in spatial arrangement but share the same connectivity.

R/S CONFIGURATION

Mnemonic: **Rank, Rotate, Assign**

R   **R**ank substituents by priority
R   **R**otate molecule
A   **A**ssign R or S based on direction

Explanation:
- Use **Cahn-Ingold-Prelog** priority rules to **Rank** groups, **Rotate** to position lowest priority at the back, and Assign **R** (clockwise) or **S** (counterclockwise) configuration.

E/Z CONFIGURATION

Mnemonic: **E for Enemies, Z for Zame**

E   Groups on **Opposite** sides
Z   Groups **on the Same** side

Explanation:
- In **E/Z configuration** for alkenes, **E** means high-priority groups are on Opposite sides, while **Z** means they are on the **Same** side.

NOMENCLATURE OF CYCLIC COMPOUNDS

Mnemonic: **Cycle Comes First**

C   **C**ycle (prefix "cyclo" before the root name)
F   **F**irst in naming

Explanation:
- For **Cyclic compounds**, add **Cyclo-** before the alkane, alkene, or alkyne name and follow IUPAC rules for substituents and numbering.

FUNCTIONAL GROUPS

Mnemonic: **Chemists Handle Cool Active Molecules**

- **C** — Carbonyl
- **H** — Hydroxyl
- **C** — Carboxyl
- **A** — Amino
- **M** — Methyl (or Thiol for sulfur-containing groups)

Explanation:
- Recognize **Functional groups** such as **Carbonyl**, **Hydroxyl**, **Carboxyl**, **Amino**, and **Methyl** (or **Thiol**) groups, as they define reactivity and properties.

NAMING COMPLEX MOLECULES

Mnemonic: **Find Chain, Name Substituents, Place Numbers**

- **F** — Find the parent chain
- **N** — Name substituents
- **P** — Place numbers

Explanation:
- For **Complex molecules**, identify the longest carbon chain, assign and name substituents, and number the chain to provide the simplest possible structure.

IUPAC NAMING RULES

Mnemonic: **Parents Add Numbers" or "P.A.N**

- **P** — Parent chain (longest carbon chain)
- **A** — Add substituents at specified positions
- **N** — Number to clarify positions

Explanation:
- When **Drawing structures**, start with the **Parent chain**, **Add** substituents, and **Number** according to the IUPAC name to accurately represent the molecule.

ISOMERS

CHARACTERISTICS OF CONFORMATIONAL ISOMERS

Mnemonic: **Rotate for Relaxed Forms**

- **R** — **R**otate (bond rotation forms conformers)
- **R** — **R**elaxed or staggered (low-energy form)
- **F** — **F**orms of same molecule

Explanation:
- **Conformational isomers** result from Rotation around single bonds, creating different forms (e.g., staggered, eclipsed) without breaking bonds.

CHARACTERISTICS OF CONFIGURATIONAL ISOMERS

Mnemonic: **Fixed Configurations**

- **C** — **F**ixed (cannot interconvert by rotation)
- **F** — **C**onfiguration is distinct

Explanation:
- **Configurational isomers** cannot Interconvert by rotation and require bond-breaking to change configurations (e.g., R/S or E/Z isomers).

CHARACTERISTICS OF ENANTIOMERS

Mnemonic: **Mirror Image Twins**

- **M** — **M**irror images
- **I** — **I**dentical properties (except optical activity)
- **T** — **T**wins (non-superimposable)

Explanation:
- **Enantiomers** are **Mirror-image** isomers that are non-superimposable, identical in physical properties except for their optical activity.

CHARACTERISTICS OF DIASTEREOMERS

Mnemonic: **Differ But Not Mirror**

- **D** Differ in configuration
- **N** Not mirror images

Explanation:
- **Diastereomers** are **Non-mirror** image stereoisomers, differing in configuration and often showing different physical and chemical properties.

CHARACTERISTICS OF MESO COMPOUNDS

Mnemonic: **Mirror in Middle**

- **M** Meso compounds
- **M** Mirror plane (internal symmetry)

Explanation:
- **Meso compounds** have Internal symmetry and are optically inactive despite having chiral centers, due to internal cancellation.

CHARACTERISTICS OF CIS-TRANS ISOMERISM

Mnemonic: **Same or Opposite Sides**

- **S** Same side (Cis)
- **O** Opposite side (Trans)

Explanation:
- **Cis-Trans isomerism** occurs in alkenes or cyclic compounds, where substituents are on the Same (Cis) or Opposite (Trans) sides.

RULES FOR DRAWING FISCHER PROJECTIONS

Mnemonic: **Vertical is Back, Horizontal is Hugs**

- **V** — Vertical lines (back or away from viewer)
- **H** — Horizontal lines (toward viewer)
- **H** — Looks like **H**ugs (towards)

Explanation:
- In **Fischer projections**, **Vertical lines** point away from the viewer, while **Horizontal lines** point towards the viewer, showing stereochemistry clearly.

RULES FOR DRAWING NEWMAN PROJECTIONS

Mnemonic: **Front Circle, Rear Hidden**

- **F** — Front carbon (shown as dot or circle)
- **R** — Rear carbon (hidden behind)

Explanation:
- **Newman projections** show the **Front carbon** as a circle with the rear carbon hidden behind, used to analyze conformations.

ISOMERIZATION REACTIONS

Mnemonic: **Heat Lights a Catalyst Shift**

- **H** — Heat (temperature affects energy)
- **L** — Light (can cause isomerization)
- **C** — Catalyst (may assist in conversion)
- **S** — Shift (to different isomer forms)

Explanation:
- **Isomerization reactions** are influenced by **Heat**, **Light**, and **Catalysts**, which can help shift molecules between different isomeric forms.

BONDING

TYPES OF BONDS BASED ON POLARITY

Mnemonic: **Non-Polar Ionic**

N — **N**onpolar (equal sharing of electrons)
P — **P**olar (unequal sharing of electrons)
I — **I**onic (complete transfer of electrons)

Explanation:
- Bonds are classified as **Nonpolar** (equal sharing), **Polar** (unequal sharing), or **Ionic** (transfer of electrons) based on the electronegativity difference between atoms.

DETERMINE MOLECULAR POLARITY

Mnemonic: **Shape Electronegativities to Symmetry**

S — **S**hape of the molecule
E — **E**lectronegativity differences
S — **S**ymmetry of distribution

Explanation:
- To determine **Molecular polarity**, assess the **Shape** of the molecule, **E**lectronegativity of atoms, and **Symmetry** of electron distribution.

TYPES OF INTERMOLECULAR FORCES

Mnemonic: **London Did Hold**

L — **L**ondon dispersion (weak, in all molecules)
D — **D**ipole-dipole (polar molecules)
H — **H**ydrogen bonding (stronger, with H-F, H-O, H-N)

Explanation:
- **Intermolecular forces** include **London dispersion** (weakest), **Dipole-dipole** (polar), and **Hydrogen bonding** (strongest, in specific cases).

RULES ON HOW TO DRAW RESONANCE STRUCTURES

Mnemonic: **Move Electrons, Not Atoms" or "M.E.N**

M — Move only Electrons (not atoms)
E — Electrons in lone pairs or pi bonds
N — Negative go on more electronegative atoms

Explanation:
- **Resonance structures** are drawn by **Moving electrons** (in lone pairs or bonds), ensuring that atoms stay fixed, and stability is maximized.

TYPES OF HYBRID ORBITALS

Mnemonic: **SP, SP2, SP3 Mix**

S — sp (linear geometry)
S — sp² (trigonal planar)
S — sp³ (tetrahedral)

Explanation:
- **Hybrid orbitals** include **sp** (linear), **sp²** (trigonal planar), and **sp³** (tetrahedral), formed by mixing different atomic orbitals.

KEY CONCEPTS IN MOLECULAR ORBITAL THEORY

Mnemonic: **A Big Active Officer**

B — Bonding orbitals (lower energy)
A — Antibonding orbitals (higher energy)
O — Overlap of atomic orbitals

Explanation:
- **Molecular Orbital Theory** explains bonding through **Bonding** and **Antibonding orbitals** formed by **Overlap of atomic orbitals**.

FORMAL CHARGE FOR STABLE LEWIS STRUCTURES

Mnemonic: **Valence Minus Sticks and Dots**

- **V** — Valence electrons (total for the atom)
- **M** — Minus Sticks (count each bond as one)
- **D** — Minus Dots (lone pair electrons)

Explanation:
- To calculate **Formal charge**, subtract the **Sticks** (bonds) and **Dots** (lone pairs) from **Valence electrons**. The **Most stable structure** minimizes formal charges, with negative charges ideally on more electronegative atoms.

HOW HYPERCONJUGATION WORKS

Mnemonic: **Sigma Overlaps to Spread Stability**

- **S** — Sigma bond electrons
- **O** — Overlap with empty p-orbital
- **S** — Spread stability through delocalization

Explanation:
- In **Hyperconjugation**, **Sigma bond** electrons **Overlap** with an empty or partially filled p-orbital, **Spreading stability** by delocalizing electrons over a larger area, which lowers the system's energy.

FACTORS AFFECTING BOND DISSOCIATION ENERGY

Mnemonic: **Bold Strong Elegant & Strong**

- **B** — Bond Strength (stronger bonds have higher dissociation energy)
- **S** — Size of atoms (smaller atoms form stronger bonds)
- **E** — Electron distribution (electronegativity differences affect stability)
- **S** — Shape and bond order (multiple bonds increase dissociation energy)

Explanation:
- **Bond Dissociation Energy** is influenced by **Bond Strength**, **Size** of atoms, **Electron distribution** (polarity), and Shape (including bond order and angle), with stronger bonds requiring more energy to break.

ANALYZING ORGANIC REACTIONS

ORGANIC REACTIONS

Mnemonic: **Always Observe Carefully**

- **A** — Analyze reactants and products
- **O** — Observe reaction mechanism
- **C** — Consider factors affecting the reaction

Explanation:
- **Analyzing Organic Reactions** involves **Observing** the reaction mechanisms, Analyzing reactants and products, and **Considering** factors like energy, rate, and selectivity.

COMMON REACTION INTERMEDIATES

Mnemonic: **Curious Chemists Find Crazy New Bonds**

- **C** — Carbocations
- **C** — Carbanions
- **F** — Free Radicals
- **C** — Carbenes
- **N** — Nitrenes
- **B** — Benzyne

Explanation:
- Common reaction intermediates include **Carbocations**, **Carbanions**, Free **Radicals**, **Carbenes**, **Nitrenes**, and **Benzyne**, each with unique stability and reactivity properties.

FACTORS AFFECTING REACTION RATES

Mnemonic: **Cats Taste Certain Salty Nuts**

- **C** — Concentration
- **T** — Temperature
- **C** — Catalyst
- **S** — Surface area
- **N** — Nature of reactants

Explanation:
- **Reaction rates** are influenced by **Concentration**, **Temperature**, **Catalysts**, **Surface area**, and **Nature of reactants**, impacting how fast a reaction proceeds.

KEY THERMODYNAMIC FUNCTIONS

Mnemonic: **Happy Students Grow**

- **H** — Enthalpy (**H**)
- **S** — Entropy (**S**)
- **G** — Gibbs Free Energy (**G**)

Explanation:
- **Thermodynamic functions** like **Enthalpy**, **Entropy**, and **Gibbs Free Energy** determine reaction spontaneity, stability, and energy changes.

AROMATIC SUBSTITUTION REACTIONS

Mnemonic: **Happy New Students Fear Chemistry**

- **H** — Halogenation
- **N** — Nitration
- **S** — Sulfonation
- **F** — Friedel-Crafts Alkylation
- **C** — Friedel-Crafts Acylation

Explanation:
- Common Electrophilic **Aromatic Substitution** reactions include **Halogenation**, **Nitration**, **Sulfonation**, and **Friedel-Crafts reactions**, modifying the aromatic ring structure.

NUCLEOPHILIC SUBSTITUTION FACTORS

Mnemonic: **Nuts Subtract Loving Solvents**

- **N** — Nature of Nucleophile
- **S** — Substrate
- **L** — Leaving Group
- **S** — Solvent

Explanation:
- **Nucleophilic substitution reactions** depend on the **Nature of the Nucleophile**, **Substrate**, **Leaving group**, and **Solvent**, each affecting reaction rate and mechanism.

FACTORS AFFECTING ELIMINATION REACTIONS

Mnemonic: **Bases Stop Leaving Soon**

- **B** — Base strength
- **S** — Substrate nature
- **L** — Leaving Group
- **S** — Solvent

Explanation:
- Factors affecting **Elimination reactions** include **Base strength**, **Substrate**, **Leaving group**, and **Solvent**, determining the likelihood of elimination over substitution.

TYPES OF PERICYCLIC REACTIONS

Mnemonic: **Exciting Cycles Spin**

- **E** — Electrocyclic reactions
- **C** — Cycloaddition reactions
- **S** — Sigmatropic rearrangements

Explanation:
- **Pericyclic reactions** include **Electrocyclic reactions**, **Cycloaddition reactions**, and **Sigmatropic rearrangements**, each involving electron rearrangements in a concerted mechanism.

WOODWARD-HOFFMANN RULES

Mnemonic: **Count Cis-Con Mode**

- **C** — Count electrons (4n or 4n+2)
- **C** — Cis or trans (stereochemistry of reactants)
- **M** — Mode (Conrotatory or Disrotatory)

Explanation:
- The **Woodward-Hoffmann Rules** rely on **Counting** electrons involved in the reaction (4n or 4n+2), assessing **Cis** or **Trans** stereochemistry, and determining the Mode of ring opening/closure as either **Conrotatory** or **Disrotatory**.

ALCOHOLS

FACTORS AFFECTING THE ACIDITY OF ALCOHOLS

Mnemonic: **Small Cats Never Miss**

- **S** — **S**ize of the alkyl group
- **C** — **C**harge distribution
- **N** — **N**eighbors (electron-withdrawing groups)
- **M** — **M**olecular structure (branching or substitution)

Explanation:
- **Small Cats Never Miss** helps remember that the **Size**, **Charge**, **Neighbors**, and **Molecular structure** of alcohols influence their acidity.

COMMON REACTIONS OF ALCOHOLS

Mnemonic: **Old Red Dragons Nap**

- **O** — **O**xidation (to aldehydes, ketones, or acids)
- **R** — **R**eduction (to alkanes)
- **D** — **D**ehydration (formation of alkenes)
- **N** — **N**ucleophilic substitution

Explanation:
- **Old Red Dragons Nap** represents **Oxidation, Reduction, Dehydration,** and **Nucleophilic substitution**, which are common reactions of alcohols.

OXIDATION OF ALCOHOLS

Mnemonic: **Primary Ages Slowly, Secondary Ages Quickly**

- **P** — **P**rimary alcohols (to aldehydes)
- **S** — **S**econdary alcohols (to ketones)

Explanation:
- **Primary Ages Slowly, Secondary Ages Quickly** reminds us that Primary alcohols oxidize to Aldehydes or Acids, while **Secondary alcohols** oxidize to **Ketones** more directly.

FACTORS AFFECTING DEHYDRATION OF ALCOHOLS

Mnemonic: **Strong Acid Triggers Steam**

S Structure of the alcohol
A Acid catalyst required
T Temperature (increases dehydration)
S Solvent (type influences reaction)

Explanation:
- **Strong Acid Triggers Steam** signifies that **Structure, Acid catalyst, Temperature,** and **Solvent** all play roles in the **Dehydration of alcohols**.

COMMON PROTECTING GROUPS FOR ALCOHOLS

Mnemonic: **Silly Elephants Enjoy"**

S Silyl ethers
E Ethers
E Esters

Explanation:
- **Silly Elephants Enjoy** reminds us of **Silyl ethers, Ethers,** and **Esters,** which are commonly used **Protecting groups for alcohols**.

REACTIONS OF GRIGNARD REAGENTS

Mnemonic: **Climb Every Hill**

C Carbonyl compounds
E Epoxides
H Halogenated compounds

Explanation:
- **Giraffes Climb Every Hill** helps us recall that **Grignard reagents** react with **Carbonyl compounds, Epoxides,** and **Halogenated compounds**.

TYPES OF PHENOLS

Mnemonic: **Simple Play**

P	**S**imple phenols (one hydroxyl group)
S	**P**olyphenols (multiple hydroxyls)

Explanation:
- **Silly Pandas Play** reminds us of **Simple phenols** (single -OH) and **Polyphenols** (multiple -OH groups), which are Types of phenols.

DIFFERENT METHODS FOR SYNTHESIZING ALCOHOLS

Mnemonic: **Hot Honey Opens Gates**

H	**H**ydration of alkenes
H	**H**ydroboration-oxidation
O	**O**xidation of alkyl halides
G	**G**rignard reaction

Explanation:
- **Hot Honey Opens Gates** represents common methods for Synthesizing alcohols: **Hydration**, **Hydroboration-oxidation**, **Oxidation**, and **Grignard reaction**.

SPECTROSCOPIC ANALYSIS OF ALCOHOLS

Mnemonic: **I Need Unique Sights**

I	**I**R spectroscopy (O-H stretch)
N	**N**MR spectroscopy (distinct shifts for -OH)
U	**U**V-Vis spectroscopy
S	**S**tructure analysis

Explanation:
- **I Need Unique Sights** refers to **IR**, **NMR**, and **UV-Vis spectroscopy**, common techniques in the Spectroscopic analysis of alcohols.

ELECTROPHILICITY & REDOX

TYPES OF ELECTROPHILES

Mnemonic: **Crazy Cats Always Leap**

- **C** — Carbocations
- **C** — Carbonyl compounds
- **A** — Alkyl halides
- **L** — Lewis acids

Explanation:
- **Crazy Cats Always Leap** helps remember the types of Electrophiles: **Carbocations**, **Carbonyl compounds**, **Alkyl halides**, and **Lewis acids**.

TYPES OF NUCLEOPHILES

Mnemonic: **Humble Owls Never Stop Calling**

- **H** — Halide ions
- **O** — Oxygen-based nucleophiles
- **N** — Nitrogen-based nucleophiles
- **S** — Sulfur-based nucleophiles
- **C** — Carbon-based nucleophiles

Explanation:
- **Humble Owls Never Stop Calling** reminds us of the types of Nucleophiles: **Halide ions, Oxygen-based, Nitrogen-based, Sulfur-based,** and **Carbon-based nucleophiles**.

COMMON EAS REACTIONS

Mnemonic: **Happy New Students Craft Double A's**

- **H** — Halogenation
- **N** — Nitration
- **S** — Sulfonation
- **A** — Friedel-Crafts Alkylation
- **A** — Friedel-Crafts Acylation

Explanation:
- **Happy New Students Study Chemistry** refers to **Halogenation, Nitration, Sulfonation, Friedel-Crafts Alkylation,** and **Acylation**, common **Electrophilic Aromatic Substitution** reactions.

TYPES OF NAS REACTIONS

Mnemonic: **Alice Eats Apples**

- **A** Acid Chloride reactions
- **E** Ester reactions
- **A** Anhydride reactions

Explanation:
- **Alice Eats Apples** stands for Nucleophilic Acyl Substitution Reactions: **Acid chloride**, **Ester**, and **Anhydride reactions**.

RULES FOR ASSIGNING OXIDATION STATES

Mnemonic: **Every Cat Sings Playful Folk Hymns Outdoors**

- **E** Elemental form = 0
- **C** Charge of monatomic ion = oxidation state
- **S** Sum in neutral compound = 0
- **P** Polyatomic ion sum = ion charge
- **F** Fluorine = -1 in compounds
- **H** Hydrogen = +1 (except -1 in metal hydrides)
- **O** Oxygen = -2 (except -1 in peroxides, -1/2 in superoxides)

Explanation:
- **Every Cat Sings Playful Folk Hymns Outdoors** captures key rules for **Assigning Oxidation States**, covering elemental forms, ions, and exceptions for **Fluorine**, **Hydrogen**, and **Oxygen**.

COMMON REDOX REACTIONS

Mnemonic: **Old Rivers Oxidize Rapidly Of course**

- **O** Oxidation of alcohols
- **R** Reduction of carbonyl compounds
- **O** Oxidation of alkenes
- **R** Reduction of alkenes and alkynes
- **O** Oxidation of alkylbenzenes

Explanation:
- **Old Rivers Oxidize Rapidly Of course** stands for common **Redox reactions**: **Oxidation** of alcohols, **Reduction** of carbonyl compounds, Oxidation of alkenes and alkylbenzenes, and **Reduction** of alkenes and alkynes.

COMMON INORGANIC OXIDIZING AGENTS

Mnemonic: **Potatoes, Potatoes, Please Help**

- **P** — Potassium permanganate ($KMnO_4$)
- **P** — Potassium dichromate ($K_2Cr_2O_7$)
- **P** — Pyridinium chlorochromate (PCC)
- **H** — Hydrogen peroxide (H_2O_2)

Explanation:
- **Potatoes, Potatoes, Please Help** represents **Common Inorganic Oxidizing Agents**: **Potassium permanganate**, **Potassium dichromate**, **Pyridinium chlorochromate**, and **Hydrogen peroxide**.

COMMON ORGANIC OXIDIZING AGENTS

Mnemonic: **Perfect Desserts**

- **P** — Peroxyacids (e.g., m-CPBA)
- **D** — Dimethyl sulfoxide (DMSO)

Explanation:
- **Perfect Desserts** represents **Common Organic Oxidizing Agents**: **Peroxyacids** (like m-CPBA) and **Dimethyl sulfoxide** (DMSO).

COMMON REDUCING AGENTS

Mnemonic: **Hot Metal Drives Zippy Hikers"**

- **H** — Hydrogen gas
- **M** — Metal hydrides
- **D** — Diisobutylaluminum hydride (DIBAL-H)
- **Z** — Zinc amalgam (Zn/Hg)
- **H** — Hydrazine (N_2H_4)

Explanation:
- **Hot Metal Drives Zippy Hikers** stands for **Common Reducing Agents**: **Hydrogen gas**, **Metal hydrides**, **DIBAL-H**, **Zinc amalgam**, and **Hydrazine**.

ENOLATES

KINETIC ENOLATE VS. THERMODYNAMIC ENOLATE

Mnemonic: **Quick Kick, Strong Stay**

- **Q** Quick formation for Kinetic enolate
- **K** Kick off from low temperatures or bulky bases
- **S** Strong stability for Thermodynamic enolate
- **S** Stay with higher temperatures and small bases

Explanation:
- **Quick Kick, Strong Stay** reminds us that **Kinetic enolates** form **Quickly** with low temperatures or bulky bases, while **Thermodynamic** enolates are more **Stable** and favored at higher temperatures with smaller bases.

COMMON REACTIONS OF ENOLATES

Mnemonic: **Alligators Act Angry Chomping Hogs**

- **A** Alkylation
- **A** Acylation
- **A** Aldol condensation
- **C** Claisen condensation
- **H** Halogenation

Explanation:
- **Alligators Act Angry Chomping Hogs** represents the **Common reactions of enolates**: **Alkylation**, **Acylation**, **Aldol condensation**, **Claisen condensation**, and **Halogenation**.

TYPES OF ALDOL CONDENSATION

Mnemonic: **Some Cats Interact**

- **S** Self-Aldol condensation
- **C** Crossed-Aldol condensation
- **I** Intramolecular Aldol condensation

Explanation:
- **Some Cats Interact** helps remember the **Types of Aldol condensation**: **Self-Aldol**, **Crossed-Aldol**, and **Intramolecular Aldol condensation**.

KEY FACTORS AFFECTING CLAISEN CONDENSATION

Mnemonic: **Bears Swim Through Snow**

- **B** — **B**ase strength
- **S** — **S**olvent
- **T** — **T**emperature
- **S** — **S**teric hindrance

Explanation:
- **Bears Swim Through Snow** represents the **Key factors affecting Claisen condensation**: **Base strength**, **Solvent**, **Temperature**, and **Steric hindrance**.

REDUCTION OF CARBONYL COMPOUNDS

Mnemonic: **All Kids Create Alcohols**

- **A** — **A**ldehydes
- **K** — **K**etones
- **C** — **C**arboxylic acids
- **A** — Reduced to **A**lcohols

Explanation:
- **All Kids Create Alcohols** reminds us that **Aldehydes**, **Ketones**, and **Carboxylic acids** are reduced to **Alcohols** with agents like **LiAlH$_4$** and **NaBH$_4$**.

REDUCTION OF ALKYNES TO ALKENES AND ALKANES

Mnemonic: **Alkyne Journey to Alkanes**

- **A** — **A**lkyne
- **J** — **J**ourney to intermediate Alkene
- **A** — Ends as **A**lkane

Explanation:
- **Alkyne Journey to Alkanes** indicates that **Alkynes** can be reduced to **Alkenes** or **Alkanes** depending on the conditions and reducing agents used.

MECHANISM OF CATALYTIC HYDROGENATION

Mnemonic: **Perfect Platinum Powers**

- **P** — Pd (palladium)
- **P** — Pt (platinum)
- **P** — Participate as Metal catalysts

Explanation:
- **Perfect Platinum Powers** highlights how **Pd** (palladium) and **Pt** (platinum), along with other catalysts, play a crucial role in **promoting** hydrogenation reactions during catalytic processes.

STEREOSELECTIVE REDUCTION REACTIONS

Mnemonic: **Cool Chefs Serve Temperature and Seasoned Enzymes**

- **C** — Chiral reducing agents
- **C** — Chiral ligands
- **S** — Substrate control
- **T** — Temperature and solvent effects
- **E** — Enzyme catalysis

Explanation:
- **Cool Chefs Serve Temperature** and **Seasoned Enzymes** helps remember factors for **Stereoselective reduction: Chiral reducing agents, Chiral ligands, Substrate control, Temperature and solvent effects,** and **Enzyme catalysis.**

WOLFF-KISHNER REDUCTION PROCESS

Mnemonic: **Hydrazine Heats High Alkanes**

- **H** — Hydrazine (N_2H_4) reacts with carbonyl
- **H** — Heat (reaction requires high temperature)
- **H** — Hydroxide (strong base like KOH)
- **A** — Converts to Alkane

Explanation:
- **Hydrazine Heats High Alkanes** represents the key steps of the **Wolff-Kishner Reduction: Hydrazine (N_2H_4)** reacts with the carbonyl group in the presence of a strong base **(Hydroxide like KOH)** and Heat to convert the carbonyl compound into an **Alkane**.

CARBOXYLIC ACID

CARBOXYLIC ACID ACIDITY FACTORS

Mnemonic: **Resonance Inspires Polarity**

R Resonance stabilization of the carboxylate ion
I Inductive effect (electron-withdrawing groups increase acidity)
P Polarity of the O-H bond

Explanation:
- **Resonance Inspires Polarity** represents **Resonance stabilization**, **Inductive effects**, and **Polarity** as factors affecting **Acidity** in carboxylic acids.

COMMON REACTIONS OF CARBOXYLIC ACIDS

Mnemonic: **Acids Never Really Dance Elegantly**

A Acid-base reactions
N Nucleophilic acyl substitution reactions
R Reduction reactions
D Decarboxylation
E Electrophilic aromatic substitution

Explanation:
- **Acids Never Really Dance Elegantly** covers **Common reactions of carboxylic acids**: **Acid-base**, **Nucleophilic acyl substitution**, **Reduction**, **Decarboxylation**, and **Electrophilic aromatic substitution**.

STEPS OF ESTERIFICATION

Mnemonic: **Peaceful Nighttime Promises Eternity**

P Protonation of the carbonyl oxygen
N Nucleophilic attack
P Proton transfer
E Elimination of water

Explanation:
- **Peaceful Nighttime Promises Eternity** helps remember the **Steps of Esterification**: **Protonation**, **Nucleophilic attack**, **Proton transfer**, and **Elimination of water**.

ACIDIC HYDROLYSIS OF ESTERS

Mnemonic: **Protons Need Proper Elimination**

- **P** — Protonation of the carbonyl oxygen
- **N** — Nucleophilic attack
- **P** — Proton transfer
- **E** — Elimination of alcohol

Explanation:
- **Protons Need Proper Elimination** represents the **Steps in Acidic Hydrolysis of Esters: Protonation, Nucleophilic attack, Proton transfer,** and **Elimination of alcohol.**

BASIC HYDROLYSIS OF ESTERS

Mnemonic: **Noble Elephants Parade**

- **N** — Nucleophilic attack
- **E** — Elimination of alkoxide
- **P** — Protonation

Explanation:
- **Noble Elephants Parade** covers the **Steps in Basic Hydrolysis of Esters: Nucleophilic attack, Elimination of alkoxide,** and **Protonation.**

REDUCTION OF CARBOXYLIC ACIDS TO ALCOHOLS

Mnemonic: **Amazing Reduction**

- **A** — Acyl intermediate formation
- **R** — Reduction of the acyl intermediate

Explanation:
- **Amazing Reduction** reminds us of the **Reduction of Carboxylic Acids to Alcohols** through **Acyl intermediate formation** and Reduction.

FACTORS AFFECTING DECARBOXYLATION

Mnemonic: **Elephants Hate Cats**

- **E** — Electron-withdrawing groups
- **H** — Heat (promotes reaction)
- **C** — Catalytic agents aid the reaction

Explanation:
- **Elephants Hate Cats** represents the **Factors Affecting Decarboxylation**: **Electron-withdrawing groups**, **Heat**, and **Catalytic agents**.

COMMON CARBOXYLIC ACID DERIVATIVES

Mnemonic: **Angry Ants Eat Apples**

- **A** — Acid chlorides (RCOCl)
- **A** — Acid anhydrides
- **E** — Esters (RCOOR')
- **A** — Amides (RCONH$_2$)

Explanation:
- **Angry Ants Eat Apples** refers to Common **Carboxylic Acid Derivatives**: **Acid chlorides**, **Acid anhydrides**, **Esters**, and **Amides**.

NUCLEOPHILIC ACYL SUBSTITUTION

Mnemonic: **Hungry Alligators Always Roar**

- **H** — Hydrolysis
- **A** — Alcoholysis
- **A** — Aminolysis
- **R** — Reduction

Explanation:
- **Hungry Alligators Always Roar** represents **Common Nucleophilic Acyl Substitution Reactions**: **Hydrolysis**, **Alcoholysis**, **Aminolysis**, and **Reduction**.

CARBOXYLIC ACID DERIVATIVES

REACTIVITY OF CARBOXYLIC ACID DERIVATIVES

Mnemonic: **Chlorides Attack Everyone Aggressively**

- **C** — Chlorides (acid chlorides; most reactive)
- **A** — Anhydrides
- **E** — Esters
- **A** — Amides (least reactive)

Explanation:
- **Chlorides Always Attack Everyone Aggressively** represents the **Relative Reactivity** of carboxylic acid derivatives, with **Chlorides** being the most reactive and **Amides** being the least reactive.

NUCLEOPHILIC ACYL SUBSTITUTION

Mnemonic: **New Attack In Chemistry**

- **N** — Nucleophile attacks
- **A** — Forms Acyl intermediate
- **I** — Intermediate reorganizes
- **C** — Completion of substitution reaction

Explanation:
- **New Attack In Chemistry** describes the **Mechanism of Nucleophilic Acyl Substitution**, involving a **Nucleophilic attack**, formation of an **Acyl intermediate**, and **Completion** of the reaction.

ACID CHLORIDE REACTIONS

Mnemonic: **All Actors Work**

- **A** — Reacts with Alcohols
- **A** — Reacts with Amines
- **W** — Reacts with Water

Explanation:
- **All Actors Work** reminds us that Acid chlorides react with **Alcohols**, **Amines**, and **Water**.

ESTER REACTIONS

Mnemonic: **Hungry Tigers Rest**

- **H** — Hydrolysis
- **T** — Transesterification
- **R** — Reduction

Explanation:
- **Hungry Tigers Rest** helps remember **Ester Reactions**: **Hydrolysis**, **Transesterification**, and **Reduction**.

AMIDE REACTIONS

Mnemonic: **Hungry Raccoons**

- **H** — Hydrolysis
- **R** — Reduction

Explanation:
- **Hungry Raccoons** reminds us of Amide Reactions, which primarily include **Hydrolysis** and **Reduction**.

NITRILES

Mnemonic: **Nice Primary Hydro**

- **N** — Nitriles
- **P** — Reduced to Primary amines
- **H** — Hydrolysis to carboxylic acids

Explanation:
- **Nice Primary Hydro** describes the **Reactions of Nitriles**: **Reduction** to **Primary amines** and **Hydrolysis** to **Carboxylic acids**.

SPECTROSCOPY OF CARBOXYLIC ACID DERIVATIVES

Mnemonic: **IR, Noticed Immediately**

- **I** — IR spectroscopy (carbonyl stretches)
- **N** — NMR spectroscopy (distinct shifts for carboxyl groups)
- **I** — Identifies Intensity of functional groups

Explanation:
- **IR, Noticed Immediately** covers the **Spectroscopic Analysis** of carboxylic acid derivatives, with IR identifying carbonyl stretches and **NMR** providing distinct shifts.

CLAISEN CONDENSATION MECHANISM

Mnemonic: **Base Attacks, Combine, Kick Out**

- **B** — Base removes an alpha hydrogen from one ester
- **A** — Attack by enolate on the carbonyl carbon of a second ester
- **C** — Combine to form a tetrahedral intermediate
- **K** — Kick out the leaving group, forming the β-keto ester

Explanation:
- **Base Attacks, Combine, Kick Out** helps remember the **Claisen Condensation steps**: **Base** forms an enolate, **Attack** on the second ester, **Combine** into a tetrahedral intermediate, and **Kick** out a leaving group to form the β-keto ester.

DIECKMANN CONDENSATION MECHANISM

Mnemonic: **Base Creates Intramolecular Cycles**

- **B** — Base
- **C** — Creates
- **I** — Intramolecular
- **C** — Cycles

Explanation:
- **Base Creates Intramolecular Cycles** summarizes the **Dieckmann Condensation**: the **Base** forms an enolate, which **Creates** an **intramolecular** attack on a carbonyl, leading to a **Cycle** and forming a Cyclic β-keto ester.

NITROGEN & PHOSPHORUS

AMINES

Mnemonic: **Basic Aliens Attack Acids**

B — **B**asicity of amines
A — **A**mines react with **A**cids
A — React with **A**lkyl halides
A — React with **A**cyl chlorides

Explanation:
- **Basic Aliens Attack Acids** reminds us that **Amines** are **Basic** and react with **Acids**, **Alkyl halides**, and **Acyl chlorides**.

AMIDES

Mnemonic: **Amides Handle Reduction**

A — **A**mides
H — Undergo **H**ydrolysis
R — Undergo **R**eduction

Explanation:
- **Amides Handle Hydrolysis** and **Reduction** helps remember the **Reactions of Amides**, including **Hydrolysis** and **Reduction**.

NITRILES

Mnemonic: **Nitriles Reduce Hardly**

N — **N**itriles
R — **R**eduction to amines
H — **H**ydrolysis to carboxylic acids

Explanation:
- **Nitriles Reduce Hardly** covers the **Reactions of Nitriles: Reduction** to amines and **Hydrolysis** to carboxylic acids.

IMINES AND ENAMINES

Mnemonic: **Imagine Enigmas Formed**

- **I** — Imines
- **E** — Enamines
- **F** — Formation and Reactivity

Explanation:
- **Imagine Enigmas Formed** represents **Imines** and **Enamines**, covering their **Formation and Reactivity**.

PHOSPHORUS COMPOUNDS

Mnemonic: **Phosphorus Plants Thrive Excellently**

- **P** — Phosphines
- **P** — Phosphites
- **T** — Thrive (reactivity)
- **E** — Esters (phosphate esters)

Explanation:
- **Phosphorus Plants Thrive Excellently** covers **Phosphorus Compounds** like **Phosphines**, **Phosphites**, and **Phosphate** esters and their reactivity.

PHOSPHORUS NUCLEOPHILIC SUBSTITUTION

Mnemonic: **New Substitute Arrives**

- **N** — Nucleophilic substitution
- **S** — Substitution mechanism
- **A** — Arbuzov reaction

Explanation:
- **New Substitute Arrives** reminds us of **Nucleophilic** substitution reactions of phosphorus compounds, particularly the **Arbuzov reaction**.

HETEROCYCLIC COMPOUNDS

Mnemonic: **Puzzling Patterns Impressed**

P Pyridine
P Pyrrole
I Imidazole

Explanation:
- **Puzzling Patterns Impressed** represents **Heterocyclic Compounds** with nitrogen, such as **Pyridine**, **Pyrrole**, and **Imidazole**.

BIOLOGICALLY IMPORTANT NITROGEN COMPOUNDS

Mnemonic: **Animals Need Nourishment**

A Amino acids
N Nucleotides
N Neurotransmitters

Explanation:
- **Animals Need Nourishment** helps recall **Biologically Important Nitrogen Compounds**: **Amino acids**, **Nucleotides**, and **Neurotransmitters**.

NITROGEN & PHOSPHORUS SPECTROSCOPY

Mnemonic: **Spectral Insights Needed**

S Spectroscopic analysis
I IR spectra (identifying N-H and P-H bonds)
N NMR spectra

Explanation:
- **Spectral Insights Needed** refers to **Spectroscopic Analysis** of nitrogen and phosphorus compounds, including **IR** and NMR spectra for identifying functional groups.

SPECTROSCOPY

INFRARED (IR) SPECTROSCOPY

Mnemonic: **Vibrant Bonds Absorb**

- **V** — Vibrations of bonds
- **B** — Bonds' vibrations relate to IR absorption
- **A** — Absorption seen in IR spectra

Explanation:
- **Vibrant Bonds Absorb** describes how **Bond Vibrations** absorb IR radiation at specific frequencies, which are detected in **IR Spectroscopy**.

FUNCTIONAL GROUP REGIONS IN IR

Mnemonic: **Alcohols, Carbonyls, Amines Shine**

- **A** — Alcohols (O-H stretch around 3200-3600 cm^{-1})
- **C** — Carbonyls (C=O stretch around 1700 cm^{-1})
- **A** — Amines (N-H stretch around 3300-3500 cm^{-1})
- **S** — Shine (distinct IR peaks)

Explanation:
- **Alcohols, Carbonyls, Amines Shine** reminds us of **Characteristic IR regions** for **Alcohols**, **Carbonyls**, and **Amines**.

NITROGEN & PHOSPHORUS SPECTROSCOPY

Mnemonic: **Chemical Shifts Inside**

- **C** — Chemical shifts
- **S** — Splitting patterns (multiplicity)
- **I** — Integration (peak areas)

Explanation:
- Chemical Shifts in New Splits covers the basics of **NMR Spectroscopy**: Chemical shifts, Integration, and **Splitting patterns**.

PROTON NMR (1H NMR)

Mnemonic: **Protons Seek Intense Splits**

P   Protons (1H nuclei in NMR)
S   Shifts (chemical shift values)
I   Integration (number of hydrogens)
S   Splits (multiplicity)

Explanation:
- **Protons Seek Intense Splits** helps us interpret **1H NMR Spectra**, focusing on **Chemical shift**, **Integration**, and **Splitting patterns**.

CARBON-13 NMR (13C NMR)

Mnemonic: **Carbon Shifts Quietly**

C   Carbon-13 nuclei
S   Shifts (chemical shift values)
Q   Quietly (no splitting due to low abundance)

Explanation:
- **Carbon Shifts Quietly** refers to **13C NMR**, where Chemical shifts are observed without **Splitting** due to the low natural abundance of **13C**.

MASS SPECTROMETRY (MS)

Mnemonic: **Ionize and Fragment**

I   Ionization techniques (EI, CI)
F   Fragmentation patterns

Explanation:
- **Ionize and Fragment** highlights the **Principles of Mass Spectrometry**: Ionization and observing **Fragmentation patterns** to identify compounds.

UV-VIS SPECTROSCOPY

Mnemonic: **Chromophores Use Vision**

- **C** — Chromophores
- **U** — UV-Vis spectra
- **V** — Visible (determines conjugated structure)

Explanation:
- **Chromophores Use Vision** refers to **UV-Vis Spectroscopy**, where **Chromophores** absorb UV-Vis light, helping determine conjugated structures.

SPECTROSCOPIC ANALYSIS OF MIXTURES

Mnemonic: **Mix, Match, Identify**

- **M** — Mixtures
- **M** — Match spectra of components
- **I** — Identify each component

Explanation:
- **Mix, Match, Identify** guides the **Spectroscopic Analysis** of **Mixtures** by Matching spectral features and Identifying components.

CORRELATION TABLES

Mnemonic: **Tables Predict Shifts**

- **T** — Tables (correlation tables)
- **P** — Predict chemical shifts
- **S** — Shifts and splitting patterns

Explanation:
- **Tables Predict Shifts Smartly** emphasizes **Using Correlation Tables** to Predict chemical shifts and **Splitting patterns** in NMR spectra.

SEPARATIONS & PURIFICATIONS

EXTRACTION

Mnemonic: **Solvents Separate Solutions**

- **S** — **S**olvents (use different solvents for separation)
- **S** — **S**eparate compounds based on solubility
- **S** — Create **S**olutions in each layer

Explanation:
- **Solvents Separate Solutions** refers to the use of different **Solvents** to **Separate** compounds based on **Solubility** in liquid-liquid Extraction.

DISTILLATION

Mnemonic: **Simple Facts Vary**

- **S** — **S**imple distillation
- **F** — **F**ractional distillation
- **V** — **V**acuum distillation

Explanation:
- **Simple Facts Vary** helps remember the Types of **Distillation**: **Simple**, **Fractional**, and **Vacuum distillation**.

CHROMATOGRAPHY

Mnemonic: **Thin Columns Gather**

- **T** — **T**hin-layer chromatography
- **C** — **C**olumn chromatography
- **G** — **G**as chromatography

Explanation:
- **Thin Columns Gather** stands for the **Types of Chromatography**: TLC, **Column chromatography**, and **Gas chromatography**, used in **Separating** and **Purifying Compounds**.

RECRYSTALLIZATION

Mnemonic: **Solvents Dissolve Crystals**

- **S** — **S**olvent selection is critical
- **D** — **D**issolve the compound
- **C** — Form **C**rystals upon cooling

Explanation:
- **Solvents Dissolve Crystals** summarizes **Recrystallization** steps: choosing a **Solvent**, **Dissolving** the compound, and forming **Crystals**.

SUBLIMATION

Mnemonic: **Solid to Gas Purifies**

- **S** — **S**olid (compound in solid form)
- **G** — **G**as phase (direct transition)
- **P** — **P**urifies the substance

Explanation:
- **Solid to Gas Purifies** describes **Sublimation**, where a **Solid** directly converts to a Gas for **Purification**.

FILTRATION

Mnemonic: **Gravity Vacuums Liquid**

- **G** — **G**ravity filtration
- **V** — **V**acuum filtration
- **L** — Separate **L**iquid from solid

Explanation:
- **Gravity Vacuums Liquid** covers **Types of Filtration**: **Gravity filtration** and **Vacuum filtration** to separate **Solids** from **Liquids**.

CENTRIFUGATION

Mnemonic: **Spin Density Separates**

- **S** — **S**pin samples in a centrifuge
- **D** — Based on **D**ensity
- **S** — **S**eparates components

Explanation:
- **Spin Density Separates** refers to **Centrifugation**, where Spinning based on **Density** allows for the **Separation** of components.

DRYING AGENTS

Mnemonic: **Sodium Might Absorb**

- **S** — **S**odium sulfate (anhydrous)
- **M** — **M**agnesium sulfate
- **A** — **A**bsorb water from organic solvents

Explanation:
- **Sodium Might Absorb** helps remember **Common Drying Agents** like **Sodium sulfate** and **Magnesium sulfate** used to **Absorb** water.

EXTRACTION EFFICIENCY

Mnemonic: **Partition Volume Matters**

- **P** — **P**artition coefficient (affects efficiency)
- **V** — **V**olume ratio of two solvents
- **M** — Efficiency **M**atters

Explanation:
- **Partition Volume Matters** relates to **Factors Affecting Extraction Efficiency**, including the **Partition coefficient** and **Volume ratio** of solvents.

CHEAT SHEET

	BIOLOGY & BEHAVIOR
Neurotransmitter Systems	• Chemical systems in the brain, such as dopamine, serotonin, acetylcholine, and norepinephrine, that influence mood, behavior, and physiological responses.
Hormonal Influences on Behavior	• Hormones like testosterone, estrogen, and oxytocin affect behavior, mood, and social bonding.
Genetics and Behavior	• Genetic makeup influences traits, predispositions, and behaviors, often interacting with environmental factors.
Evolutionary Psychology	• A field that explores how evolutionary pressures have shaped behaviors like mate selection, aggression, and altruism.
Sociocultural Influences on Behavior	• Cultural norms, societal expectations, and social influences shape individual behaviors and attitudes.
The Role of the Environment in Behavior	• Environmental factors such as stress, nutrition, and exposure to toxins significantly affect brain development and behavior.
Neuroimaging Techniques	• Methods like fMRI and PET scans are used to visualize brain activity and study its relationship to behavior.
Sleep and Behavior	• Sleep quality and duration directly impact cognitive function, mood, and behavioral performance.
The Role of the Autonomic Nervous System	• The autonomic nervous system regulates involuntary physiological responses through its sympathetic (fight or flight) and parasympathetic (rest and digest) branches.
Plasticity of the Brain	• The brain's ability to adapt and reorganize itself by forming new neural connections in response to learning, experience, or injury.
Endocrine System and Behavior	• The endocrine system regulates behavior through hormone secretion, influencing stress, metabolism, growth, and reproduction.

Behavioral Genetics	- The study of how genetic and environmental factors contribute to individual differences in behavior and personality.
Learning and Memory	- Processes by which behaviors are acquired through experiences and retained over time, involving brain structures like the hippocampus.

SENSATION & PERCEPTION	
Sensory Adaptation	- The process where sensory receptors become less sensitive to constant stimuli over time.
Sensory Habituation	- The reduction in response to a stimulus after repeated exposure, driven by cognitive processing.
Psychophysics	- The study of the relationship between physical stimuli and the sensations and perceptions they produce.
Bottom-Up and Top-Down Processing	- Bottom-up processing relies on data from the senses, while top-down processing uses prior knowledge to interpret sensory information.
Perceptual Illusions	- Misinterpretations or distortions of sensory input that reveal how the brain processes perception.
Depth Perception	- The ability to perceive the world in three dimensions using cues from both eyes (binocular) and one eye (monocular).
Gestalt Principles	- Perceptual rules like proximity, similarity, continuity, and closure that describe how we organize sensory information into meaningful patterns.
Sensory Integration	- The process of combining information from multiple sensory modalities into a cohesive perceptual experience.
Cross-Modal Perception	- The interaction between different sensory modalities, where one sense influences or enhances the perception of another.
Absolute Threshold	- The minimum level of stimulus intensity required to detect a stimulus 50% of the time.
Difference Threshold	- The smallest detectable difference between two stimuli that a person can perceive.

Weber's Law	• The principle that the just noticeable difference between two stimuli is proportional to the magnitude of the stimuli.
Selective Attention	• The process of focusing on specific stimuli while ignoring others, allowing for efficient information processing.
Signal Detection Theory	• A framework for understanding how individuals detect faint stimuli under uncertain conditions, accounting for both sensory and decision-making factors.

LEARNING & MEMORY	
State-Dependent Memory	• The retrieval of information is easier when a person is in the same internal state as during encoding.
Context-Dependent Memory	• Information is more easily recalled when a person is in the same physical environment where the memory was encoded.
Encoding Specificity Principle	• Memory retrieval is most effective when the conditions at retrieval match those during encoding.
Implicit Memory	• A type of long-term memory involving skills and habits that can be recalled without conscious awareness.
Semantic Memory	• A category of long-term memory that stores general world knowledge, concepts, and facts.
Flashbulb Memory	• A vivid, detailed memory of an emotionally significant event.
Memory Consolidation	• The process by which short-term memories are stabilized and stored as long-term memories.
Forgetting Curve	• A graphical representation of the decline in memory retention over time, with rapid initial forgetting.
Mnemonic Devices	• Techniques, such as acronyms or imagery, used to enhance memory retention and recall.
Working Memory	• A cognitive system responsible for temporarily holding and processing information needed for reasoning and decision-making.
Episodic Memory	• A type of long-term memory that involves recollection of specific personal experiences and events.

COGNITION, CONSCIOUSNESS & LANGUAGE

Theory of Mind	• The ability to understand and attribute beliefs, desires, and intentions to oneself and others.
Consciousness and Attention	• Consciousness refers to awareness of surroundings and internal states, while attention involves focusing selectively on specific stimuli.
Language Acquisition	• The process through which individuals learn and develop language, influenced by both biological predispositions and environmental factors.
Language Disorders	• Impairments in language abilities, such as aphasia and dyslexia, affecting speech, reading, or comprehension.
Problem-Solving Strategies	• Methods like algorithms, heuristics, and insight used to resolve challenges and make decisions.
Cognitive Biases	• Systematic patterns of deviation from rational judgment, such as confirmation bias, anchoring bias, and the availability heuristic.
Cognitive Control	• The ability to regulate thoughts and behaviors, often involving the prefrontal cortex for planning and decision-making.
Working Memory	• A system for temporarily holding and manipulating information necessary for complex cognitive tasks.
Consciousness and Sleep	• Sleep involves different stages of consciousness, including REM and non-REM sleep, crucial for rest and dreaming.
Metacognition	• The awareness and understanding of one's own thought processes, including the ability to monitor and regulate them.
Executive Functions	• Higher-level cognitive processes such as planning, decision-making, and problem-solving, primarily governed by the prefrontal cortex.
Linguistic Relativity	• The theory that the structure of a language influences the way its speakers think and perceive the world.
Neuroplasticity	• The brain's ability to adapt and reorganize itself by forming new neural connections in response to learning or injury.

MOTIVATION, EMOTION & STRESS

Self-Efficacy	• The belief in one's ability to successfully perform and achieve specific goals.
Intrinsic and Extrinsic Motivation	• Intrinsic motivation arises from internal satisfaction, while extrinsic motivation is driven by external rewards.
Emotion Regulation	• The process of managing and modifying emotional responses through strategies like cognitive reappraisal or suppression.
Theories of Emotion	• Frameworks explaining emotion, such as James-Lange (emotion follows physiological response), Cannon-Bard (simultaneous emotion and response), and Schachter-Singer (emotion influenced by arousal and interpretation).
Stress Response	• The body's reaction to stress, including the immediate fight-or-flight response and the long-term activation of the HPA axis.
Coping Mechanisms	• Strategies to handle stress, including problem-focused coping (addressing stressors) and emotion-focused coping (managing feelings).
Social Support and Stress	• The availability of social relationships that reduce the psychological and physiological impact of stress.
Post-Traumatic Stress Disorder (PTSD)	• A mental health condition triggered by traumatic events, characterized by flashbacks, anxiety, and prolonged stress responses.
Positive Psychology	• A field focusing on strengths, virtues, and practices that enhance well-being and resilience.
Dual-Process Theory	• A cognitive model explaining decision-making and reasoning through two systems: fast, automatic (System 1) and slow, deliberate (System 2).
Selective and Divided Attention	• Selective attention focuses on specific stimuli, while divided attention involves multitasking and managing multiple inputs simultaneously.
Broca's and Wernicke's Areas	• Brain regions critical for language, with Broca's area involved in speech production and Wernicke's area in language comprehension.

IDENTITY & PERSONALITY	
Social Identity Theory	- A theory that explains how an individual's identity is shaped by group membership and the associated norms, values, and behaviors.
Self-Concept	- The collection of beliefs, evaluations, and perceptions an individual has about themselves, including self-esteem, self-efficacy, and self-schema.
Personality Traits (Five-Factor Model)	- A widely accepted model describing personality using five traits: openness, conscientiousness, extraversion, agreeableness, and neuroticism.
Psychoanalytic Theory	- Freud's theory of personality, emphasizing the interaction of the id, ego, and superego in shaping behavior and desires.
Humanistic Psychology	- A perspective focusing on personal growth, self-actualization, and the inherent potential for positive change in individuals.
Social Cognitive Theory	- A framework explaining how personality is influenced by the reciprocal interaction of cognitive processes, behaviors, and environmental factors.
Cultural Influences on Identity	- The impact of cultural norms, values, and practices on shaping an individual's sense of self and behavior.
Gender Identity and Role	- The understanding and expression of oneself in terms of gender, influenced by societal roles and stereotypes.
Identity Crisis	- A period of uncertainty and exploration of values, beliefs, and roles, often leading to the development of a clearer sense of self.
Erikson's Stages of Psychosocial Development	- A theory outlining eight stages across the lifespan, each presenting a unique psychosocial conflict that influences identity formation.
Big Five and Behavioral Outcomes	- Research linking personality traits from the Five-Factor Model to behavioral patterns, mental health, and life outcomes.
Collective Identity	- An individual's sense of belonging to a collective group, shaped by shared goals, values, and cultural heritage.

PSYCHOLOGICAL DISORDERS

Major Depressive Disorder (MDD)	• A mood disorder characterized by persistent feelings of sadness, loss of interest, and significant impairment in daily functioning.
Bipolar Disorder	• A mood disorder involving episodes of mania or hypomania alternating with episodes of depression.
Obsessive-Compulsive Disorder (OCD)	• A disorder characterized by intrusive, repetitive thoughts (obsessions) and ritualistic behaviors (compulsions) performed to reduce anxiety.
Schizophrenia	• A severe mental disorder marked by distorted thoughts, perceptions, and behaviors, often including hallucinations and delusions.
Postpartum Depression	• A form of depression occurring after childbirth, involving mood swings, anxiety, and difficulties bonding with the baby.
Generalized Anxiety Disorder (GAD)	• A disorder characterized by excessive, uncontrollable worry about various aspects of daily life.
Phobias (Specific and Social)	• Intense, irrational fears of specific objects, situations, or social interactions that lead to avoidance behavior.
Panic Disorder	• A disorder involving recurrent and unexpected panic attacks, accompanied by persistent fear of future attacks.
Substance Use Disorders	• Disorders involving problematic patterns of substance use leading to significant impairment or distress.
Eating Disorders (Anorexia and Bulimia)	• Disorders characterized by unhealthy eating behaviors, such as extreme restriction (anorexia) or bingeing and purging (bulimia).
Adjustment Disorder	• A stress-related condition where emotional or behavioral symptoms develop in response to a significant life change or stressor.
Histrionic Personality Disorder	• A personality disorder characterized by excessive emotionality and attention-seeking behavior, often with a need for approval.

SOCIAL PROCESSES, ATTITUDE & BEHAVIOR

Social Cognition	• The process of interpreting, analyzing, and remembering information about social interactions and environments.
Attitudes and Persuasion	• Attitudes encompass thoughts, feelings, and behaviors toward an object or idea, while persuasion involves efforts to change these attitudes through communication.
Cognitive Dissonance	• The mental discomfort experienced when holding conflicting beliefs or engaging in behaviors inconsistent with personal values.
Social Influence	• The effects of social norms, conformity, and authority on individual behaviors and decision-making.
Group Processes	• The dynamics within groups, including phenomena like groupthink, social facilitation, and social loafing.
Altruism and Prosocial Behavior	• Voluntary actions intended to benefit others, often motivated by empathy or societal norms.
Aggression and Violence	• Behaviors intended to cause harm or assert dominance, influenced by biological, psychological, and social factors.
Prejudice and Discrimination	• Prejudice involves unfounded negative attitudes toward a group, while discrimination refers to unfair actions based on these biases.
Social Identity Theory	• A theory that explains how group membership shapes self-concept and influences intergroup behavior and attitudes.
Social Facilitation	• The phenomenon where individuals perform better on simple or well-learned tasks in the presence of others but may struggle with complex tasks under observation.
Deindividuation	• A psychological state where individuals lose self-awareness and accountability in group settings, leading to behavior that may deviate from personal norms.
Social Comparison Theory	• The idea that individuals evaluate their own abilities, opinions, and self-worth by comparing themselves to others.
Normative and Informational Social Influence	• Normative influence occurs when individuals conform to be liked or accepted, while informational influence arises from a desire to act correctly in uncertain situations.

SOCIAL INTERACTIONS	
Social Exchange Theory	• Proposes that social interactions are driven by the desire to maximize rewards and minimize costs.
Equity Theory	• Suggests individuals assess fairness in relationships by comparing their contributions and benefits to those of others.
Social Comparison Theory	• Explains that individuals evaluate their own abilities and opinions by comparing themselves to others.
Impression Management	• Refers to strategies individuals use to influence how others perceive them.
Nonverbal Communication	• Involves transmitting information without words through body language, facial expressions, gestures, and tone.
Social Facilitation and Inhibition	• Describes how the presence of others can enhance or impair individual performance depending on the task's difficulty.
Groupthink	• Occurs when the desire for harmony or conformity in a group leads to poor decision-making.
Bystander Effect	• The tendency for individuals to be less likely to help in an emergency when others are present.
Social Loafing	• The phenomenon where individuals exert less effort when working in a group compared to working alone.
Role Conflict	• Occurs when competing demands from different social roles create tension or difficulty in fulfilling them.
Deindividuation	• A psychological state where individuals lose their sense of self-awareness and responsibility in group settings, often leading to impulsive behavior.
Social Norms	• Shared expectations and rules that guide behavior within a group or society.
Status and Role	• Refers to an individual's position within a social hierarchy (status) and the expected behaviors associated with that position (role).
Power Dynamics	• Explores how power is distributed and exercised in relationships and groups, influencing interactions and outcomes.

SOCIAL THINKING

Attribution Theory	• Explains behavior by attributing it to internal dispositions or external situations.
Fundamental Attribution Error	• The tendency to overemphasize internal factors and underestimate external factors when explaining others' behaviors.
Self-Serving Bias	• A cognitive bias where successes are attributed to internal factors and failures to external ones.
Just-World Hypothesis	• The belief that people get what they deserve and deserve what they get.
Confirmation Bias	• The tendency to seek and favor information that confirms one's preexisting beliefs while ignoring contradictory evidence.
Hindsight Bias	• The inclination to see events as predictable after they have occurred.
Counterfactual Thinking	• The mental process of imagining alternative outcomes to events that have already happened.
Social Cognition	• The process of perceiving, interpreting, and responding to social information and cues.
Stereotypes and Prejudice	• Generalized cognitive beliefs (stereotypes) and emotional reactions (prejudice) that can lead to biased behavior.
Actor-Observer Bias	• The tendency to attribute one's own actions to external factors while attributing others' actions to internal factors.
False Consensus Effect	• The belief that others share the same opinions, beliefs, or behaviors as oneself more often than they actually do.
Optimism Bias	• The tendency to overestimate the likelihood of positive outcomes and underestimate the likelihood of negative ones.
Halo Effect	• A cognitive bias where the perception of one positive trait influences the perception of other unrelated traits.
Self-Fulfilling Prophecy	• A phenomenon where an individual's expectations about someone lead that person to behave in ways that confirm those expectations.

SOCIAL STRUCTURE & DEMOGRAPHICS

Social Stratification	• The hierarchical organization of society based on wealth, power, and prestige.
Social Inequality	• The unequal distribution of resources and opportunities across class, race, gender, and age groups.
Social Mobility	• The movement of individuals or groups within the social hierarchy, either upward or downward.
Cultural Diversity	• The coexistence of multiple cultural groups within a society, influencing social dynamics and interactions.
Globalization	• The increasing interconnectedness of cultures, economies, and societies on a global scale.
Urbanization	• The growth and expansion of urban areas, leading to changes in social structure, economy, and demographics.
Demographic Transition Model	• A model that describes the transition of population growth patterns through stages of development, based on birth and death rates.
Social Change	• Transformations in society driven by cultural shifts, technological advancements, and evolving trends.
Social Institutions	• Established structures like family, education, religion, and government that govern societal behavior and interactions.
Population Aging	• The increasing proportion of older individuals in the population, impacting economic, healthcare, and social policies.
Intersectionality	• The concept that social categories such as race, gender, class, and sexuality intersect to create unique systems of discrimination or privilege for individuals.
Migration Patterns	• The movement of people between regions or countries, influencing demographic shifts, cultural exchanges, and economic development.
Environmental Justice	• The fair treatment and meaningful involvement of all individuals, regardless of race or income, in environmental policies and practices that affect their communities.

SOCIAL STRATIFICATIONS DEFINITIONS	
Social Class	• A hierarchical division of society based on factors like wealth, education, and occupation, influencing life opportunities and status.
Socioeconomic Status (SES)	• A composite measure that combines income, education level, and occupational prestige to determine an individual's position in society.
Cultural Capital	• Non-financial social assets such as knowledge, education, and skills that promote social mobility within a stratified society.
Social Reproduction	• The perpetuation of social inequalities across generations through institutions such as family and education.
Intersectionality	• The framework that examines how different aspects of identity, such as race, gender, and class, combine to create unique experiences of discrimination or privilege.
Global Inequality	• The unequal distribution of resources, wealth, and opportunities among individuals and nations worldwide.
Poverty and Inequality	• The state where individuals or groups lack access to basic resources, services, and opportunities, perpetuating disparities in health, education, and social outcomes.
Social Mobility	• The ability of individuals or groups to move up or down the social hierarchy, either within their lifetime or across generations.
Social Exclusion	• The process by which certain groups are systematically marginalized and denied access to full participation in society.

BIOLOGY & BEHAVIOR

NEUROTRANSMITTER SYSTEMS

Mnemonic: **Dancing Stars Always Nod**

- **D** **D**opamine (involved in reward and pleasure)
- **S** **S**erotonin (affects mood and sleep)
- **A** **A**cetylcholine (involved in learning and memory)
- **N** **N**orepinephrine (influences alertness and arousal)

Explanation:
- **Dancing Stars Always Nod** represents key **Neurotransmitters**: **Dopamine, Serotonin, Acetylcholine**, and **Norepinephrine**, each with specific roles in behavior and mood.

HORMONAL INFLUENCES ON BEHAVIOR

Mnemonic: **Test Every Opportunity**

- **T** **T**estosterone (influences aggression and mood)
- **E** **E**strogen (affects mood and social bonding)
- **O** **O**xytocin (related to bonding and trust)

Explanation:
- **Test Every Opportunity** covers **Hormonal Influences** on **Behavior**, including **Testosterone, Estrogen**, and **Oxytocin**.

GENETICS AND BEHAVIOR

Mnemonic: **Genes Shape Personality**

- **G** **G**enetics influence on behavior
- **S** **S**pecific genes linked to traits and disorders
- **P** **P**ersonality and behavioral traits

Explanation:
- **Genes Shape Personality** emphasizes the role of **Genetics** in **Behavior**, linking specific genes to **Personality** and behavioral traits.

EVOLUTIONARY PSYCHOLOGY

Mnemonic: **Mates Act Altruistic**

M — Mate selection
A — Aggression
A — Altruism

Explanation:
- **Mates Act Altruistic** highlights **Evolutionary Psychology** concepts such as **Mate selection**, **Aggression**, and **Altruism** as behaviors shaped by evolutionary principles.

SOCIOCULTURAL INFLUENCES ON BEHAVIOR

Mnemonic: **Culture Shapes Society**

C — Culture
S — Social norms
S — Societal expectations

Explanation:
- **Culture Shapes Society** emphasizes **Sociocultural Influences** on **Behavior**, where **Culture**, **Social norms**, and **Societal expectations** shape individual behavior.

THE ROLE OF THE ENVIRONMENT IN BEHAVIOR

Mnemonic: **Stressful Nutrition Toxicity**

S — Stress
N — Nutrition
T — Toxins

Explanation:
- **Stressful Nutrition Toxicity** reflects **Environmental Influences** on **Behavior** through **Stress**, **Nutrition**, and **Toxins** impacting brain development and behavior.

NEUROIMAGING TECHNIQUES

Mnemonic: **Fun Pictures**

    F   fMRI (functional magnetic resonance imaging)
    P   PET scans (positron emission tomography)

Explanation:
- **Fun Pictures** represents **Neuroimaging Techniques** such as **fMRI** and **PET scans** used to study brain function and behavior.

SLEEP AND BEHAVIOR

Mnemonic: **Sleep Deprivation Hurts**

    S   Sleep affects behavior
    D   Deprivation impacts cognitive function
    H   Hurts mood and performance

Explanation:
- **Sleep Deprivation Hurts** reminds us of **Sleep's Impact** on **Behavior**, as lack of sleep affects cognition, mood, and overall behavior

ROLE OF THE AUTONOMIC NERVOUS SYSTEM

Mnemonic: **Sympathetic Parasympathetic Balances**

    S   Sympathetic nervous system (fight or flight)
    P   Parasympathetic nervous system
    B   Balances physiological responses

Explanation:
- **Sympathetic Parasympathetic Balances** highlights the **Role** of the **Autonomic Nervous System** in **Balancing** physiological responses through **Sympathetic** and **Parasympathetic** branches.

SENSATION & PERCEPTION

SENSORY ADAPTATION

Mnemonic: **Adjust After Exposure**

A — **A**djust to constant stimuli
A — **A**fter prolonged exposure
E — Leads to **E**xposure desensitization

Explanation:
- **Adjust After Exposure** captures **Sensory Adaptation**, where senses **Adjust** to **Constant Stimuli** and sensitivity decreases over time.

SENSORY HABITUATION

Mnemonic: **Habitual Sounds Fade**

H — **H**abituation reduces response
S — To repeated **S**ounds or stimuli
F — **F**ade with repeated exposure

Explanation:
- **Habitual Sounds Fade** represents **Sensory Habituation**, where repeated exposure to a stimulus leads to a **Fading** response over time.

PSYCHOPHYSICS

Mnemonic: **Absolute Differences Work**

A — **A**bsolute threshold (minimum detectable level)
D — **D**ifference threshold (just noticeable difference)
W — **W**eber's Law (proportional change detection)

Explanation:
- **Absolute Differences Work** helps remember the key concepts in **Psychophysics**: **Absolute threshold**, **Difference threshold**, and **Weber's Law**.

BOTTOM-UP AND TOP-DOWN PROCESSING

Mnemonic: **Bottom First, Top Tunes**

- **B** — Bottom-Up processing starts with data
- **T** — Top-Down processing applies prior knowledge
- **T** — Tunes perception through both processes

Explanation:
- **Bottom First, Top Tunes** emphasizes the difference between **Bottom-Up** (data-driven) and **Top-Down** (knowledge-driven) processing and how they tune perception.

PERCEPTUAL ILLUSIONS

Mnemonic: **Illusions Trick Eyes**

- **I** — Illusions
- **T** — Trick the mind's perception
- **E** — Exploit perceptual Errors

Explanation:
- **Illusions Trick Eyes** reminds us that **Perceptual Illusions Trick** our eyes and mind, often due to underlying psychological mechanisms.

DEPTH PERCEPTION

Mnemonic: **Both Cues Make Depth Clear**

- **B** — Binocular cues (disparity and convergence)
- **C** — Cues from monocular sources
- **M** — Make Depth perception clearer

Explanation:
- **Both Cues Make Depth Clear** indicates the role of **Binocular** and **Monocular Cues** in creating a sense of **Depth Perception**.

GESTALT PRINCIPLES

Mnemonic: **People See Complex Closures**

- **P** — Proximity (grouping by closeness)
- **S** — Similarity (grouping by likeness)
- **C** — Continuity (following smooth paths)
- **C** — Closure (perceiving complete shapes)

Explanation:
- **People See Complex Closures** covers key **Gestalt Principles**: **Proximity**, **Similarity**, **Continuity**, and **Closure** in perception.

SENSORY INTEGRATION

Mnemonic: **Senses Unite Smoothly**

- **S** — Senses combine (vision, hearing, touch, etc.)
- **U** — Unite to form a single perception
- **S** — Smoothly integrates experiences

Explanation:
- **Senses Unite Smoothly** represents **Sensory Integration**, where multiple senses **Combine** to create a unified perceptual experience.

CROSS-MODAL PERCEPTION

Mnemonic: **Crossing Modalities Connects**

- **C** — Crossing sensory modalities
- **M** — Modalities interact
- **C** — Connects perceptions (e.g., McGurk effect)

Explanation:
- **Crossing Modalities Connects** refers to **Cross-Modal Perception**, where one sense **Influences** another, as seen in effects like the **McGurk Effect**.

LEARNING & MEMORY

STATE-DEPENDENT MEMORY

Mnemonic: **Mood Matches Memory**

M — **M**ood or internal **S**tate at the time of learning
M — **M**atches the **M**emory retrieval state

Explanation:
- **Mood Matches Memory** helps us remember that **State-Dependent Memory** involves retrieving information more easily when in the same internal state as when it was encoded.

CONTEXT-DEPENDENT MEMORY

Mnemonic: **Context Completes Cues**

C — **C**ontext where information was learned
C — **C**ompletes the retrieval **C**ues

Explanation:
- **Context Completes Cues** indicates that **Context-Dependent Memory** retrieval is easier when in the same physical environment or **Context** as when learning occurred.

ENCODING SPECIFICITY PRINCIPLE

Mnemonic: **Exact Setting Helps**

E — **E**xact encoding conditions
S — Retrieval matches **S**etting of encoding
H — **H**elps with memory recall

Explanation:
- **Exact Setting Helps** represents the **Encoding Specificity Principle**, where **Exact** conditions of encoding enhance **Memory Retrieval** if similar at recall.

30 Day MCAT

IMPLICIT MEMORY

Ingrained Skills Stay

Mnemonic:

I	**I**mplicit memory
S	**S**kills and procedural habits
S	**S**tay without conscious recall

Explanation:

- **Ingrained Skills Stay** highlights **Implicit Memory**, which involves procedural **Skills** and habits that **Stay** without needing conscious recall.

SEMANTIC MEMORY

Semantic is Shared Knowledge

Mnemonic:

S	**S**emantic memory
S	**S**tores Shared knowledge
K	Different from **K**nowledge of personal experiences

Explanation:

- **Semantic is Shared Knowledge** distinguishes **Semantic Memory** (general knowledge) from **Episodic Memory** (personal experiences).

FLASHBULB MEMORY

Flashes of Emotion

Mnemonic:

F	**F**lashbulb memory
E	Vivid due to **E**motion

Explanation:

- **Flashes of Emotion** describes **Flashbulb Memory** as vivid and highly detailed memories triggered by emotionally significant events.

MEMORY CONSOLIDATION

Mnemonic: **Converts Short to Strong**

- **C** — **C**onverts memories
- **S** — From **S**hort-term to long-term
- **S** — Into **S**trong, lasting memories

Explanation:
- **Converts Short to Strong** represents **Memory Consolidation**, where **Short-term** memories are **Converted** into **Long-term** memories.

FORGETTING CURVE

Mnemonic: **Forgetting Drops Fast**

- **F** — **F**orgetting
- **D** — **D**rops over time
- **F** — **F**ast initial decline

Explanation:
- **Forgetting Drops Fast** illustrates the **Forgetting Curve**, where **Memory Declines** quickly at first and then levels off over time.

MNEMONIC DEVICES

Mnemonic: **Memories Need Tricks**

- **M** — **M**nemonic devices
- **N** — Improve **N**ew memories
- **T** — Through **T**ricks like acronyms and acrostics

Explanation:
- **Forgetting Drops Fast** illustrates the **Forgetting Curve**, where **Memory Declines** quickly at first and then levels off over time.

COGNITION & LANGUAGE

THEORY OF MIND

Mnemonic: **Beliefs Drive Intentions**

- **B** — **B**eliefs (understanding others' beliefs)
- **D** — **D**esires (recognizing others' desires)
- **I** — **I**ntentions (understanding others' intentions)

Explanation:
- **Beliefs Drive Intentions** represents **Theory of Mind**, the ability to attribute **Beliefs**, **Desires**, and **Intentions** to oneself and others.

CONSCIOUSNESS AND ATTENTION

Mnemonic: **Focus Alters States**

- **F** — **F**ocus through attention
- **A** — **A**lters perception
- **S** — **S**tates of consciousness (e.g., alertness, sleep)

Explanation:
- **Focus Alters States** helps us remember that **Consciousness** and **Attention** involve **Focusing** on stimuli and experiencing various **States** of awareness.

LANGUAGE ACQUISITION

Mnemonic: **Nature Nurtures Language**

- **N** — **N**ature (biological predispositions)
- **N** — **N**urture (environmental influence)
- **L** — **L**anguage development stages

Explanation:
- **Nature Nurtures Language** reflects **Language Acquisition** and the interplay between **Nature** and **Nurture** in the development of language.

LANGUAGE DISORDERS

Mnemonic: **Aphasia Disrupts Speech**

- **A** Aphasia (impairs language ability)
- **D** Dyslexia (affects reading)
- **S** Speech and language impairments

Explanation:
- **Aphasia Disrupts Speech** covers **Language Disorders** like **Aphasia** and **Dyslexia** and their effects on **Speech** and language processing.

PROBLEM-SOLVING STRATEGIES

Mnemonic: **All Hints Inspire**

- **A** Algorithms (step-by-step solutions)
- **H** Heuristics (mental shortcuts)
- **I** Insight (sudden realization)

Explanation:
- **All Hints Inspire** summarizes **Problem-Solving Strategies**: **Algorithms**, **Heuristics**, and **Insight**.

COGNITIVE BIASES

Mnemonic: **Confirm Anchors Available**

- **C** Confirmation bias
- **A** Anchoring bias
- **A** Availability heuristic

Explanation:
- **Confirm Anchors Available** covers key **Cognitive Biases** that influence decision-making, such as **Confirmation bias, Anchoring**, and **Availability heuristic**.

COGNITIVE CONTROL

Mnemonic: ## Prefrontal Plans Decisions

- **P** — Prefrontal cortex
- **P** — Plans
- **D** — Decision-making and impulse control

Explanation:
- **Prefrontal Plans Decisions** represents **Cognitive Control**, emphasizing the **Prefrontal Cortex's** role in **Planning** and **Decision-Making**.

WORKING MEMORY

Mnemonic: ## Work Holds Ideas

- **W** — Working memory
- **H** — Holds information temporarily
- **I** — Ideas manipulated in short-term memory

Explanation:
- **Work Holds Ideas** describes **Working Memory** as it **Holds** and manipulates information for short-term tasks.

CONSCIOUSNESS AND SLEEP

Mnemonic: ## Sleep Dreams Cycle

- **S** — Sleep stages (various stages including REM)
- **D** — Dream states
- **C** — Cycles through different Consciousness levels

Explanation:
- **Sleep Dreams Cycle** covers **Consciousness** and **Sleep** by highlighting **Sleep Stages**, **Dreams**, and the **Cycle** of consciousness during sleep.

MOTIVATION & STRESS

BELIEVE TO ACHIEVE

Mnemonic: **Adjust After Exposure**

- **B** — **B**elief in one's abilities
- **A** — Impacts **A**chievement and motivation

Explanation:
- **Believe to Achieve** captures **Self-Efficacy**, where **Belief** in one's capabilities boosts **Motivation** and **Achievement**.

INTRINSIC AND EXTRINSIC MOTIVATION

Mnemonic: **Inside or External Drive**

- **I** — **I**ntrinsic motivation (internal satisfaction)
- **E** — **Ex**trinsic motivation (external rewards)
- **D** — **D**rive for behavior

Explanation:
- **Inside or External Drive** helps differentiate between **Intrinsic** motivation (from within) and **Extrinsic** motivation (from outside rewards).

EMOTION REGULATION

Mnemonic: **Calm and Control**

- **C** — **C**ognitive reappraisal (reframing thoughts)
- **C** — **C**ontrol through emotional suppression

Explanation:
- **Calm and Control** refers to **Emotion Regulation** strategies like **Cognitive Reappraisal** and **Emotional Suppression** to manage emotions.

THEORIES OF EMOTION

Mnemonic: **Just Can't Stay Still**

J — **J**ames-Lange theory (emotion from physiological response)

C — **C**annon-Bard theory (emotion and physiology simultaneous)

S — **S**chachter-Singer two-factor theory (emotion based on arousal and interpretation)

Explanation:
- **Just Can't Stay Still** covers the **Theories of Emotion: James-Lange, Cannon-Bard,** and **Schachter-Singer.**

STRESS RESPONSE

Mnemonic: **Fight or HPA Axis**

F — **F**ight-or-flight response (immediate stress response)

HPA — **H**ypothalamic-**P**ituitary-**A**drenal axis (long-term stress response)

Explanation:
- **Fight or HPA Axis** represents **Stress Responses: Fight-or-flight** for immediate reaction, and **HPA axis** for extended stress regulation.

COPING MECHANISMS

Mnemonic: **Problems Ease Emotions**

P — **P**roblem-focused coping (tackling stressors directly)

E — **E**motion-focused coping (managing feelings)

Explanation:
- **Problems Ease Emotions** represents **Coping Mechanisms: Problem-focused** and **Emotion-focused** coping for managing stress.

SOCIAL SUPPORT AND STRESS

Mnemonic: **Support Soothes Stress**

- **S** — Social Support
- **S** — Soothes and mitigates
- **S** — Negative effects of Stress

Explanation:
- **Support Soothes Stress** highlights the role of **Social Support** in reducing the **Impact of Stress**.

POST-TRAUMATIC STRESS DISORDER

Mnemonic: **Trauma's Lingering Stress**

- **T** — Trauma leads to PTSD
- **L** — Lingering symptoms (flashbacks, anxiety)
- **S** — Ongoing Stress response

Explanation:
- **Trauma's Lingering Stress** helps remember **PTSD** as prolonged stress and symptoms following Trauma.

POSITIVE PSYCHOLOGY

Mnemonic: **Strengths Build Resilience**

- **S** — Strengths and virtues focus
- **B** — Build well-being
- **R** — Resilience and mental health

Explanation:
- **Strengths Build Resilience** captures the **Essence of Positive Psychology**, emphasizing **Strengths** and **Well-being** to foster **Resilience**.

IDENTITY & PERSONALITY

SOCIAL IDENTITY THEORY

Mnemonic: **Group Belonging Matters**

G — **G**roup membership shapes identity
B — Influences **B**eliefs and behaviors
M — **M**atters for social identity formation

Explanation:
- **Group Belonging Matters** represents **Social Identity Theory**, where **Group membership** forms an individual's sense of identity.

SELF-CONCEPT

Mnemonic: **Esteem, Efficacy, Schema**

E — Self-**E**steem (overall value of oneself)
E — Self-**E**fficacy (belief in one's abilities)
S — Self-**S**chema (mental representations of oneself)

Explanation:
- **Esteem, Efficacy, Schema** highlights the components of **Self-Concept**: **Self-Esteem**, **Self-Efficacy**, and **Self-Schema**.

PERSONALITY TRAITS (FIVE-FACTOR MODEL)

Mnemonic: **OCEAN**

O — **O**penness (open-mindedness and curiosity)
C — **C**onscientiousness
E — **E**xtraversion (sociability and assertiveness)
A — **A**greeableness (cooperativeness and empathy)
N — **N**euroticism (emotional stability)

Explanation:
- **OCEAN** represents the **Five-Factor Model of Personality**: **Openness**, **Conscientiousness**, **Extraversion**, **Agreeableness**, and **Neuroticism**.

PSYCHOANALYTIC THEORY

Mnemonic: **I Eat Supper**

- **I** — Id (primitive desires)
- **E** — Ego (reality-oriented mediator)
- **S** — Superego (moral standards)

Explanation:
- **I Eat Supper** represents Freud's **Psychoanalytic Theory**: the **Id**, **Ego**, and **Superego** in personality structure.

HUMANISTIC PSYCHOLOGY

Mnemonic: **Grow Towards Positive**

- **G** — Emphasis on Growth
- **T** — Towards self-actualization
- **P** — Focus on Positive psychology

Explanation:
- **Grow Towards Positive** reflects **Humanistic Psychology's** focus on **Growth**, **Self-Actualization**, and **Positive Psychology**.

SOCIAL COGNITIVE THEORY

Mnemonic: **Cognition Behaves Environmentally**

- **C** — Cognitive processes affect learning
- **B** — Behavior (personal actions)
- **E** — Interaction with the Environment

Explanation:
- **Cognition Behaves Environmentally** covers **Social Cognitive Theory**, where **Cognition**, **Behavior**, and **Environment** interact in shaping personality.

CULTURAL INFLUENCES ON IDENTITY

Mnemonic: **Culture Shapes Values**

C — **C**ulture influences identity
S — **S**hapes beliefs
V — Determines **V**alues and behaviors

Explanation:
- **Culture Shapes Values** signifies **Cultural Influences** on **Identity** by shaping **Values**, **Beliefs**, and behaviors.

GENDER IDENTITY AND ROLE

Mnemonic: **Gender Roles Influence Identity**

G — **G**ender identity
R — **R**oles and stereotypes
I — Affect **I**dentity and behavior

Explanation:
- **Gender Roles Influence Identity** represents **Gender Identity** and **Role**, where **Gender Roles** and **Stereotypes** impact **Identity**.

IDENTITY CRISIS

Mnemonic: **Exploring Self**

E — **E**xploring values and beliefs
S — Occurs during periods of **S**elf-exploration

Explanation:
- **Exploring Self** describes **Identity Crisis**, a period of **Self-Exploration** that often occurs during adolescence as individuals explore their beliefs and values.

PSYCHOLOGICAL DISORDERS

SOMATIC SYMPTOM DISORDER

Mnemonic: **Somatic Symptoms Worry**

- **S** — **S**omatic or physical symptoms
- **S** — Excessive **S**ymptom focus
- **W** — Constant **W**orry about health

Explanation:
- **Somatic Symptoms Worry** describes **Somatic Symptom Disorder**, where individuals experience **Physical Symptoms** and excessive **Worry** about their health.

ILLNESS ANXIETY DISORDER

Mnemonic: **Illness Anxiety Ahead**

- **I** — Excessive **I**llness worry
- **A** — **A**nxiety about getting ill
- **A** — Focused on **A**head (future illnesses)

Explanation:
- **Illness Anxiety Ahead** captures **Illness Anxiety** Disorder, where individuals worry about potential **Future Illnesses** rather than current symptoms.

CONVERSION DISORDER

Mnemonic: **Convert Stress to Symptoms**

- **C** — **C**onversion of stress
- **S** — **S**tress becomes physical symptoms
- **S** — **S**ymptoms like paralysis or blindness

Explanation:
- **Convert Stress to Symptoms** represents **Conversion Disorder**, where **Stress** is converted into **Physical Symptoms**.

DISSOCIATIVE DISORDERS

Mnemonic: **Different Selves**

- **D** — **D**issociative Identity Disorder
- **S** — **S**elves or identities (multiple identities)

Explanation:
- **Different Selves** covers **Dissociative Disorders**, such as **Dissociative Identity Disorder** and **Dissociative Amnesia**, where there is a disruption in Self or memory.

PERSONALITY DISORDERS (CLUSTERS)

Mnemonic: **Odd Drama Anxiety**

- **O** — Cluster A: **O**dd-Eccentric (e.g., paranoid)
- **D** — Cluster B: **D**ramatic-Emotional (e.g., borderline)
- **A** — Cluster C: **A**nxious-Fearful (e.g., avoidant)

Explanation:
- **Odd Drama Anxiety** represents the Personality Disorder Clusters: **Odd-Eccentric** (A), **Dramatic-Emotional** (B), and **Anxious-Fearful** (C).

BORDERLINE PERSONALITY DISORDER

Mnemonic: **Borderline Boundaries Broken**

- **B** — **B**orderline instability
- **B** — Poor **B**oundaries in relationships
- **B** — **B**roken relationships and impulsivity

Explanation:
- **Borderline Boundaries Broken** describes **Borderline Personality Disorder**, where emotional instability, impulsivity, and intense relationships are common.

ANTISOCIAL PERSONALITY DISORDER

Mnemonic: **Against Social Rules**

- **A** — Antisocial behavior
- **S** — Social disregard
- **R** — Lack of Remorse for actions

Explanation:
- **Against Social Rules** captures **Antisocial Personality Disorder**, where individuals often disregard **Social Norms** and lack **Remorse**.

NEURODEVELOPMENTAL DISORDERS

Mnemonic: **Autism Attention Develops**

- **A** — Autism Spectrum Disorder
- **A** — ADHD
- **D** — Disorders Develop in childhood

Explanation:
- **Autism Attention Develops** represents **Neurodevelopmental Disorders**, such as **Autism** and **ADHD**, which develop in early childhood.

NEUROCOGNITIVE DISORDERS

Mnemonic: **Aging Memory Declines**

- **A** — Alzheimer's disease
- **M** — Memory Decline
- **D** — Other Dementias

Explanation:
- **Aging Memory Declines** covers **Neurocognitive Disorders**, particularly **Alzheimer's** and other forms of **Dementia**.

SOCIAL BEHAVIOR & ATTITUDES

SOCIAL COGNITION

Mnemonic: **Social Schemas Shape Stereotypes**

- **S** — **S**ocial information processing
- **S** — **S**chemas (mental frameworks)
- **S** — Form **S**tereotypes and attributions

Explanation:
- **Social Schemas Shape Stereotypes** represents Social Cognition, which involves using **Schemas** and **Stereotypes** to perceive and interpret social information.

ATTITUDES AND PERSUASION

Mnemonic: **CAB Persuades**

- **C** — **C**ognitive component (thoughts/beliefs)
- **A** — **A**ffective component (feelings/emotions)
- **B** — **B**ehavioral component (actions)

Explanation:
- **CAB Persuades** helps recall the **Components** of **Attitudes**: **Cognitive**, **Affective**, and **Behavioral**, which are targeted in **Persuasion** techniques.

COGNITIVE DISSONANCE

Mnemonic: **Conflict Drives Change**

- **C** — **C**onflict between beliefs and behaviors
- **D** — Leads to **D**issonance (discomfort)
- **C** — **C**hange in beliefs or behaviors to reduce discomfort

Explanation:
- **Conflict Drives Change** captures **Cognitive Dissonance**, where conflicting beliefs and behaviors drive individuals to change their attitudes or actions.

SOCIAL INFLUENCE

Mnemonic: **Conform to Social Orders**

- **C** — Conformity (adjusting to group norms)
- **S** — Social norms influence behavior
- **O** — Obedience to authority figures

Explanation:
- **Conform to Social Orders** represents **Social Influence**, including **Conformity**, **Social Norms**, and **Obedience**.

GROUP PROCESSES

Mnemonic: **Groups Share Goals**

- **G** — Groupthink (desire for harmony in groups)
- **S** — Social loafing (reduced effort in groups)
- **G** — Goals achieved through Social Facilitation

Explanation:
- **Groups Share Goals** highlights **Group Processes** such as **Groupthink**, **Social Loafing**, and **Social Facilitation**.

ALTRUISM AND PROSOCIAL BEHAVIOR

Mnemonic: **Empathy Guides Help**

- **E** — Empathy encourages helping
- **G** — Guided by social norms
- **H** — Leads to Helping behavior

Explanation:
- **Empathy Guides Help** describes **Altruism** and **Prosocial Behavior**, driven by **Empathy** and social norms to help others.

AGGRESSION AND VIOLENCE

Mnemonic: **Bio-Psycho-Social Anger**

- **B** — **B**iological factors (genetics, hormones)
- **P** — **P**sychological factors (frustration, anger)
- **S** — **S**ocial factors (cultural influences)

Explanation:
- **Bio-Psycho-Social Anger** represents factors contributing to **Aggression** and **Violence**: **Biological**, **Psychological**, and **Social**.

PREJUDICE AND DISCRIMINATION

Mnemonic: **Prejudice Divides People**

- **P** — **P**rejudice (unfounded attitudes)
- **D** — Leads to **D**iscrimination (biased actions)
- **P** — Creates division and **P**eople inequality

Explanation:
- **Prejudice Divides People** represents **Prejudice** and **Discrimination**, where biased attitudes lead to **Discrimination** and social inequality.

SOCIAL IDENTITY THEORY

Mnemonic: **Groups Influence Identity**

- **G** — **G**roup membership
- **I** — **I**nfluences self-concept and identity
- **I** — Affects **I**ntergroup relations

Explanation:
- **Groups Influence Identity** highlights **Social Identity Theory**, where group membership impacts self-concept and **Intergroup Relations**.

SOCIAL INTERACTIONS

SOCIAL EXCHANGE THEORY

Mnemonic: **Maximize Rewards, Cut Costs**

M — **M**aximize Rewards
C — **C**ut Costs in interactions

Explanation:
- **Maximize Rewards, Cut Costs** describes **Social Exchange Theory**, where individuals seek to **Maximize** rewards and **Minimize** costs in social interactions.

EQUITY THEORY

Mnemonic: **Fair Input Output**

F — **F**airness in relationships
I — **I**nput (what individuals contribute)
O — **O**utput (what they receive)

Explanation:
- **Fair Input Output** represents **Equity Theory**, where individuals evaluate relationship **Fairness** based on the balance of **Inputs** and **Outputs**.

SOCIAL COMPARISON THEORY

Mnemonic: **Compare to Evaluate**

C — **C**ompare oneself with others
E — To **E**valuate abilities and opinions

Explanation:
- **Compare to Evaluate** describes **Social Comparison Theory**, where individuals **Compare** themselves to others to **Evaluate** their own abilities and opinions.

IMPRESSION MANAGEMENT

Mnemonic: **Present Positive Image**

P — Presentation of self
P — Positive image management
I — Influence others' perceptions

Explanation:
- **Present Positive Image** represents **Impression Management**, where people use strategies to Present a **Positive Image** and influence how others see them.

NONVERBAL COMMUNICATION

Mnemonic: **Body, Face, Tone**

B — Body language
F — Facial expressions
T — Tone of voice

Explanation:
- **Body, Face, Tone** highlights **Nonverbal Communication** cues, including **Body Language**, **Facial Expressions**, and **Tone**.

SOCIAL FACILITATION AND INHIBITION

Mnemonic: **Others Help or Hinder**

O — Others' presence
H — Can Help (facilitation) performance
H — Or Hinder (inhibition) performance

Explanation:
- **Others Help** or **Hinder** describes **Social Facilitation** and **Inhibition**, where the presence of **Others** can **Help** or **Hinder** performance.

GROUPTHINK

Mnemonic: **Harmony Hurts Judgment**

- **H** — Harmony within the group
- **H** — Hurts critical thinking
- **J** — Leads to poor Judgment

Explanation:
- **Harmony Hurts Judgment** represents **Groupthink**, where the desire for **Harmony Hurts** critical thinking and **Judgment**.

BYSTANDER EFFECT

Mnemonic: **Others Wait, I Wait**

- **O** — Presence of Others
- **W** — Leads to Waiting for someone else to act
- **I** — Individual hesitation

Explanation:
- **Others Wait, I Wait** captures the **Bystander Effect**, where the presence of **Others** leads individuals to delay or avoid helping.

SOCIAL LOAFING

Mnemonic: **Less Effort in Groups**

- **L** — Less effort
- **G** — When working in Groups

Explanation:
- **Less Effort in Groups** describes **Social Loafing**, where individuals exert **Less Effort** when working collectively.

SOCIAL THINKING

ATTRIBUTION THEORY

Mnemonic: **Internal or External Causes**

- **I** — Internal attributions (dispositional factors)
- **E** — External attributions (situational factors)
- **C** — Explaining Causes of behavior

Explanation:
- **Internal or External Causes** covers **Attribution Theory**, where people explain behavior through **Internal** or **External** factors.

FUNDAMENTAL ATTRIBUTION ERROR

Mnemonic: **Faults Internally Attributed**

- **F** — Faults in others' behavior
- **I** — Overemphasis on Internal factors
- **A** — Attributed more than external factors

Explanation:
- **Faults Internally Attributed** describes the **Fundamental Attribution Error**, where people tend to blame **Internal** factors for others' actions.

SELF-SERVING BIAS

Mnemonic: **Success Inside, Fail Outside**

- **S** — Success attributed to internal factors
- **I** — Inside (internal success)
- **F** — Failures blamed on external factors

Explanation:
- **Success Inside, Fail Outside** represents the **Self-Serving Bias**, where successes are attributed to **Internal** factors, and failures to **External**.

JUST-WORLD HYPOTHESIS

Mnemonic: Justice for All

- **J** — **J**ustice or fairness belief
- **A** — **A**ll get what they deserve

Explanation:
- **Justice for All** captures the **Just-World Hypothesis**, the belief that people ultimately **Deserve** their outcomes, good or bad.

CONFIRMATION BIAS

Mnemonic: Confirm Only Beliefs

- **C** — **C**onfirm one's beliefs
- **O** — **O**nly seeking supportive information
- **B** — Ignorin**g** **c**ontradictory **B**eliefs

Explanation:
- **Confirm Only Beliefs** describes **Confirmation Bias**, where people seek information that **Confirms** their **Beliefs** and disregard opposing evidence.

HINDSIGHT BIAS

Mnemonic: Knew It All Along

- **K** — **K**new outcome seemed predictable
- **I** — **I**t was obvious, in hindsight
- **A** — **A**long (after the event)

Explanation:
- **Knew It All Along** captures **Hindsight Bias**, the tendency to feel that one could have predicted the outcome after it has happened.

COUNTERFACTUAL THINKING

Mnemonic: **Could've Been Different**

- **C** — Counterfactual thoughts
- **B** — Imagine it Been differently
- **D** — Different outcomes in mind

Explanation:
- **Could've Been Different** describes **Counterfactual Thinking**, where individuals imagine alternative scenarios or outcomes.

SOCIAL COGNITION

Mnemonic: **Perceive, Interpret, Respond**

- **P** — Perceiving social cues
- **I** — Interpreting information
- **R** — Responding to social interactions

Explanation:
- **Perceive, Interpret, Respond** covers **Social Cognition**, which involves **Perceiving**, **Interpreting**, and **Responding** to social information.

STEREOTYPES AND PREJUDICE

Mnemonic: **Stereotypes Produce Bias**

- **S** — Stereotypes (cognitive beliefs)
- **P** — Lead to Prejudice (emotional reaction)
- **B** — Can result in Bias and discrimination

Explanation:
- **Stereotypes Produce Bias** represents **Stereotypes** and **Prejudice**, where **Stereotypes** lead to **Prejudice** and potentially **Discrimination**.

SOCIETY & DEMOGRAPHICS

SOCIAL STRATIFICATION

Mnemonic: **Wealth Power Prestige**

W — **W**ealth (economic resources)
P — **P**ower (influence over others)
P — **P**restige (social respect)

Explanation:
- **Wealth Power Prestige** represents **Social Stratification**, the hierarchical organization of society based on **Wealth**, **Power**, and **Prestige**.

SOCIAL INEQUALITY

Mnemonic: **Class Race Gender Age**

C — **C**lass inequality
R — **R**ace disparities
G — **G**ender discrimination
A — **A**ge differences

Explanation:
- **Class Race Gender Age** describes forms of **Social Inequality** based on **Class**, **Race**, **Gender**, and **Age**.

SOCIAL MOBILITY

Mnemonic: **Moving Up or Down**

M — **M**oving Up or Down
U — **U**pward mobility
D — **D**ownward mobility

Explanation:
- **Moving Up** or **Down** captures **Social Mobility**, where individuals experience Upward or **Downward** movement in social status.

30 Day MCAT

CULTURAL DIVERSITY

Mnemonic: **Many Cultures Matter**

M	**M**any different cultures
C	Recognizing **C**ultural differences
M	**M**atters for social interaction

Explanation:
- **Many Cultures Matter** represents **Cultural b**, where multiple cultures coexist, influencing behavior and social harmony.

GLOBALIZATION

Mnemonic: **Global Links Grow**

G	**G**lobal connections
L	**L**inks cultures and economies
G	Leads to growth and **G**lobalization

Explanation:
- **Global Links Grow** covers **Globalization**, which connects cultures and economies, fostering **Global** relationships and impacts.

URBANIZATION

Mnemonic: **City Growth Changes**

C	**C**ity development
G	**G**rowth in urban areas
C	Leads to social **C**hanges

Explanation:
- **City Growth Changes** describes **Urbanization**, which affects **Social Structures**, crime rates, and mental health as cities expand.

DEMOGRAPHIC TRANSITION MODEL

Mnemonic: **Stages for Population Shift**

S — Stages of demographic change
P — Population growth and decline
S — Reflect Shift in age and birth/death rates

Explanation:
- **Stages for Population Shift** represents the **Demographic Transition Model**, which illustrates **Population** growth patterns across Stages.

SOCIAL CHANGE

Mnemonic: **Tech, Trends, Transform**

T — Technological advances
T — Trends in culture
T — Transform society

Explanation:
- **Tech, Trends, Transform** highlights **Social Change** drivers, such as **Technology**, **Cultural Trends**, and social transformations.

SOCIAL INSTITUTIONS

Mnemonic: **Family Educates Religion Governs**

F — Family structures
E — Education system
R — Religion and beliefs
G — Government roles

Explanation:
- **Family Educates Religion Governs** represents key **Social Institutions** that shape behavior: **Family**, **Education**, **Religion**, and **Government**.

SOCIAL STRATIFICATIONS

SOCIAL CLASS

Mnemonic: **Class Impacts Life**

C — Class and social hierarchy
I — Impacts life aspects like education
L — Life expectancy and healthcare access

Explanation:
- **Class Impacts Life** represents **Social Class**, highlighting how class affects **Education**, **Healthcare**, and **Life Expectancy**.

SOCIOECONOMIC STATUS (SES)

Mnemonic: **Income, Education, Occupation**

I — Income level
E — Education achievement
O — Occupation type

Explanation:
- **Income, Education, Occupation** outlines the components of **Socioeconomic Status** (SES), which influence social outcomes.

CULTURAL CAPITAL

Mnemonic: **Knowledge Skills Behavior**

K — Knowledge valued in society
S — Skills that provide advantages
B — Socially valued Behaviors

Explanation:
- **Knowledge Skills Behavior** describes **Cultural Capital**, where **Knowledge**, **Skills**, and **Behaviors** are valued within a society.

SOCIAL REPRODUCTION

Mnemonic: **Class Transfers Through Generations**

- **C** — **C**lass status
- **T** — **T**ransfers through family and education
- **G** — Across **G**enerations

Explanation:
- **Class Transfers Through Generations** captures **Social Reproduction**, where social class is passed on through Generations.

INTERSECTIONALITY

Mnemonic: **Identities Shape Experiences**

- **I** — Multiple **I**dentities like race and gender
- **S** — **S**hape individual experiences
- **E** — Influence **E**xperiences and opportunities

Explanation:
- **Identities Shape Experiences** reflects Intersectionality, where **Social Identities** intersect to affect **Opportunities**.

GLOBAL INEQUALITY

Mnemonic: **Wealth Power Gaps**

- **W** — **W**ealth disparities
- **P** — Unequal **P**ower
- **G** — **G**lobal Gaps in resources

Explanation:
- **Wealth Power Gaps** represents Global Inequality, highlighting the unequal distribution of Wealth, Power, and resources globally.

POVERTY AND INEQUALITY

Mnemonic: **Lacking Health Education Crime**

- **L** — Lacking resources (poverty)
- **H** — Affects Health and access to services
- **E** — Impacts Education opportunities
- **C** — Leads to higher Crime rates

Explanation:
- **Lacking Health Education Crime** represents Poverty and Inequality, covering the **Health**, **Education**, and **Crime** impacts of limited resources.

SOCIAL MOBILITY

Mnemonic: **Move Up or Across Generations**

- **M** — Move socially
- **U** — Upward or Downward mobility
- **A** — Across generations (intergenerational)

Explanation:
- **Move Up or Across Generations** describes **Social Mobility**, encompassing **Upward**, **Downward**, and **Intergenerational** movement within social hierarchies.

SOCIAL EXCLUSION

Mnemonic: **Marginalized Groups Left Out**

- **M** — Marginalized populations (poor, elderly)
- **G** — Vulnerable Groups
- **L** — Feel Left Out and isolated

Explanation:
- **Marginalized Groups Left Out** highlights **Social Exclusion**, where **Marginalized Groups** experience isolation and restricted opportunities.

CHEAT SHEET

KINEMATICS & DYNAMICS

Kinematics & Dynamics	• The study of motion and the forces that cause it.
Projectile Motion	• The motion of an object under the influence of gravity with an initial velocity in two dimensions.
Circular Motion	• The movement of an object along a circular path due to centripetal force.
Work-Energy Theorem	• The principle that work done on an object changes its kinetic energy.
Conservation of Mechanical Energy	• In a closed system without external forces, the total mechanical energy remains constant.
Impulse-Momentum Theorem	• Impulse applied to an object results in a change in its momentum.
Friction	• The resistive force opposing relative motion between two surfaces in contact.
Non-Inertial Reference Frames	• Reference frames where apparent forces arise due to acceleration, such as centrifugal and Coriolis forces.
Rigid Body Motion	• The study of motion and forces in objects that do not deform under stress.
Simple Harmonic Motion	• Oscillatory motion where the restoring force is proportional to displacement and directed toward equilibrium.
Newton's Laws of Motion	• Three fundamental principles that describe the relationship between motion and forces acting on a body.
Center of Mass	• The point in a system or body where its total mass is considered to be concentrated for motion analysis.
Rotational Kinematics	• The study of angular motion parameters such as angular velocity and angular acceleration without considering the forces causing the motion.

Energy Conservation	• Energy cannot be created or destroyed but only transformed from one form to another in an isolated system.
Elastic and Inelastic Collisions	• Elastic collisions conserve kinetic energy, while inelastic collisions result in a loss of kinetic energy to other forms.

WORK & ENERGY

Conservative vs. Non-Conservative Forces	• Conservative forces are path-independent and conserve mechanical energy, while non-conservative forces, like friction, are path-dependent and dissipate energy.
Potential Energy Functions	• Functions that describe the potential energy stored in a system due to its position or configuration.
Power	• The rate at which work is performed or energy is transferred over time.
Work-Energy Theorem with Non-Conservative Forces	• The total work done, including contributions from non-conservative forces, results in a change in the system's mechanical energy.
Energy Diagrams	• Visual representations of potential and kinetic energy changes in a system, often illustrating energy barriers like activation energy.
Efficiency	• The ratio of useful energy output to the total energy input in a system.
Conservation of Energy in Open Systems	• In open systems, energy conservation accounts for energy transfer across system boundaries as heat and work.
Energy Transformations	• The process by which energy changes forms, such as from kinetic to thermal or potential to electrical.
Energy in Biological Systems	• The storage, transformation, and usage of energy in living organisms, often mediated by ATP.
Kinetic Energy	• The energy an object has due to its motion.

Elastic Potential Energy	• The energy stored in a stretched or compressed spring or elastic material.
Mechanical Advantage	• A measure of how much a machine amplifies the input force.
Power in Rotational Systems	• The rate at which work is done in rotational motion.
Thermal Energy	• The energy within a system due to the movement of its particles, often produced by friction.

THERMODYNAMICS

Heat Capacity and Specific Heat	• Heat capacity is the total energy required to change a system's temperature, while specific heat is the energy needed per unit mass.
Latent Heat	• The energy absorbed or released during a phase change without a change in temperature.
Second Law of Thermodynamics and Entropy	• Entropy in an isolated system always increases, guiding spontaneous processes and energy dispersal.
Carnot Cycle	• A theoretical thermodynamic cycle consisting of isothermal and adiabatic processes, representing the most efficient heat engine.
Heat Engines and Refrigerators	• Devices that transfer heat between reservoirs through cyclic processes to perform work or cool spaces.
Adiabatic Processes	• Processes in which no heat is transferred to or from the system, with changes in pressure, volume, and temperature.
Thermodynamic Potentials	• Quantities like internal energy, enthalpy, Helmholtz free energy, and Gibbs free energy that describe a system's energy states.

Phase Diagrams	• Graphical representations showing the states of matter of a substance as functions of pressure and temperature.
Statistical Mechanics	• The study of how microscopic particle behavior determines macroscopic thermodynamic properties.

FLUIDS

Viscosity	• The measure of a fluid's resistance to flow due to internal friction.
Surface Tension	• The cohesive force at the surface of a fluid that causes it to behave like a stretched elastic sheet.
Buoyancy Force	• The upward force exerted by a fluid on an object submerged in it, as described by Archimedes' Principle.
Fluid Pressure	• The force exerted by a fluid per unit area, increasing with depth due to the weight of the fluid above.
Pascal's Principle	• A pressure change applied to an enclosed fluid is transmitted equally in all directions throughout the fluid.
Bernoulli's Principle	• Processes in which no heat is transferred to or from the system, with changes in pressure, volume, and temperature.
Thermodynamic Potentials	• In a moving fluid, an increase in velocity results in a decrease in pressure.
Fluid Flow Rate	• The volume of fluid passing through a cross-sectional area per unit time.
Turbulent Flow	• A type of fluid flow characterized by chaotic changes in pressure and velocity, with swirling and irregular patterns.

ELECTROSTATICS AND MAGNETISM

Electric Potential Energy	• The energy a charged object possesses due to its position in an electric field.
Electric Dipoles	• A system of two equal but opposite charges separated by a distance, creating an electric field.
Gauss's Law	• The net electric flux through a closed surface is proportional to the charge enclosed within it.
Magnetic Field Lines	• Imaginary lines representing the direction and strength of a magnetic field, denser where the field is stronger.
Faraday's Law of Induction	• A changing magnetic field in a circuit induces an electromotive force and current.
Lenz's Law	• The direction of an induced current opposes the change in magnetic flux that caused it.
Magnetic Force on a Moving Charge	• A force experienced by a moving charge in a magnetic field, perpendicular to its velocity and the field.
Electromagnetic Waves	• Oscillating electric and magnetic fields that propagate through space at the speed of light.
Maxwell's Equations	• Four fundamental equations that describe the behavior of electric and magnetic fields and their interactions.
Coulomb's Law	• The force between two point charges is directly proportional to the product of their charges and inversely proportional to the square of the distance between them.
Electric Field	• A region around a charged object where other charges experience an electrostatic force.
Magnetic Flux	• The measure of the total magnetic field passing through a given area.
Ampere's Law	• The magnetic field around a closed loop is proportional to the electric current passing through the loop.

CIRCUITS

Kirchhoff's Laws	• Rules stating that the sum of currents entering a junction equals the sum leaving it, and the sum of voltage drops in a loop equals the total voltage supplied.
Equivalent Resistance and Capacitance	• The total resistance or capacitance in a circuit, simplified using specific rules for series and parallel configurations.
RC Circuits	• Circuits consisting of a resistor and capacitor that charge or discharge with a characteristic time constant.
RL Circuits	• Circuits containing a resistor and inductor where current grows or decays over time due to inductance.
RLC Circuits	• Circuits with a resistor, inductor, and capacitor that exhibit resonance at a specific frequency.
AC Circuits	• Circuits powered by alternating current, characterized by impedance, which opposes current flow and affects phase angles.
Transformers	• Devices that change the voltage level of alternating current for efficient power transmission
Diodes and Transistors	• Diodes allow current to flow in one direction, while transistors act as switches or amplifiers in circuits.
Operational Amplifiers (Op-Amps)	• Components used to amplify, filter, or compare electrical signals in circuits.
Ohm's Law	• The relationship between voltage, current, and resistance in a circuit, stating that V=IRV = IRV=IR.
Capacitive Reactance	• The opposition to alternating current by a capacitor, dependent on the frequency of the current.
Inductive Reactance	• The opposition to alternating current by an inductor, also dependent on the frequency of the current.
Superposition Theorem	• A method for analyzing circuits with multiple independent sources by considering the effect of each source individually.

WAVES AND SOUNDS

Wave Interference	• The phenomenon where two waves overlap, resulting in constructive or destructive interference.
Doppler Effect	• The change in frequency or wavelength of a wave due to the relative motion between the source and observer.
Sound Intensity and Decibel Scale	• A logarithmic measure of sound power per unit area, perceived as loudness.
Standing Waves	• A wave pattern formed by the interference of two waves traveling in opposite directions, creating nodes and antinodes.
Sound Quality (Timbre)	• The characteristic of sound determined by the combination of its frequencies and amplitudes.
Ultrasound	• High-frequency sound waves beyond the range of human hearing, commonly used in medical imaging.
Shock Waves and Sonic Booms	• High-pressure waves and loud booms produced when an object travels faster than the speed of sound.
Acoustic Resonance	• The amplification of sound at specific frequencies due to constructive interference within a system.
Binaural Hearing	• The ability to localize sound sources using input from both ears.
Wave Speed	• The speed at which a wave propagates through a medium, determined by the medium's properties.
Frequency and Wavelength Relationship	• The relationship stating that the speed of a wave is the product of its frequency and wavelength.
Reflection and Refraction of Waves	• Reflection is the bouncing back of waves at a boundary, while refraction is the bending of waves as they pass between different media.

LIGHT AND OPTICS

Dispersion of Light	• The separation of light into its constituent wavelengths as it passes through a medium, forming a spectrum.
Polarization of Light	• The process of aligning light waves in a specific direction, often using polarizing filters.
Diffraction and Interference	• Diffraction is the bending of waves around obstacles, while interference is the combination of waves to form patterns.
Geometric Optics	• The study of light propagation through lenses and mirrors using the principles of reflection and refraction.
Optical Instruments	• Devices like microscopes, telescopes, and cameras that use lenses or mirrors to manipulate light for specific purposes.
Fiber Optics	• The transmission of light through thin, flexible fibers using total internal reflection for communication.
Doppler Effect for Light	• The change in light's frequency and wavelength due to the relative motion of the source and observer, observed as redshift or blueshift.
Photoelectric Effect	• The emission of electrons from a material when light of sufficient energy strikes its surface.
Blackbody Radiation	• The emission of electromagnetic radiation from an object due to its temperature, characterized by quantized energy levels.
Snell's Law	• The relationship between the angles of incidence and refraction when light passes between two media with different refractive indices.
Critical Angle and Total Internal Reflection	• The angle of incidence beyond which light is entirely reflected within a medium rather than refracted.
Huygens' Principle	• A principle stating that every point on a wavefront acts as a source of secondary spherical wavelets, explaining diffraction and refraction.

ATOMIC NUCLEAR & PHENOMENA

Quantum Tunneling	• A quantum phenomenon where particles pass through energy barriers they classically cannot overcome.
Photoelectric Effect	• The emission of electrons from a material when it is exposed to light of sufficient energy.
Blackbody Radiation	• The emission of electromagnetic radiation by an object based on its temperature, with quantized energy levels.
Atomic Spectra	• The unique spectral lines emitted by atoms due to electron transitions between energy levels.
Radioactive Decay	• The process by which unstable atomic nuclei lose energy by emitting radiation such as alpha particles, beta particles, or gamma rays.
Nuclear Fission and Fusion	• Fission is the splitting of heavy atomic nuclei, while fusion is the joining of light nuclei, both releasing significant energy.
Half-Life	• The time required for half of a radioactive substance to decay into its daughter products.
Nuclear Binding Energy	• The energy that holds protons and neutrons together in a nucleus, contributing to its stability.
Quantum Mechanics	• The branch of physics describing the behavior of particles at atomic and subatomic scales, including wave-particle duality and uncertainty.
Isotopes	• Variants of an element with the same number of protons but different numbers of neutrons, resulting in varying atomic masses.
Mass-Energy Equivalence	• A principle stating that mass and energy are interchangeable.
Chain Reactions	• A self-sustaining nuclear reaction where the products of one reaction initiate further reactions, critical in fission processes.

30 Day MCAT

MATHEMATICS

Logarithms and Exponentials	• Logarithms and exponentials describe the inverse relationship between powers and their bases.
Trigonometry	• The study of relationships between angles and sides in triangles, often using sine, cosine, and tangent functions.
Unit Conversions	• The process of converting quantities from one unit to another, ensuring measurements are consistent.
Dimensional Analysis	• A method to check the validity of equations by ensuring consistent units across calculations.
Algebraic Manipulation	• The process of rearranging, factoring, and solving equations to isolate variables or simplify expressions.
Functions and Graphs	• Functions represent relationships between variables, and graphs visualize these relationships.
Rates and Ratios	• Mathematical comparisons of two quantities, often used to express proportions, speeds, or percentages.
Statistical Concepts	• Includes measures like mean, median, mode, and spread to describe and analyze data distributions.
Geometric Formulas	• Equations used to calculate areas, volumes, and surface areas of various 2D and 3D shapes.
Probability	• The study of the likelihood of events occurring, expressed as a number between 0 and 1.
Limits and Continuity	• Concepts in calculus that determine the behavior of a function as it approaches a specific point or infinity.
Derivatives	• A measure of how a function changes as its input changes, representing the slope of the function at any point.
Integrals	• The process of finding the area under a curve, representing accumulation or total change.

DESIGN REASONING & RESEARCH EXECUTION

Scientific Method	• A systematic process involving observation, hypothesis formulation, experimentation, analysis, and conclusion to investigate phenomena.
Experimental Design	• The planning of experiments to test hypotheses by controlling variables and ensuring accurate data collection.
Data Analysis and Interpretation	• The process of organizing, summarizing, and drawing conclusions from collected data.
Data Visualization	• The representation of data through graphs, charts, and other visual formats to identify patterns and trends.
Hypothesis Testing	• A method of testing whether a proposed explanation or hypothesis is supported by experimental data.
Error Analysis	• The evaluation and quantification of errors in data to improve accuracy and reliability of results.
Ethical Considerations in Research	• Principles ensuring the protection, consent, and confidentiality of research subjects and integrity in research practices.
Critical Thinking	• The ability to objectively analyze and evaluate information to make reasoned judgments.
Problem-Solving	• The process of identifying, analyzing, and resolving issues systematically and creatively.
Control Groups	• Groups in experiments that do not receive the treatment, serving as a baseline to compare the effects of the variable being tested.
Replication	• Repeating experiments to ensure consistency and reliability of results, minimizing the impact of random errors.
Literature Review	• A comprehensive survey of existing research to identify gaps, establish context, and justify the research question or hypothesis.

DATA BASE & STATISTICAL REASONING

Statistical Significance	• A measure of whether a result is likely due to chance, determined by comparing the p-value to a significance threshold (alpha level).
Type I and Type II Errors	• A Type I error is a false positive, while a Type II error is a false negative in hypothesis testing.
Correlation vs. Causation	• Correlation indicates an association between variables, but it does not establish a cause-and-effect relationship.
Sampling Bias	• A bias introduced when a sample is not representative of the population, leading to skewed results.
Confounding Variables	• Variables that affect both the independent and dependent variables, potentially distorting the observed relationship.
Effect Size	• A quantitative measure of the strength of a relationship or the magnitude of an effect in a study.
Meta-Analysis	• A statistical method of combining results from multiple studies to draw a more robust conclusion.
Data Visualization	• The graphical representation of data to identify patterns, trends, and distributions.
Bayesian Statistics	• A statistical approach that updates the probability of a hypothesis based on new evidence using Bayes' theorem.
Standard Deviation and Variance	• Measures of data dispersion, with variance quantifying the average squared deviations from the mean, and standard deviation as its square root.
Confidence Intervals	• A range of values within which a population parameter is likely to lie, based on sample data and a given confidence level.
Regression Analysis	• A statistical method to model and analyze the relationships between dependent and independent variables.
Null and Alternative Hypotheses	• The null hypothesis states no effect or relationship exists, while the alternative hypothesis suggests the presence of an effect or relationship.

KINEMATICS & DYNAMICS

PROJECTILE MOTION

Mnemonic: **Range Height Time**

- **R** — Range (horizontal distance)
- **H** — Height (maximum vertical reach)
- **T** — Time of flight

Explanation:
- **Range Height Time** helps remember the key aspects of **Projectile Motion**: calculating Range, Maximum Height, and Time of flight

CIRCULAR MOTION

Mnemonic: **Centripetal Acceleration and Force**

- **C** — Centripetal acceleration (points to center)
- **A** — Acceleration (changes direction)
- **F** — Force directed inward

Explanation:
- **Centripetal Acceleration** and **Force** covers **Circular Motion**, focusing on **Centripetal Acceleration**, **Force**, and Angular Velocity.

WORK-ENERGY THEOREM

Mnemonic: **Work Equals Energy Change**

- **W** — Work done on an object
- **E** — Equals change in Energy (kinetic or potential)
- **C** — Change in energy

Explanation:
- **Work Equals Energy Change** captures the Work-Energy Theorem, where Work done on a system results in a Change in its Energy.

CONSERVATION OF MECHANICAL ENERGY

Mnemonic: **Energy Stays Constant**

- **E** — Energy (mechanical) is conserved
- **S** — Stays constant without external work
- **C** — Constant in a closed system

Explanation:
- **Energy Stays Constant** represents **Conservation** of **Mechanical Energy**, where total Mechanical Energy remains constant in a closed system without external forces.

IMPULSE-MOMENTUM THEOREM

Mnemonic: **Impulse Makes Momentum**

- **I** — Impulse (force applied over time)
- **M** — Causes a change in Momentum

Explanation:
- **Impulse Makes Momentum** helps recall the **Impulse-Momentum Theorem**, where **Impulse** causes a change in **Momentum** during collisions.

FRICTION

Mnemonic: **Static Kinetic Friction**

- **S** — Static friction (before motion)
- **K** — Kinetic friction (during motion)
- **F** — Frictional force calculation

Explanation:
- **Static Kinetic Friction** describes **Friction**, focusing on **Static** and **Kinetic Friction** types and how to calculate **Frictional Forces**.

NON-INERTIAL REFERENCE FRAMES

Mnemonic: **Apparent Centrifugal Coriolis**

- **A** — **A**pparent forces appear in non-inertial frames
- **C** — **C**entrifugal force (outward force in a rotating frame)
- **C** — **C**oriolis force (affects moving objects in rotating frames)

Explanation:
- **Apparent Centrifugal Coriolis** covers **Non-Inertial Reference Frames**, focusing on **Apparent Forces** like **Centrifugal** and **Coriolis**.

RIGID BODY MOTION

Mnemonic: **Torque and Rotation**

- **T** — **T**orque (rotational force)
- **R** — Leads to **R**otation and angular motion
- **M** — Includes **M**oment of inertia

Explanation:
- **Torque** and **Rotation** represents **Rigid Body Motion**, covering **Torque**, **Rotational Motion**, and **Moment** of **Inertia**.

SIMPLE HARMONIC MOTION

Mnemonic: **Amplitude Period Frequency**

- **A** — **A**mplitude (maximum displacement)
- **P** — **P**eriod (time for one cycle)
- **F** — **F**requency (cycles per second)

Explanation:
- **Amplitude Period Frequency** describes **Simple Harmonic Motion**, focusing on **Amplitude**, **Period**, and **Frequency** characteristics.

WORK & ENERGY

CONSERVATIVE VS. NON-CONSERVATIVE FORCES

Mnemonic: **Gravity Conserves, Friction Fails**

- **G** — Gravity (conservative force)
- **C** — Conserves energy (path-independent)
- **F** — Friction (non-conservative force)
- **F** — Fails to conserve energy (path-dependent)

Explanation:
- **Gravity Conserves, Friction Fails** helps differentiate between **Conservative** forces (like Gravity) and **Non-Conservative** forces (like **Friction**).

POTENTIAL ENERGY FUNCTIONS

Mnemonic: **Potential from Conservative Force**

- **P** — Potential energy derivation
- **C** — Comes from Conservative Forces
- **F** — Calculating Function differences

Explanation:
- **Potential** from **Conservative Force** describes **Potential Energy** Functions derived from **Conservative Forces** to calculate energy differences.

POWER

Mnemonic: **Work Rate Equals Power**

- **W** — Work done
- **R** — Rate of work
- **P** — Equals Power

Explanation:
- **Work Rate Equals Power** represents **Power** as the **Rate of Work** done or energy transfer.

WORK-ENERGY WITH NON-CONSERVATIVE FORCES

Mnemonic: **Non-Conservatives Add Work**

- **N** — **N**on-Conservative forces (e.g., friction)
- **A** — **A**dd additional work to the system
- **W** — Affect **W**ork-Energy calculations

Explanation:
- **Non-Conservatives Add Work** applies the **Work-Energy** Theorem in systems with **Non-Conservative** forces, which add work to the system.

ENERGY DIAGRAMS

Mnemonic: **Plot Potential Kinetic Activation**

- **P** — **P**otential energy changes
- **K** — **K**inetic energy representation
- **A** — **A**ctivation energy barrier

Explanation:
- **Plot Potential Kinetic Activation** represents **Energy Diagrams**, visualizing **Potential**, **Kinetic**, and **Activation** energy

EFFICIENCY

Mnemonic: **Useful Output Over Input**

- **U** — **U**seful work or energy output
- **O** — **O**ver total energy input
- **I** — Determines **I**nput efficiency

Explanation:
- **Useful Output Over Input** describes **Efficiency**, the ratio of **Useful Work Output** to **Total Energy** Input.

CONSERVATION OF ENERGY IN OPEN SYSTEMS

Mnemonic: **Heat and Work Transfer**

- **H** — Heat added or removed
- **W** — Work done on or by the system
- **T** — Transfer of energy across system boundaries

Explanation:
- **Heat and Work Transfer** applies **Conservation** of **Energy** to **Open Systems**, where energy is transferred as **Heat** or **Work**.

ENERGY TRANSFORMATIONS

Mnemonic: **Kinetic Potential Thermal Electric**

- **K** — Kinetic energy (motion)
- **P** — Potential energy (position-based)
- **T** — Thermal energy (heat)
- **E** — Electrical energy (charge flow)

Explanation:
- **Kinetic Potential Thermal Electric** helps remember **Energy Transformations** between forms like **Kinetic**, **Potential**, **Thermal**, and **Electrical** energy.

ENERGY IN BIOLOGICAL SYSTEMS

Mnemonic: **ATP Powers Cells**

- **A** — ATP (adenosine triphosphate)
- **P** — Provides energy for Processes
- **C** — In Cells and biological systems

Explanation:
- **ATP Powers Cells** highlights **Energy** in **Biological Systems**, where ATP provides energy for cellular processes, including **Photosynthesis** and **Metabolism**.

THERMODYNAMICS

HEAT CAPACITY AND SPECIFIC HEAT

Mnemonic: **Capacity Covers All, Specific Splits Units**

- **C** — **C**apacity (total energy to heat entire system)
- **A** — **A**ll energy in a material
- **S** — **S**pecific heat (energy per unit mass)
- **S** — **S**plits energy by mass or volume units

Explanation:
- **Capacity Covers All, Specific Splits Units** helps remember that **Heat Capacity** measures total energy change, while **Specific Heat** measures energy change per unit.

LATENT HEAT

Mnemonic: **Phase Heat Hidden**

- **P** — **P**hase transitions (melting, vaporization)
- **H** — **H**eat added or removed
- **H** — **H**idden (does not change temperature)

Explanation:
- **Phase Heat Hidden** describes **Latent Heat**, the energy required for **Phase Changes** without changing temperature.

SECOND LAW OF THERMODYNAMICS AND ENTROPY

Mnemonic: **Entropy Always Spreads**

- **E** — **E**ntropy (measure of disorder)
- **A** — **A**lways increases in isolated systems
- **S** — **S**preads energy, driving spontaneous processes

Explanation:
- **Entropy Always Spreads** captures the **Second Law** of **Thermodynamics**, where **Entropy** naturally increases, guiding spontaneous processes.

CARNOT CYCLE

Mnemonic: **Isothermal Adiabatic Repeat**

- **I** — Isothermal expansion
- **A** — Adiabatic expansion
- **R** — Repeat with compression stages

Explanation:
- **Heat** and **Work Transfer** applies **Conservation** of **Energy** to **Open Systems**, where energy is transferred as **Heat** or **Work**.

HEAT ENGINES AND REFRIGERATORS

Mnemonic: **Cycle Moves Heat**

- **C** — Cycle of processes
- **M** — Moves energy
- **H** — Transfers Heat between reservoirs

Explanation:
- **Cycle Moves Heat** describes **Heat Engines** and **Refrigerators**, which rely on **Cyclic Processes** to transfer **Heat** between sources.

ADIABATIC PROCESSES

Mnemonic: **No Heat Transfer**

- **N** — No heat added or removed
- **H** — Heat Transfer is zero

Explanation:
- **No Heat Transfer** captures **Adiabatic Processes**, where there is No **Heat Transfer** even as pressure, volume, and temperature change.

THERMODYNAMIC POTENTIALS

Mnemonic: Energy Types Include Gibbs

E	Energy types (internal, potential)
T	Types of thermodynamic potentials
I	Include internal energy, enthalpy, Helmholtz free energy, and Gibbs free energy

Explanation:
- **Energy Types Include Gibbs** represents **Thermodynamic Potentials**, which include **Internal Energy, Enthalpy, Helmholtz Free Energy**, and **Gibbs Free Energy**.

PHASE DIAGRAMS

Mnemonic: Phase Pressure Temperature

P	Phase determination
P	By Pressure
T	And Temperature

Explanation:
- **Phase Pressure Temperature** highlights **Phase Diagrams**, which show how **Phase** changes with **Pressure** and **Temperature**.

STATISTICAL MECHANICS

Mnemonic: Micro Makes Macro

M	Microscopic states
M	Define Macroscopic properties

Explanation:
- **Micro Makes Macro** represents **Statistical Mechanics**, where **Microscopic States** collectively determine **Macroscopic Properties** in thermodynamics.

FLUIDS

VISCOSITY

Mnemonic: **Resistance Slows Flow**

- **R** — **R**esistance to flow
- **S** — **S**lows down Flow in fluids

Explanation:
- **Resistance Slows Flow** captures **Viscosity**, the internal **Resistance** in fluids that slows **Flow**, especially relevant in narrow passages like blood vessels.

SURFACE TENSION

Mnemonic: **Tiny Forces, Big Effects**

- **T** — **T**iny molecular Forces
- **B** — Create **B**ig effects like droplets
- **E** — **E**ffects in capillary action

Explanation:
- **Tiny Forces, Big Effects** describes **Surface Tension**, where small intermolecular forces create significant effects, like droplet formation and capillary action.

BUOYANCY FORCE

Mnemonic: **Buoyant Archimedes Pushes**

- **B** — **B**uoyant force
- **A** — **A**rchimedes' Principle
- **P** — **P**ushes objects up in fluids

Explanation:
- **Buoyant Archimedes Pushes** represents the **Buoyant Force** and **Archimedes' Principle**, which explains how fluids exert an upward **Push** on submerged objects.

FLUID PRESSURE

Mnemonic: **Pressure Deepens Downward**

- **P** — Pressure in fluids
- **D** — Deepens with increased Depth

Explanation:
- **Pressure Deepens Downward** describes **Fluid Pressure**, which increases with **Depth** due to the weight of the fluid above.

PASCAL'S PRINCIPLE

Mnemonic: **Pressure Passes Equally**

- **P** — Pressure applied to a fluid
- **P** — Passes undiminished
- **E** — Equally in all directions

Explanation:
- **Pressure Passes Equally** represents **Pascal's Principle**, where a change in **Pressure** applied to an enclosed fluid is transmitted Equally throughout the fluid.

BERNOULLI'S PRINCIPLE

Mnemonic: **Fast Flow Low Pressure**

- **F** — Fast moving fluid
- **L** — Results in Low pressure
- **P** — Pressure decreases with speed

Explanation:
- **Fast Flow Low Pressure** covers **Bernoulli's Principle**, which states that faster fluid flow results in Lower **Pressure**, applied in contexts like lift on airplane wings.

FLUID FLOW RATE

Mnemonic: **Area Times Velocity**

- **A** — **A**rea of cross-section
- **T** — Multiplied by **T**imes
- **V** — **V**elocity of fluid

Explanation:
- **Area Times Velocity** describes **Flow Rate**, calculated as the product of cross-sectional **Area** and **Velocity** of the fluid.

TURBULENT FLOW

Mnemonic: **Chaotic Swirls Flow**

- **C** — **C**haotic fluid movement
- **S** — Full of **S**wirls and eddies
- **F** — Irregular **F**low pattern

Explanation:
- **Chaotic Swirls Flow** represents **Turbulent Flow**, characterized by chaotic swirls and irregular flow, as opposed to smooth **Laminar Flow**.

FLUID DYNAMICS IN BIOLOGICAL SYSTEMS

Mnemonic: **Flow Keeps Life**

- **F** — **F**low of blood and air
- **K** — **K**eeps body functions working
- **L** — Essential for **L**ife processes

Explanation:
- **Flow Keeps Life** describes **Fluid Dynamics** in **Biological Systems**, where fluid flow (e.g., blood, air) is crucial for sustaining **Life** in systems like circulation and respiration.

ELECTROSTATIC AND MAGNETISM

ELECTRIC POTENTIAL ENERGY

Mnemonic: **Potential Powers Energy**

- **P** — **P**otential energy in an electric field
- **P** — Related to **P**otential difference
- **E** — **E**nergy of charge in the field

Explanation:
- **Potential Powers Energy** captures **Electric Potential Energy**, where **Potential** difference powers the **Energy** of charges in an electric field.

ELECTRIC DIPOLES

Mnemonic: **Dipoles Point Opposite**

- **D** — **D**ipoles have positive and negative charges
- **P** — **P**oint toward opposite poles in a field
- **O** — **O**pposite charges create a field

Explanation:
- **Dipoles Point Opposite** represents **Electric Dipoles**, where opposite charges in a dipole interact with external **Electric Fields**.

GAUSS'S LAW

Mnemonic: **Surface Counts Charge**

- **S** — Electric **S**urface
- **C** — **C**ounts enclosed Charge
- **C** — To **C**alculate Electric Field

Explanation:
- **Surface Counts Charge** describes **Gauss's Law**, which calculates the **Electric Field** based on the **Surface** enclosing **Charge**.

MAGNETIC FIELD LINES

Mnemonic: **Lines Show Strength**

- **L** — Lines represent magnetic fields
- **S** — Show direction and density
- **S** — Density indicates Strength

Explanation:
- **Lines Show Strength** represents **Magnetic Field Lines**, where the density and direction of lines indicate **Field Strength**.

FARADAY'S LAW OF INDUCTION

Mnemonic: **Induction Generates Current**

- **I** — Induction in a changing magnetic field
- **G** — Generates electric current
- **C** — Resulting Current flows in the circuit

Explanation:
- **Induction Generates Current** describes **Faraday's Law** of Induction, where **Magnetic** Induction generates **Current** in a circuit.

LENZ'S LAW

Mnemonic: **Opposes Change in Field**

- **O** — Opposes change in magnetic field
- **C** — Creates a Current to oppose it
- **F** — Ensures Field direction resists change

Explanation:
- **Opposes Change** in **Field** represents Lenz's Law, which states that an induced current flows to oppose the change in **Magnetic Field**.

MAGNETIC FORCE ON A MOVING CHARGE

Mnemonic: **Charge Crosses Field**

- **C** — Charge moving in a field
- **C** — Crosses magnetic field lines
- **F** — Experiences a Force

Explanation:
- **Charge Crosses Field** captures the concept of **Magnetic Force** on a **Moving Charge**, where a **Charge** moving across field lines experiences a Force.

ELECTROMAGNETIC WAVES

Mnemonic: **Speedy Waves of Light**

- **S** — Speed of light
- **W** — Properties of Waves (frequency, wavelength)
- **L** — Light as an example of electromagnetic waves

Explanation:
- **Speedy Waves of Light** describes **Electromagnetic Waves**, which travel at the **Speed** of light and have specific **Wavelength** and **Frequency**.

MAXWELL'S EQUATIONS

Mnemonic: **Electromagnetic Equations Rule**

- **E** — Electromagnetic fields
- **E** — Four fundamental Equations
- **R** — Govern and Rule over electromagnetism

Explanation:
- **Electromagnetic Equations Rule** represents **Maxwell's Equations**, the four fundamental equations that govern **Electromagnetism**.

CIRCUITS

KIRCHHOFF'S LAWS

Mnemonic: **Current and Voltage Keep Constant**

- **C** — **C**urrent Law (sum of currents = 0 at a junction)
- **V** — **V**oltage Law (sum of voltages = 0 in a loop)
- **K** — **K**eep conservation of energy and charge

Explanation:
- **Current and Voltage Keep Constant** captures **Kirchhoff's Laws**, which state that **Current** is conserved at junctions and **Voltage** is conserved in loops.

EQUIVALENT RESISTANCE AND CAPACITANCE

Mnemonic: **Series Sum, Parallel Product**

- **S** — **S**eries: add resistances/capacitances directly
- **P** — **P**arallel: product-over-sum for resistances
- **P** — **P**roduct of capacitances for parallel

Explanation:
- **Series Sum, Parallel Product** helps remember that **Series** components are summed, while **Parallel** components use different rules for resistance and capacitance.

RC CIRCUITS

Mnemonic: **Resistor Charges, Capacitor Changes**

- **R** — **R**esistor controls charge rate
- **C** — **C**apacitor stores charge
- **C** — **C**hanges with time constant

Explanation:
- **Resistor Charges, Capacitor Changes** describes **RC Circuits**, where the **Resistor** affects charging, and the **Capacitor** changes voltage over time.

RL CIRCUITS

Mnemonic: **Resistor Inducts Current**

- **R** — **R**esistor limits current growth
- **I** — **I**nductor stores energy in a magnetic field
- **C** — **C**urrent Changes with time

Explanation:
- **Resistor Limits Inductor Current** represents **RL Circuits**, where the **Inductor** affects current growth and decay with the **Resistor** limiting the current.

RLC CIRCUITS

Mnemonic: **Resonance Leads Circuit**

- **R** — **R**esonance frequency
- **L** — **L**eads to minimal impedance
- **C** — Phase angle in the **C**ircuit

Explanation:
- **Resonance Leads Circuit** represents **RLC Circuits**, where **Resonance** minimizes impedance and affects **Phase Angle**.

AC CIRCUITS

Mnemonic: **Impedance Affects Current**

- **I** — **I**mpedance (opposition to AC)
- **A** — **A**ffects current and phase
- **C** — **C**urrent and Phase angle

Explanation:
- **Impedance Affects Current** describes **AC Circuits**, where Impedance affects current flow and **Phase Angle**.

TRANSFORMERS

Mnemonic: **Step Voltage Up or Down**

S	**S**tep up or down voltage
V	**V**oltage adjustment
U/D	Controls power **U**p or **D**own

Explanation:
- **Step Voltage Up or Down** describes **Transformers**, which adjust **Voltage** for efficient power transmission by **Stepping** it up or down.

DIODES AND TRANSISTORS

Mnemonic: **Diodes Direct, Transistors Toggle**

D	**D**iodes allow one-way current flow
T	**T**ransistors act as switches/amplifiers
T	**T**oggle current or amplify signals

Explanation:
- **Diodes Direct, Transistors Toggle** represents **Diodes** (for directing current) and **Transistors** (for toggling and amplifying in circuits).

OPERATIONAL AMPLIFIERS (OP-AMPS)

Mnemonic: **Amplify, Filter, Compare**

A	**A**mplify signals
F	**F**ilter frequencies
C	**C**ompare voltages

Explanation:
- **Amplify, Filter, Compare** covers **Op-Amps**, which are used to **Amplify** signals, **Filter** frequencies, and **Compare** voltages in circuits.

WAVES AND SOUNDS

WAVE INTERFERENCE

Mnemonic: **Construct or Destroy Waves**

C	**C**onstructive interference (waves add up)
D	**D**estructive interference (waves cancel out)
W	Forms **W**aves like standing waves and beats

Explanation:
- **Construct or Destroy Waves** represents **Wave Interference**, where waves **Constructively** or **Destructively** interfere, affecting wave patterns.

DOPPLER EFFECT

Mnemonic: **Close High yet Far and Low**

C	**C**loser source increases frequency
H	**H**igher pitch when moving toward
F	**F**urther source decreases frequency
L	**L**ower pitch when moving away

Explanation:
- **Closer, Higher, Further, Lower** captures the **Doppler Effect**, where frequency and pitch change based on relative movement of source and observer.

SOUND INTENSITY AND DECIBEL SCALE

Mnemonic: **Loud Logarithmic Levels" or "Triple L**

L	**L**oudness perception
L	**L**ogarithmic decibel scale
L	Measures sound **L**evels

Explanation:
- **Loud Logarithmic Levels** represents **Sound Intensity** and **Decibel Scale**, where sound intensity is measured on a **Logarithmic** scale for **Loudness**.

STANDING WAVES

Mnemonic: **Nodes and Antinodes Align**

N Nodes (points of no movement)
A Antinodes (points of max movement)
A Align to form harmonics and overtones

Explanation:
- **Nodes and Antinodes Align** describes **Standing Waves**, where Nodes and Antinodes create harmonics on strings and in pipes.

SOUND QUALITY (TIMBRE)

Mnemonic: **Tones Blend Frequencies**

T Tones combine
B Blend different frequencies and amplitudes
F Forms Frequencies that define sound quality

Explanation:
- **Tones Blend Frequencies** represents **Sound Quality** (Timbre), defined by the **Blend** of frequencies and amplitudes in a sound wave.

ULTRASOUND

Mnemonic: **Beyond Hearing, Medical Imaging**

B Beyond normal hearing range
H High-frequency Hearing
M Used in Medical Imaging

Explanation:
- **Beyond Hearing, Medical Imaging** captures **Ultrasound**, where high-frequency sound waves are used for **Medical Imaging** beyond human hearing range.

SHOCK WAVES AND SONIC BOOMS

Mnemonic: **Speed Breaks Sound Barrier**

- **S** — High **S**peed object
- **B** — **B**reaks the sound barrier
- **S** — Causes **S**onic Boom

Explanation:
- **Speed Breaks Sound Barrier** represents **Shock Waves** and **Sonic Booms**, formed when an object travels faster than the speed of sound.

ACOUSTIC RESONANCE

Mnemonic: **Sound Resonates Clearly**

- **S** — **S**ound waves in a structure
- **R** — **R**esonates at specific frequencies
- **C** — Enhances **C**larity in musical instruments

Explanation:
- **Sound Resonates Clearly** describes **Acoustic Resonance**, where sound waves resonate to amplify clarity in instruments and architectural spaces.

BINAURAL HEARING

Mnemonic: **Both Ears Locate Sound**

- **B** — **B**oth ears receive sound
- **E** — **E**ars help to Locate
- **S** — **S**ound source by processing differences

Explanation:
- **Both Ears Locate Sound** represents **Binaural Hearing**, where the brain processes input from **Both Ears** to localize sound sources.

LIGHT AND OPTICS

DISPERSION OF LIGHT

Mnemonic: **Different Wavelengths Spread**

D — **D**ifferent wavelengths of light
W — **W**avelengths refract at unique angles
S — **S**pread out to form a spectrum

Explanation:
- **Different Wavelengths Spread** describes **Dispersion** of **Light**, where different **Wavelengths** refract at unique angles, creating a **Spectrum**.

POLARIZATION OF LIGHT

Mnemonic: **Align Light Waves**

A — **A**lign light waves in a specific direction
L — **L**ight passing through polarizers
W — **W**aves filtered by alignment

Explanation:
- **Align Light Waves** represents **Polarization** of **Light**, where light waves are filtered and **Aligned** in one direction by polarizers.

DIFFRACTION AND INTERFERENCE

Mnemonic: **Waves Bend and Combine**

W — **W**aves spread or Bend around obstacles
C — **C**ombine to form patterns

Explanation:
- **Waves Bend and Combine** describes **Diffraction** and **Interference**, where **Waves** bend around edges and combine, forming patterns in applications like gratings and interferometers.

GEOMETRIC OPTICS

Mnemonic: **Reflect and Refract for Images**

- **R** — Reflect using mirrors
- **R** — Refract using lenses
- **I** — Forms Images in optical systems

Explanation:
- **Reflect and Refract for Images** represents **Geometric Optics**, where **Reflection** and **Refraction** are used to create **Images** with lenses and mirrors.

OPTICAL INSTRUMENTS

Mnemonic: **Microscopes, Telescopes, Cameras**

- **M** — Microscopes for small details
- **T** — Telescopes for distant objects
- **C** — Cameras capture images

Explanation:
- **Microscopes, Telescopes, Cameras** captures key **Optical Instruments** and their functions, focusing on **Image Formation** in devices.

FIBER OPTICS

Mnemonic: **Total Internal Reflection**

- **T** — Total internal reflection
- **I** — Used in Internal communication systems
- **R** — Reflection keeps light within fibers

Explanation:
- **Total Internal Reflection** represents **Fiber Optics**, where light is contained within fibers due to Total **Internal Reflection** for communication.

DOPPLER EFFECT FOR LIGHT

Mnemonic: **Shift Colors with Motion**

S Shift in light frequency
C Colors change (redshift/blueshift)
M Motion of light source affects color

Explanation:
- **Shift Colors with Motion** represents the **Doppler Effect for Light**, where **Motion** changes the **Color** (frequency) observed, such as **Redshift** and **Blueshift** in astronomy.

PHOTOELECTRIC EFFECT

Mnemonic: **Light Ejects Electrons**

L Light as particles (photons)
E Ejects electrons from material

Explanation:
- **Light Ejects Electrons** describes the **Photoelectric Effect**, where **Light** photons cause **Electrons** to be ejected, showing light's particle nature.

BLACKBODY RADIATION

Mnemonic: **Quantized Energy Glow**

Q Quantized energy levels
E Energy emitted as radiation
G Glow as temperature increases

Explanation:
- **Quantized Energy Glow** represents **Blackbody Radiation**, where objects emit radiation in **Quantized** energy levels, producing a characteristic **Glow**.

ATOMIC NUCLEAR & PHENOMENA

QUANTUM TUNNELING

Mnemonic: **Particles Cross Barriers**

- **P** — Particles (small, like electrons)
- **C** — Cross barriers they normally can't
- **B** — Quantum Barriers in physical

Explanation:
- **Particles Cross Barriers** represents **Quantum Tunneling**, where **Particles** can cross energy barriers despite not having enough classical energy.

PHOTOELECTRIC EFFECT

Mnemonic: **Light Ejects Electrons**

- **L** — Light as photons
- **E** — Ejects electrons from a surface

Explanation:
- **Light Ejects Electrons** describes the **Photoelectric Effect**, where **Light** photons cause **Electrons** to be ejected, showing light's particle nature.

BLACKBODY RADIATION

Mnemonic: **Energy Quantized Glow**

- **E** — Energy emitted as radiation
- **Q** — Quantized in specific levels
- **G** — Glow with temperature increase

Explanation:
- **Energy Quantized Glow** represents **Blackbody Radiation**, where **Quantized Energy** levels lead to emission as an object heats up and **Glows**.

ATOMIC SPECTRA

Mnemonic: **Spectra Identify Elements**

- **S** — **S**pectra from electrons transitioning
- **I** — **I**dentify unique patterns for each element
- **E** — Used to detect **E**lements

Explanation:
- **Spectra Identify Elements** describes **Atomic Spectra**, where unique **Spectral** Lines are produced by each **Element**, allowing identification.

RADIOACTIVE DECAY

Mnemonic: **Alpha, Beta, Gamma Decay**

- **A** — **A**lpha particles emitted
- **B** — **B**eta particles or electrons emitted
- **G** — **G**amma rays as high-energy radiation

Explanation:
- **Alpha, Beta, Gamma Decay** captures **Radioactive Decay**, with **Alpha**, **Beta**, and **Gamma** as primary decay types, each with distinct characteristics.

NUCLEAR FISSION AND FUSION

Mnemonic: **Fission Splits, Fusion Joins**

- **F** — **F**ission splits heavy nuclei
- **S** — **S**plits atoms to release energy
- **F** — **F**usion joins small nuclei
- **J** — **J**oins to form heavier atoms

Explanation:
- **Fission Splits, Fusion Joins** represents **Nuclear Fission** (splitting nuclei) and **Fusion** (joining nuclei), both releasing energy.

HALF-LIFE

Mnemonic: **Time to Decay Half**

- **T** — Time for decay process
- **D** — Amount Decays to half its quantity
- **H** — Represents Half of original substance

Explanation:
- **Time to Decay Half** describes **Half-Life**, the time required for half of a radioactive sample to decay.

NUCLEAR BINDING ENERGY

Mnemonic: **Binding Strength for Stability**

- **B** — Binding energy in nucleus
- **S** — Provides Strength for nuclear stability
- **S** — Related to nuclear Stability

Explanation:
- **Binding Strength** for **Stability** describes **Nuclear Binding Energy**, the energy that binds protons and neutrons, determining nuclear **Stability**.

QUANTUM MECHANICS

Mnemonic: **Particles Wave Uncertainly**

- **P** — Particles exhibit wave behavior
- **W** — Waveparticle duality
- **U** — Uncertainty principle governs behavior

Explanation:
- **Particles Wave Uncertainly** captures **Quantum Mechanics**, highlighting **Wave-Particle Duality** and the **Uncertainty Principle** in quantum phenomena.

MATHEMATICS

LOGARITHMS AND EXPONENTIALS

Mnemonic: **Logs Expose Powers**

L — **L**ogarithms break down exponents
E — **E**xpose the relationship to exponents
P — Work with **P**owers and exponential equations

Explanation:
- **Logs Expose Powers** represents **Logarithms** and **Exponentials**, focusing on how **Logarithms** relate to **Exponents**.

TRIGONOMETRY

Mnemonic: **SOH CAH TOA**

S — **S**ine = Opposite / Hypotenuse
C — **C**osine = Adjacent / Hypotenuse
T — **T**angent = Opposite / Adjacent

Explanation:
- **SOH CAH TOA** is the classic mnemonic to remember **Trigonometric Functions** for right triangles.

UNIT CONVERSIONS

Mnemonic: **Metric Inches Feet Scale**

M — **M**etric (centimeters, meters)
I — **I**nches for smaller imperial units
F — **F**eet for larger imperial units
S — **S**cale conversions

Explanation:
- **Metric Inches Feet Scale** helps recall **Unit Conversions**, especially between metric and imperial systems.

DIMENSIONAL ANALYSIS

Mnemonic: **Units Must Match**

- **U** — **U**nits in equations
- **M** — **M**ust be consistent
- **M** — **M**atch for valid results

Explanation:
- **Units Must Match** represents **Dimensional Analysis**, ensuring Units are consistent to validate equations.

ALGEBRAIC MANIPULATION

Mnemonic: **Factor Solve Rearrange**

- **F** — **F**actor polynomials
- **S** — **S**olve for variables
- **R** — **R**earrange equations

Explanation:
- **Factor Solve Rearrange** describes **Algebraic Manipulation**, focusing on skills to **Solve**, **Factor**, and **Rearrange** equations.

FUNCTIONS AND GRAPHS

Mnemonic: **Graphs Show Function Patterns**

- **G** — **G**raphs visualize functions
- **S** — **S**how relationships
- **F** — Different **F**unction types
- **P** — Reveal **P**atterns in behavior

Explanation:
- **Graphs Show Function Patterns** represents **Functions** and **Graphs**, emphasizing how **Graphs** reveal **Patterns** in functions.

RATES AND RATIOS

Mnemonic: **Proportions in Ratios**

- **P** Proportions in different units
- **I** Used for Interest and percentages
- **R** Ratios relate values

Explanation:
- **Proportions in Ratios** helps recall **Rates** and **Ratios**, where ratios are used to find **Proportions** in different contexts.

STATISTICAL CONCEPTS

Mnemonic: **Mean, Mode, Median, Spread**

- **M** Mean (average value)
- **M** Mode (most common value)
- **M** Median (middle value)
- **S** Spread measures variation

Explanation:
- **Mean, Mode, Median, Spread** captures **Statistical Concepts**, including measures of central tendency and variation.

GEOMETRIC FORMULAS

Mnemonic: **Areas Volumes Shapes**

- **A** Areas of 2D shapes
- **V** Volumes of 3D shapes
- **S** Common Shapes formulas

Explanation:
- **Areas Volumes Shapes** covers **Geometric Formulas** needed for **Areas, Volumes,** and **Surface Areas** of common shapes.

DESIGN & RESEARCH

SCIENTIFIC METHOD

Mnemonic: **Observe Hypothesize Experiment Analyze Conclude**

- **O** — **O**bserve phenomena
- **H** — Form a **H**ypothesis
- **E** — **E**xperiment to test the hypothesis
- **A** — **A**nalyze data
- **C** — Draw a **C**onclusion

Explanation:
- **Observe Hypothesize Experiment Analyze Conclude** covers the **Scientific Method** steps from **Observation** to **Conclusion**.

EXPERIMENTAL DESIGN

Mnemonic: **Identify Control Variables**

- **I** — **I**dentify independent and dependent variables
- **C** — **C**ontrol other variables to ensure accuracy
- **V** — Select appropriate **V**ariables and techniques

Explanation:
- **Identify Control Variables** helps remember **Experimental Design**, including selecting variables and controlling conditions.

DATA ANALYSIS AND INTERPRETATION

Mnemonic: **Mean Spread Correlate**

- **M** — Calculate the **M**ean for central tendency
- **S** — **S**pread measures like variance
- **C** — Determine **C**orrelation between variables

Explanation:
- **Mean Spread Correlate** represents **Data Analysis** and **Interpretation**, covering **Mean**, **Spread**, and **Correlation** for interpreting data.

DATA VISUALIZATION

Mnemonic: **Graphs Chart Trends**

- **G** — **G**raphs display data visually
- **C** — **C**hart results in easy-to-read forms
- **T** — Identify **T**rends and patterns

Explanation:
- **Graphs Chart Trends** captures **Data Visualization**, focusing on using **Graphs** and **Charts** to identify **Trends**.

HYPOTHESIS TESTING

Mnemonic: **Form Test Conclude**

- **F** — **F**ormulate a hypothesis
- **T** — **T**est it with experiments
- **C** — **C**onclude based on results

Explanation:
- **Form Test Conclude** describes **Hypothesis Testing**, where a hypothesis is **Formulated**, **Tested**, and **Conclusions** are drawn.

ERROR ANALYSIS

Mnemonic: **Minimize Measurement Mistakes**

- **M** — **M**inimize sources of error
- **M** — Focus on accurate **M**easurement
- **M** — Reduce **M**istakes in data collection

Explanation:
- **Minimize Measurement Mistakes** covers **Error Analysis**, emphasizing minimizing **Measurement** Errors for accurate results.

ETHICAL CONSIDERATIONS IN RESEARCH

Mnemonic: **Consent Confidential Care**

- **C**   Obtain informed **C**onsent
- **C**   Maintain **C**onfidentiality
- **C**   Ensure **C**are for subjects

Explanation:
- **Consent Confidential Care** represents **Ethical Considerations**, ensuring Informed **Consent**, **Confidentiality**, and **Welfare** in research.

CRITICAL THINKING

Mnemonic: **Evaluate Facts Critically**

- **E**   **E**valuate information
- **F**   Distinguish **F**acts from opinion
- **C**   Think **C**ritically and identify fallacies

Explanation:
- **Evaluate Facts Critically** describes **Critical Thinking**, which involves evaluating **Facts** and identifying logical **Fallacies**.

PROBLEM-SOLVING

Mnemonic: **Break Steps Solve**

- **B**   **Break** down complex problems
- **S**   Identify **S**teps to solve them
- **S**   **S**olve using logic and creativity

Explanation:
- **Break Steps Solve** represents **Problem-Solving**, focusing on breaking problems into smaller Steps for easier solutions.

DATA BASE & STATISTICAL

STATISTICAL SIGNIFICANCE

Mnemonic: **Alpha Protects P-Values**

A — **A**lpha level sets the threshold
P — Determines if **P**-Values are significant

Explanation:
- **Alpha Protects P-Values** captures **Statistical Significance**, where the Alpha level (often 0.05) helps decide if **P-Values** indicate significance.

TYPE I AND TYPE II ERRORS

Mnemonic: **Cry False, Miss True**

C — **C**ry False: Type I error (false positive)
M — **M**iss True: Type II error (false negative)

Explanation:
- **Cry False, Miss True** represents **Type I** (false positive) and **Type II** (false negative) errors, differentiating False Alarms and **Missed Signals**.

CORRELATION VS. CAUSATION

Mnemonic: **Correlation Can't Cause**

C — **C**orrelation only shows association
C — **C**an't imply Cause

Explanation:
- **Correlation Can't Cause** reminds us that **Correlation** does not imply **Causation**, highlighting limits in correlational studies

SAMPLING BIAS

Mnemonic: **Biased Samples Skew Results**

- **B** — **B**iased selections
- **S** — Create **S**kewed findings
- **R** — Affect study **R**esults

Explanation:
- **Biased Samples Skew Results** describes **Sampling Bias**, where unrepresentative samples produce **Skewed Results**.

CONFOUNDING VARIABLES

Mnemonic: **Confound Clouds Connection**

- **C** — **C**onfounding variables
- **C** — **C**louds relationships between variables
- **C** — Affects **C**onnection in studies

Explanation:
- **Confound Clouds Connection** represents **Confounding Variables**, which **Cloud** relationships between variables in research.

EFFECT SIZE

Mnemonic: **Size Shows Strength**

- **S** — **S**ize of effect
- **S** — **S**hows strength of relationship

Explanation:
- **Size Shows Strength** covers **Effect Size**, which measures the **Strength** of a relationship in research findings.

META-ANALYSIS

Mnemonic: **Many Studies Stronger**

- **M** — **M**any studies combined
- **S** — Yield a **S**tronger conclusion

Explanation:
- **Many Studies Stronger** represents **Meta-Analysis**, where results from **Many Studies** are combined to enhance conclusions.

DATA VISUALIZATION

Mnemonic: **Histograms Show Plots**

- **H** — **H**istograms visualize distributions
- **S** — **S**how data distribution and patterns
- **P** — Includes different types of **P**lots

Explanation:
- **Histograms Show Plots** covers **Data Visualization**, with various types of **Plots** like histograms, scatter, and box plots used to display data.

BAYESIAN STATISTICS

Mnemonic: **Bayes Updates Beliefs**

- **B** — **B**ayes' theorem
- **U** — **U**pdates probabilities
- **B** — **B**ased on new **B**eliefs or data

Explanation:
- **Bayes Updates Beliefs** represents **Bayesian Statistics**, where **Bayes' Theorem** helps update probabilities with new information.

Made in the USA
Coppell, TX
06 March 2025